T. E. Lawrence by His Friends, A. W. Lawrence

"The portrait thus collectively painted is clear
in outline, vivid and brilliantly penetrating.
It is difficult to imagine that a better study of
Lawrence's character could be produced by
any single man." Listener

"Those who have written their impressions
have been asked to be candid, critical and
personal; and they have all obeyed. The result
is a 'gallery of partial portraits', perfectly
arranged and left to speak for themselves.
It was a fine idea, and it has been finely
executed. That is a bare minimum of praise."
Observer

McGRAW-HILL PAPERBACKS
FICTION, POETRY, BIOGRAPHY AND CRITICISM

Prices subject to change without notice.

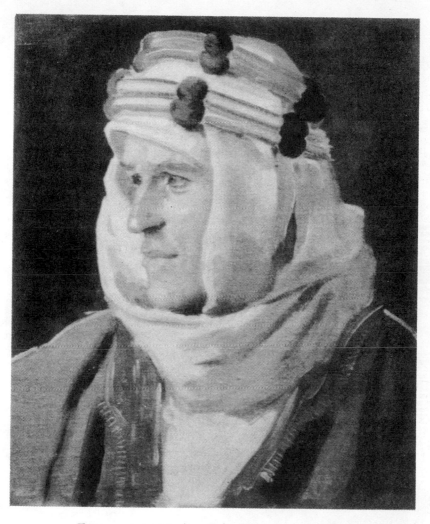

From a painting (in oils) of T. E. Lawrence
by Augustus John, 1919

T. E. Lawrence by His Friends

A new selection of memoirs

edited by A. W. Lawrence

McGraw-Hill Book Company, Inc.

New York   Toronto   London

PREFACE TO THE NEW EDITION

W<small>HEN</small> first published in 1937, two years after my brother's death, this book included some ninety opinions by persons who knew him intimately in one aspect or another. As his literary executor I had decided that, in the case of a man with so many facets, a collection of first-hand material would be more illuminating, as well as more authoritative, than an official biography. I also thought it would help all future biographers to check the validity of their own judgments: I now find, however, that I did not make sufficient allowance for intellectual perversity.

In the course of his contribution to this book the late Field-Marshal Earl Wavell observed:

> He (T. E. Lawrence) will always have his detractors, those who sneer at the 'Lawrence legend'; who ascribe his successes with the Arabs to gold; who view the man as a charlatan in search of notoriety by seeming to seek obscurity; who regard his descent from colonel to private as evidence of some morbid *nostalgie de la boue*. They knew not the man. . . .

From press cuttings which reached me in West Africa I gather that a book is expected to appear in which a detractor of the kind Lord Wavell had in mind has devoted his abilities as a novelist to a steady denigration of my brother.

Clearly no such attack can be restricted to the target of a single dead man; those who spoke well of him from their personal knowledge may well be made to appear fools, hypocrites or partners in a fraud. In their defence and his, therefore, this abridged edition of *T. E. Lawrence by his Friends* is being published sooner than had been intended.

A. W. L<small>AWRENCE</small>

Achimota, Gold Coast
April 1954

CONTENTS

CONTENTS

THE WAR: HIS COMMANDERS

THE WAR: IN ACTION

THE WAR AND AFTER

PUBLICITY

EASTERN POLITICS

POST-WAR GENERAL VIEWS

PERSONAL CRISIS

CONTENTS

DATES IN THE LIFE OF T. E. LAWRENCE

Born 1888
Oxford High School, September 1896 to July 1907
    In northern France studying castles, summers of 1906 and 1907
Jesus College, Oxford, October 1907 to June 1910
    In France studying castles, summer of 1908
    In Syria studying castles, summer of 1909
    Wrote *Crusader Castles*, winter of 1909-1910
In France studying medieval pottery, summer of 1910
At Jebail in Syria studying Arabic, winter of 1910-1911
Excavating at Carchemish (Jerablus) under D. G. Hogarth and R.
    Campbell Thompson, March and April 1911; under Campbell
    Thompson, April to July 1911
    Walk through northern Mesopotamia, summer of 1911
Excavating in Egypt under Flinders Petrie, beginning of 1912
Excavating at Carchemish under C. L. Woolley, spring 1912 to
    spring 1914
    At home in Oxford, summer of 1913
    Survey of Sinai, January to February 1914
At Oxford and London, summer of 1914, completing *Wilderness of*
    Zin (report on Sinai work), eventually at the War Office
In Egypt, December 1914 to October 1916
    Journey to 'Iraq, March to May 1916
With Arab forces, October 1916 to October 1918
In London and Oxford, October to December 1918
In Paris for Peace Conference, January to October 1919
    By air to Egypt, May 1919
At All Souls College, Oxford, and in London, October 1919-1921
Adviser, Colonial Office, 1921-1922.
    On missions to Aden, Jedda and Transjordan, August to December 1921
Aircraftman Ross, Royal Air Force, latter half of 1922 to January
    1923
    Discharged on discovery of his identity
Private Shaw, Royal Tank Corps, March 1923 to August 1925
    Acquired cottage at Clouds Hill, Dorset
    Transferred to Royal Air Force
Aircraftman Shaw, Royal Air Force, August 1925 to March 1935
    Seven Pillars of Wisdom published 1926, at 30 guineas.
    In India, January 1927 to 1928; *Revolt in the Desert* published
        and withdrawn in British Empire; *The Mint* completed;
        Marine Craft (speed boats) 1930-1935
Died after motor-cycling accident near Clouds Hill, May 1935

INTRODUCTORY

LORD HALIFAX

An address delivered in St. Paul's Cathedral, London, on the occasion of the unveiling of a bust of T. E. Lawrence on January 29th, 1936.

THE RIGHT HON. THE EARL OF HALIFAX,
K.G., G.C.S.I., P.C., O.M. Born 1881. Parliamentary Under-
Secretary for the Colonies, 1921-22 (when T. E. L. was in
Colonial Office); Viceroy of India (as Lord Irwin), 1926-31;
President of Board of Education, 1932-35; Secretary of State
for War, 1935; Lord Privy Seal, 1935-37; Leader of the House
of Lords, 1935-38 and 1940; Lord President of Council, 1937-
38; Secretary of State for Foreign Affairs, 1938-40; British
Ambassador at Washington, 1941-46; Chancellor of Oxford
University and of Sheffield University.

I TAKE it as an honour paid to the University of Oxford
that her Chancellor should have been selected to perform
this ceremony, and to say something about one of the most
remarkable of Oxford's sons. It is my misfortune that it
never fell to me to enjoy that close friendship with him, the
memory of which is the possession of many here, so it cannot
be of their Lawrence that I must principally try to speak.
Rather from a standpoint more detached must I make some
attempt to appraise the character and performance which we
here commemorate.

It is significant how strongly the personality of Lawrence
has gripped the imagination of his countrymen. To comparatively few was he intimately known; his fame rested upon
achievement in distant corners of the world; to the vast
majority he was a figure, legendary, elusive, whose master
motives lay far outside their cognizance. So true it is that men
often admire most what they are least able to understand.

There has been no character in our generation which has
more deeply impressed itself upon the mind of youth. Many
of us can remember, when we began to be told stories, how
impatiently we used to ask the teller if it were really true;
and Lawrence's life is better than any fairy story. As we
hear it we are transported back to the days of medieval
chivalry, and then we remember that these things happened
not yet twenty years ago, and were mainly due to a force present
in one man, that we acknowledge under the title of personality.

To Lawrence in an especial sense Oxford played the part
of understanding guardian. Trained of old to discern the

14

signs, she readily knew in him the divine spark that men call genius, tended and breathed upon it, until self-taught, it kindled into flame. And it is perhaps not untrue to say that the discovery by Lawrence himself of his own powers and destiny was in no small measure due to their earlier recognition at Oxford by Dr. Hogarth, whom he was accustomed to describe as a great man and the best friend he ever had. So, with the stamp of her approval, Lawrence set forth from Oxford eastwards, a crusader of the twentieth century on behalf of peoples and causes which must remain for ever associated with his name.

It was an accident that this phase of Lawrence's life should have synchronized with that most searching trial of his country which was the occasion of his rendering her such signal service. He had long dreamed of the restoration to freedom of the inhabitants of Palestine and Arabia, and it was through the reactions of the great war upon those lands that the chance came to realize his dreams. Others worked with him through the perils of the strangest warfare that those years witnessed, and share with him the glory of achievement. But he, as his collaborators were first to own, was the inspiration and fiery soul of the revolt which shattered Turkish misrule and made freemen of the children of the desert.

In 1914 Lawrence was barely twenty-six, known only to Oxford and the small circle of his friends; when the war ended his name was on the lips of all the world. For nearly three years he had organized and directed against the enemy a race of nomadic tribesmen, difficult of combination in sustained military effort, and, great captain that he was, had turned what might have seemed their chief disadvantage to the invention of a new strategy. Conscious that he had at last found a cause to which he could consecrate all his energies, privation and physical danger became only incidents in the attainment of the great end of his endeavour. By true gift of leadership he was able to communicate to others his own standard of achievement. Each man who looked to Lawrence for instructions knew that he was asked to undertake no duty that his leader would not, and could not better, discharge himself. Small wonder that he could count upon a devoted loyalty almost unique in the annals of military adventure, a loyalty which over and over again carried forlorn hopes to complete success.

The campaign ended, Lawrence found himself engaged in what was for him the more arduous struggle of the peace. Even before the war ended questions to which for him only one answer could be given were being caught up in cross-currents of international policy and rival national interests. The mark that these days left upon him was deep and ineffaceable. The strain of their anxieties was heightened by the strain of writing his own record of events, to which at whatever cost he felt impelled by historical necessity.

Even at Oxford, where he sought in All Souls to find the rest that the University offers to her returning sons, he found himself unable to escape the burden that pressed upon his soul. Relentless his fame pursued him, forced him from Oxford, made him fly even from himself, to find in change of name, scene, and occupation that loss of identity through which he hoped to win reprieve from his distress.

Thus he came to join the humblest ranks of the Royal Air Force, the youngest of the Services. The future lay with youth, and here for Lawrence was the very embodiment of youth, with all its life before it. His imagination became suddenly on fire with the thought of what the air should be. Sharing its fortunes on terms of simple comradeship, he might inspire the young Service upon whose quality he felt that some day the safety of his country might depend. He called the conquest of the air the one big thing left for our generation to do. To his decision we owe it that he was able to put into final form the narrative of those desert days, in prose which will live so long as men read the English language, and give Lawrence yet another claim to immortality.

These years from 1922 to 1934 among the unnamed rank and file were perhaps the happiest of his life. Both his mechanical and creative sense were satisfied in the work of perfecting the new speed-boats for the Air Force, and when he returned to private life it was a man restored, desiring yet doubting the taste of leisure, who went to make a quiet home for himself deep in the land of Wessex, beloved of that other master of the English tongue whom he so much revered. Here it was that after a few brief weeks he met catastrophe in what seems to have been characteristic sacrifice of self to avoid collision, and a week later died.

So passed Lawrence of Arabia, leaving behind him a memory and an example. For he always maintained that he was no more than the average of his time; what he could do another might, granted the will and the opportunity.

What was the secret of the almost mesmeric power that he exerted? So different was he from other men that they could often only catch part of his singularly complex personality, and it is perhaps just in this difficulty of judging the man whole that lies the true evidence and measure of his greatness. Nor, with his strain of puckishness, was Lawrence himself averse from deepening a mystery, at times not less baffling to himself than to many of his friends. No one can read his private letters, in some ways the most arresting of his literary work, without being conscious of sharply alternating moods, almost the conflict of competing personalities.

But, this said, there are certain fixed points that hold firm in contemporary judgment. All those who knew him agree that he possessed some quality to be best described as mastery over life. While, like all men, he owed much to the influence of heredity and environment, he, more than most men, had or acquired the capacity to mould life instead of lending himself to be moulded by it. Here lay the secret of his command over affairs, over others, and last, but not least, over himself. It is seldom that the direction of world events can be so clearly attributed to the dynamic force of a single individual. He saw a vision which to the ordinary man would have seemed like fantasy, and by the sheer force of his character made it real. From his fellows he drew without exertion an allegiance unquestioning and absolute. Most men when they are asked to give are tempted, like Ananias, to keep something back, but Lawrence asked everything, and, because of the authority with which the demand was made, everything was given. Many elements contributed to the acceptance of this superiority, unchallenged and unsought. Great powers of intellect, of imagination, of intuitive understanding of other men's thought, but above all else must rank the overwhelming conviction that he gave of moral purpose.

It was not merely that he brought to bear upon life the concentrated strength of all his being, but that this faculty was eloquent of victory in the stern struggle for self-conquest. All the things that clog — ambition, the competitive race, possessions, the appetites of the natural man — all must give way if real freedom is to be won. Life, free, unhampered, unalloyed, alone deserves the name. As he said: 'The gospel of bareness in materials is a good one.'

I cannot tell what fed the consuming fire that made him so different from the common run of men. It has been said of him that no man was ever more faithful at any cost to the inner voice of conscience. Everything he did fell under the lash of his own self-criticism, and the praise of men was unsatisfying and distasteful. But I cannot doubt some deep religious impulse moved him; not, I suppose, that which for others is interpreted through systems of belief and practice, but rather some craving for the perfect synthesis of thought and action which alone could satisfy his test of ultimate truth and his conception of life's purpose.

Strange how he loved the naked places of the earth, which seemed to match the austerity of life as he thought that it should be lived. And so he loved the desert where wide spaces are lost in distance, and, wanderer himself, found natural kinship with the wandering peoples of his adopted home.

His was the cry of Paracelsus:

I am a wanderer: I remember well
One journey, how I feared the track was missed
So long the city I desired to reach

Lay hid: when suddenly its spires afar
Flashed through the circling clouds: you may conceive
My transport: soon the vapours closed again:
But I had seen the city: and one such glance
No darkness could obscure.

Yet side by side with this craving to accomplish ran
another strand of feeling that lifts the veil from the inner
struggle which I suppose grew harder in his later years.
In August 1934 he was writing to a friend about his own
disquiet: 'I think it is in part because I am sorry to be dropping
out. One of the sorest things in life is to come to realize that
one is just not good enough. Better perhaps than some, than
many almost. But I do not care for relatives, for matching
myself against my kind. There is an ideal standard somewhere,
and only that matters, and I cannot find it. . . .'

There we must leave it, for the waters of genius run too
deep for human measure.

Lawrence himself was never free from the challenge of
his nature's secret. Perhaps he came nearer to the answer
during those last days when he lay in the uncharted land
between life and death, and saw his life no longer in part,
but whole before him. Once more, it may be, he visited the
Norman castles which first in boyhood had excited his romantic
sense, or walked again amid the ancient works of Palestine.
Or there came back to him the vision of the endless desert,
rocking in the mirage of the fierce heat of noontide, and once
more he trod the dusty ways of Akaba, Azrak, and the city of
the Caliphs, and last of all, of his beloved Damascus, with her
green gardens by the river, these fading in turn before the
places of his spiritual hermitage, Henlow, Bovington, Cranwell, and the Air Force stations of India — Peshawar, Miranshah, Karachi. And before the end came, I like to think that
he saw again the spires of Oxford, unearthly in their beauty,
set in the misty blue of early May, until at last he reached no
earthly city, but that city of his vision where he might see no
longer as through a glass darkly, and know at length as he was
known.

HOME

S. LAWRENCE
M. R. LAWRENCE
ERNEST W. COX

MY second son Thomas Edward was born at Tremadoc, Carnarvonshire, in the early hours of August 16th, 1888. He was a big, strong, active child; constantly on the move. He could pull himself up over the nursery gate some months before he could walk. When he was thirteen months old we left Wales and took a house at Kirkcudbright in the south of Scotland, where we remained till he was nearly three. During the time we were there he learned the alphabet without a single lesson from hearing his elder brother taught. The house we were in was sold, so we had to move. We went to the Isle of Man for a few weeks, where he had his third birthday; then on to Jersey for three months, and in December 1891 we went to Dinard. They had lessons from an English governess and he learned to read well. For a short time towards the end of 1893 they went to the Frères school which was close to where we lived, for an hour in the mornings. Twice a week he and his elder brother went with three other little English boys to a private gymnastic class in St. Malo that he greatly enjoyed. In the spring of 1894 we left France and took a small place at Langley on the borders of the New Forest; there they led a very free, happy life for over two years. They had lessons from a governess, and the schoolmaster gave them lessons in Latin, to prepare them for going to school; he could read English easily and his memory was remarkable, any book he took up he seemed to read at a glance, but he knew it all, as I soon found out. No tree was too high for him to climb and I never knew him to have a fall. He learned to swim, and to ride a pony while at Langley. There was a brick-pit near; he got clay from it and made some cups which he baked in the kitchen oven, and was so disappointed when he found they were porous. When the Fleet was at Spithead we took him on a steamer to see the ships. I missed him on deck, and found him curled up in the saloon reading Macaulay's *Introduction to the History of England*. When he was eight years old we moved to Oxford, September 1896, and he became a day pupil at the City of Oxford High School for Boys, where he remained till he went to Jesus College. The late Mr. A. W. Cave, M.A., was the headmaster; he was a man entirely devoted to his work, who did his utmost to bring out the best in every boy. The school had a wonderful list of open scholarships to the University, gained while he was headmaster. Lessons were never any trouble to Ned, he won prizes every year, and as they were allowed to choose the books they liked, he got two on the history of Egypt. He was constantly reading the Oxford *Helps to the Study of the Bible*. He bought two second-hand books on Layard's Excavations of Nineveh: they had a great influence on him; he almost knew them by heart. In the Senior Locals in 1906 he came first in English Language and Literature out of all the many thousands. He passed in nineteen papers, getting distinction in Scripture (3rd place) and was placed 13th in the First Class. As far as I can remember there were only 120 got Firsts that year, out of some 10,000. The Locals were very different then from what they are now. I mention these things because it has often been said that he did not like being at school; he always took a keen interest in his work and was very happy. When out in the playground one day at 11 o'clock, he saw a small boy being bullied by a bigger one; he went to the rescue. They had a struggle and fell and one of the bones in Ned's leg got broken near the ankle; he was wearing boots that day which helped to support it. He walked into the school, supporting himself by the wall, and did his mathematics till 1 o'clock. He told his brothers that he had hurt his leg and could not walk home, so they put him on a bicycle and wheeled him back. From our description the doctor gathered it was broken, and brought up a splint and set it. He was out of school for a term; it took a long time to get right. He never grew much after that — he had grown very fast just before (three inches in a year), so evidently the bones were not strong. During his convalescence he read extensively, and for a change he did a lot of poker work. From the time he was quite a small boy he was very interested in brass-rubbing, and went to all the churches in and around Oxford; and when he got older made long journeys on his cycle to every place in England which had famous brasses of Knights; he covered the walls of his bedroom with them, and they made a wonderful show, especially by firelight: some of them were over life size. He took the greatest pains over everything he did, and was always full of enthusiasm about all he was doing in work or play, and was always so good and kind to everyone.

He was for many years a constant worshipper at St. Aldate's Church and taught in the Sunday School there twice every Sunday. He had the great privilege of Canon A. M. W. Christopher's gospel teaching from his early years till he left Oxford in 1910. After the Canon retired from St. Aldate's all my sons went to a class for students which he held in his home every Sunday afternoon during Term.

During the Christmas holidays one year Ned and another schoolfellow determined to try to canoe up the Cherwell to Banbury; the river was in flood, and they just managed to get the Rob Roy through Magdalen Bridge. All went well till they got above the mill at Islip, when the strong current swept the boat under a tree, and it turned over. Ned had a thick rug wound round his legs, and he sank. When he came up, his friend caught him, and they got safe to land. They walked back in the dusk to Polstead Road, going to the miller on the way to let him know they were safe, and asking him to keep a look-out for the boat. Next day they returned and found it and the paddles and rug, but his companion had had enough and would not go into it again, so Ned and his brother Will took the boat back to Salters, but he did not give up his project. During the Easter holidays, he and Will succeeded in doing so. I think it took them three days. They left the canoe each night near one of the L.N.W. stations, returning home by train to sleep, and the next day going by train to the place they had left it. They sent us a wire from Banbury to let us know they had accomplished their self-imposed task.

When he began history a separate study was needed, so we had a very pretty well-built bungalow of two rooms made for him at the end of the garden. It had a Devon grate, electric light, and water laid on, and a telephone to the house. He hung the walls of the sitting-room with fine green bolton sheeting, which dulled the sounds and made it a very quiet room: there he did all his University work, wrote the Thesis, and also in August 1914 wrote *The Wilderness of Zin*.

There is not a word of truth in the story that he used to stay out at night till all hours, and come back and get in by a window to his room. He had lessons from a history coach, Mr. L. C. Jane, who began teaching him during his last year at school; he continued going to him till he took his Finals in June 1910. They arranged during the last year that he was always to be the last pupil, so as to give him extra time. He usually got home about 11 to 11.30. The outer door was always left unlocked and the key of the inner one was kept on a ledge over a window in the porch. When he came in he locked the outer door and passed through the house into the garden. He never did any of the stupid things attributed to him — they are pure inventions. He was most orderly and punctual: if he said he would be back at a certain hour, even if he was going on a long cycle ride, he was always there at the time.

For about three years he gave up eating meat, and lived on a vegetable, milk and egg diet. For breakfast he always had porridge and milk, never touched tea or coffee; sometimes if he was going for a long ride he would ask us to have porridge ready for him on his return. Cakes and fruit he liked. He was very strong and healthy, and could ride over a hundred miles a day on his bicycle (not a motor bicycle). He was always so full of life and told us of everything he was doing, or intending to do. We never had a dull moment when he and his brother Will were in the house, they discussed all the topics of the day. They were a most happy band of brothers. When the youngest was a tiny child, our faithful old nurse turned ill and had to go home. Ned delighted to help me to look after him; he used to come back on half holidays and say 'Mother, may I take him out?' and it was the greatest pleasure for him to wheel him down to the football field (he was nearly twelve years older than the baby). When the child was about three he took him to the Ashmolean Museum. The little boy clasped him round the neck and said, 'Are they all alive?' when he saw the statues. After they got home Ned carved a face on a stone in the garden and then gave the child a hammer to break it up, so that he would not be afraid.

He was never idle — brass-rubbing, wood carving, putting old pottery together, etc.; he brought back quantities of it, which he got the men engaged on digging deep foundations for houses in the city to keep for him. He put the fragments together with plasticine, and built up many fine pots and jugs, etc., of things broken and thrown away hundreds of years before. A lot was found under the present Masonic Hall and also in Cornmarket Street, when they were building a big shop; he paid the workmen to keep every morsel they found. A number of these pots are now in the Ashmolean Museum at Oxford. The study of old pottery took him constantly to the Ashmolean, and it was while arranging the medieval cases there with the Assistant Keeper that he first came in contact with Mr. D. G. Hogarth, who had just become Keeper. In the summer holidays of 1906-7-8 he cycled all over France, visiting the old ruined castles, photographing, drawing, and planning them; he sent us long letters describing all he saw and did. After he got home he had a bad attack of Mediter-ranean fever from drinking goats' milk. In June 1909 he went to Syria, and walked about the country for three months. He had spoken about lessons in Arabic to Prof. Margoliouth, who gave him the name of Mr. Odeh, who lived in Oxford. Ned was with him only a short time and knew very little when he started for Syria, but he studied hard on the way out. Mr. Hogarth had given him an introduction to Mr. Doughty who very kindly gave him much useful information about the Arabs; and he almost knew *Arabia Deserta* by heart. Lord Curzon obtained an *Iradé* from the Turkish Government for him which proved most valuable. It gave him many privileges, entry to buildings, safe conduct, etc., etc. He visited all the important ruined castles of the Crusading periods; many of these were in places most difficult to get at up in the hills. He had a suit of strong lightweight material made with many pockets, in which he carried all' his things. His shirts were made of thin delaine fastened by tiny glove buttons; he carried a spare one and a spare pair of stockings, a camera and many packets of films, of a sort now unobtainable — they were excellent. The photos are as good now as the day he took them. We have just had a new set printed from them. He ran many risks, once a man tried to murder him, robbing, and leaving him insensible. He had several bad attacks of fever, and towards the end his camera was stolen out of a carriage which he had hired to take him to Urfa, the farthest point he reached: to all the other places he went on foot. As a rule he was treated everywhere with great kindness by the people; and often spent some days with them. Missionaries were all very good, and gave him much help. The results of his research were summed up in the Thesis he wrote for his Finals. He got a First Class in the Honours School of History in 1910.

So much has been written about his doings after this period that I will not add more.

He was a most loving son and brother, kind and unselfish, always doing kind deeds in a quiet way; everything that was beautiful in nature or art appealed to him. *Sans peur et sans reproche.*

M . R . L A W R E N C E , b.m., b.ch., m.a. Born 1885, eldest
brother ('Bob') of T.E.L. At Oxford High School with him
1896–1904 ; St. John's College, Oxford; Royal Army Medical
Corps (in France), 1916–1919. China Inland Mission, 1921.

I WAS two years and eight months older than my brother
Ned, and as all five of us were educated at the City of
Oxford High School we were always together. He was
remarkably quick at learning and I was slow, so we were more
companionable than most brothers. We had a very happy
childhood, which was never marred by a single quarrel
between any of us. Our parents were constantly with us, to our
great delight and profit, for they shared in our progress,
made the home the place of peace it was, planned the future
and our education, and were the greatest influences in our
lives.

We were always busy and the days were never too long.
Although I was older, he was the leader in all our games.
This included, one day, jumping down from the loft of a wood
shed on to the grass, and mother from the house was horrified
to see Will, then not six, following us down this twelve foot
high jump! Truly there is a Guardian watching over children,
otherwise they would never survive their actions! And Ned
himself, before he was two, followed his father up a steep
ladder into a loft and a little voice calling 'Daddy' gave the
first indication of his safely accomplished feat!

When we were small and shared a large bedroom, he used
to tell a story which went on night after night without any end.
It was a story of adventure, and successful defence of a tower
against numerous foes, and the chief characters were Fizzy-
Fuz, Pompey, and Pete — fur animal dolls that my brothers
had. Long pieces of rhyme telling of the exploits and achievements were composed by him, and this was before he was
nine!

We used to go round this room springing from one bed to

27

the next via the three chests of drawers without touching the floor. Sitting up and swinging our bodies backwards and forwards we became quite adept in propelling the beds all over the room. We were taught privately by governesses till we went to school in Oxford. When he was about five he was able to read the *Standard* newspaper upside down; and in after life he told us he could always read the newspaper of the man opposite him in the train. He was five and a half years old when we left France and settled in Langley on the borders of the New Forest, within easy reach of the Solent at Lepe. There we got to know by sight all the boats that passed, and the large racing yachts from Cowes were always a source of interest and beauty. Among the stones of the beach were fossils, and after the rest of us had been hunting hard, he used to pick up the best ones seemingly without any trouble. We went down to the shore one evening to see the illuminations of the Fleet at Spithead. A heavy thunderstorm came on and drenched us till we took refuge in the Lepe coastguard station, where they kindly fitted us out with varied kinds of clothing. As may be imagined some garments were far too big for us, and my brother kept the whole party, parents included, in fits of laughter at his antics all the way back. In the garden of the house were two high fir trees into which we dragged up boards to make look-out places. When going to Langley Lodge for the first time Father and Mother took T.E. (we always called him Ned) with them to look after him, leaving the rest of us with our nurse in Southampton to follow later. In the course of the morning Mother mentioned that she thought she had heard thunder. He said, 'No, it is guns firing'. On asking, 'How do you know?' his reply was, 'Because I climbed to the top of the tree and saw the smoke'. My third brother, W.G. (Will), was only sixteen months younger, and they were almost like twins and devoted to one another. Later we spent several summer holidays in Langley, and had a tent close to the shore in which we slept.

In August 1898 and 1899 Father took a thatched cottage outside Yarmouth in the Isle of Wight on the hill-side west of the bridge over the Yar. It was in a field touching a wood in which we roamed at will, and not far from the beach beyond the harbour where we bathed and played on the sands. We always enjoyed visits to Alum Bay to see the coloured cliffs, and it was he who came across 'Mother Large's Well', a spring of fresh water at the foot of the rocks far round to the western side of the bay. The poet Tennyson's house and monument on top of the Downs above Freshwater, and Carisbrooke Castle with its memories of King Charles I, we knew well and he took great notice of the donkey which drew up the water from the deep well of the keep by walking in the large wheel. Unfortunately for us Myrtle Cottage was sold and enlarged, and our times there came to an end.

We also learnt to sew by making large flags of various countries in real bunting, and to scale.

In September 1896, when he was eight years old, Father brought us to Oxford for education. Soon afterwards Ned and Will were together at the end of the garden in a one-room outhouse intended for a laundry (his own house in the garden was not built till years later). Will said, 'I wonder what is in that pipe, Ned'. He replied, 'I do not know, but we will soon see', and thereupon took a hammer and drove a nail into it! Father was soused with water before he succeeded in stopping the hole with a plug of wood, and then had to get a man sent up to do the necessary repair. There was reason for his disgust as he told Mother, 'Bother take the little brat! He has gone and put a nail into the pipe!'

In spite of the above, Ned was always the one to mend any object, or find out what was wrong with the electric light, etc. When sent for anything Will never waited to hear half the directions, but was off like an arrow from the bow, but after searching round had to come back wondering for what he had been looking! My errands, too, were often fruitless, but Ned was sure to bring exactly what was needed.

Polstead Road was so close to Port Meadow that we often went there for a walk, and when the floods came, took canoes and paddled over it as far up as the Green Mound. Ned and

Will began to excavate this one day, thinking it might be a barrow, but did not get far enough to find anything. At the Oxford High School we were under Mr. A. W. Cave, to whose memory we owe a great debt of gratitude for the care and attention he gave to us individually. He was a marvellous headmaster, and knew exactly how each boy was doing. He simply lived for his work, and if any of the boys got into trouble or difficulties he spared no pains to help them. He was ably assisted by an excellent and willing staff of assistant masters. At that time the school had a splendid governing body composed of senior members of the University. The statement has been made that Ned did not enjoy his school-days, but that is quite a mistake. He was happy, good at gymnastics, and took part in games in the playground, but cricket and football had no interest for him. In addition he and Will were the leading spirits in a long series of cross-country paperchases. He was always unselfish, as the following will show. In my last term I was doing special work, but was reckoned to be still in the Fifth Form. In the Scripture examination Ned left the paper unfinished on purpose to let me get the prize, and was very disappointed when he found he was first with 86 marks; I came next with 80. During his last year (May 1907) he discovered that the Headmaster was completing twenty-one years at the school, and enthusiastically took up the idea of making him a presentation from every boy then in the school. They got a gold watch and chain which came as a great surprise to Mr. Cave. This watch is still going perfectly.

There was another figure, every remembrance of whom is a delight, and it will be long before Oxford sees his like again. The beloved Canon Christopher was completing his forty-six years at St. Aldate's, and as we attended there Ned knew him well, and while still at school began to have a Sunday School class. This involved walking down to Folly Bridge twice each Sunday (five miles in all). The class became devoted to him and he had the same boys for the next three or four years and corresponded with them when he was on his cycle tours.

Each summer he took them for an afternoon on the upper river to Godstow. This they enjoyed immensely for they did the rowing — such as it was — themselves. There was never any accident, but we were relieved to get them all back safely. Then in the winter they came up to the house for an evening, and one of the games was to pick up sixpences lying in a bath of warm water two inches deep. They knelt beside the bath, locked their hands behind them, and had to get the sixpences with their mouths under water. Some got quite expert and fished for those who could not manage it.

He was also for two to three years an officer in the St. Aldate's Company of the Church Lads' Brigade.

One day a magnificent blue Persian cat appeared on the wall and took up his abode with us. Repeated attempts to return him to his home were met by teeth and claws vigorously applied. Eventually his owner — then a small boy — gave him to us in exchange for a bicycle, which he thought was much the better part of the bargain. Accustomed as he was to the savage dogs of the East we wondered whether Ned would take to him. But we found him with the cat on his knees stroking it, and he remarked, 'I think this is the most beautiful animal I have ever seen'.

ERNEST W. COX, M.A.OXON. Assistant Master at Oxford
High School, 1882-1902. Vicar of Steyning, Sussex, 1919-45.

GENIUS is a thing apart — yet in the making of a man
much depends upon the stock from which he has sprung,
and the environment which has surrounded his early
days.

The Lawrence family were all boys — five of them altogether.
And manly boys they were; yet each was possessed of a certain
gentleness of disposition which made up for any possible lack
of a sister's influence. They owed much to the quality of the
home in which they were reared; and far more to the loving
devotion of their father and their mother, for it was they who
so firmly implanted in each of their boys that high sense of the
unfailing duty which they owed alike to God and to their
neighbour.

After a lapse of some six and thirty years the remembrance
of each of them still remains distinct in the memory of one
who was favoured to be not only their schoolmaster, but also
their neighbour and their friend; and yet — though each one
stands out clear — it has always been difficult to think of those
boys apart, so real was the influence which each had upon the
character development of the others.

The eldest four were not far separated in age; but that short
priority which nature conferred in the order of their birth was
continually recognized in the precedence which the younger
ones ever yielded to those who were older. This was, perhaps,
an early mark of that discipline of character which strengthened
them in the later hour of national need; but there was a certain
quaintness in the way in which this seniority was respected by
those four young boys as they bicycled every day to school.
They formed an attractive group, for their mother had obtained
for each of them a jersey of alternating bands of white and
navy blue, and thus uniformly clad the four every morning rode
to school in orderly formation, in evenly spaced single file,

well in on the near side of the road, and always in that same descending order — the eldest in front and the youngest last.

The eldest of the family was Bob — conscientious, solicitous, always kind; one in whom even in those early days spiritual values had a place. Of those four he now alone survives; and to him the other three owed far more than they ever knew.

And then there was Ned — one of few words, self-possessed, purposeful, inscrutable. He was just like other boys in most things, but differed from them mainly in that he gave rise to a sense of hidden possibilities — a feeling that there was a latent something just out of reach. He was clear of mind and not readily perturbed; but he was self-reliant and one could feel in him an instinctive recoil when he was being pressed into a way that he did not feel inclined to go. There was no robustness of body to suggest those future powers of physical endurance; but that short quick step with which he walked told of an alertness of mind and body; whilst there was depth and seriousness of purpose in that steady and unyielding gaze with which, with head slightly bowed, he looked up into the eyes of those who spoke with him.

And next after him came Will — one beautiful to look upon; and already as a boy possessed of a certain gravity of mind and character which gave full promise of that fine early manhood which was cut off so early in the War.

And then last of the four was Frank — a dear boy; lovable and greatly loved; one whose happiness and radiant smile remain an enduring and ever helpful memory. He joined the Army in August 1914, and was killed in France on the 9th of the following May.

Here then was an ideal family of boys, a very band of brothers — united, conscientious, strong in character, clean alike in limb and in life; each influencing and shaping the others in ways that he knew not of; boys in whom the affections, too, were kept strong and active by the presence in their home of their brother Arnold — some years younger than themselves.

THE BOY AND THE MAN

T. W. CHAUNDY

E. F. HALL

E. T. LEEDS

C. F. C. BEESON

ERNEST BARKER

T. W. C H A U N D Y, Lecturer in Mathematics, Student and Tutor of Christ Church, Oxford. Born 1889. At Oxford High School (with T.E.L.) 1896-1906; lecturer, 1910; Ministry of Munitions, Inventions Department, 1915-18.

AT school the Lawrences first began to impress my awakening consciousness by the regularity with which new members of the family appeared, in seemingly inexhaustible supply: each in a dark blue-and-white striped jersey that became almost a uniform, the softness of the wool matching a certain gentleness of speech and fairness of face. Out of this prolonged family Lawrence II gradually became distinct by a spareness of body and a pithy energy of speech. Our paths did not much overlap, I think, till we reached the fifth form: there, with some glee, he encouraged me to work all his algebra for him, in return flattering any attempts of mine to write English. He was then best known, almost to notoriety, for his archaeological rummagings (with C. F. C. Beeson) in and about Oxford. Every excavation and rebuilding in the city was penetrated, and fragments of glass and stoneware zealously recovered: a cellar in the old wall bounding the school was identified as a one-time place of confinement for 'hussies'; and we became familiar with medieval names of the Oxford streets, Fish Street, Canditch, Horsemonger Street, one of which the soldier burnt down through over-roasting a pig. The country churches round were ransacked for brasses, and his schoolfellows learnt the virtues of heel-ball. In one such ransacking I took part. In Waterperry Church there were brasses inaccessible behind some pews. Lawrence, already ruthless, made short work of the obstruction, and I still hear the splintering woodwork and his short laugh, almost sinister to my timorous ears.

As an undergraduate our subjects and colleges lay apart. It seemed a little odd, I remember, to find him in our company of scholarship-hunters; though obviously an 'intellectual', he lacked, we thought, our narrower devotion to things academically profitable. Such contacts as we had were mainly

35

literary: he awakened my attention to medieval literature and to fine printing.

When, after taking our degrees, he moved down to Magdalen and I to Christ Church, I began to hear from him of his work at Carchemish, of the mysteries of the Hittite language and of the crucial virtues of a bi-lingual inscription.

Under his guidance I made the passage of the Trill Mill stream. This stream, which had medieval importance, now runs underground from 'The Friars' and emerges in the Christ Church memorial garden: our equipment included candles for the darkness, and a pistol to waken the echoes beneath St. Aldate's. As I embarked, very much a 'passenger', Lawrence said: 'Be careful: you have there the most precious life in Oxford!' I did not miss either the irony or the friendliness of the remark.

During the war years I did not see him, but when he returned to Oxford with an All Souls Fellowship, we met fairly often. He came to lunch: and talked of the many tastes of water. At tea in his rooms he showed us, rather proudly, a scrap of Elizabethan wall-paper he had found in some corner of the college. He told us there of his ideal library: a bare minimum (it seemed almost a nudist ideal!) of some hundred and fifty books, each a paragon of print and binding. To move toward this ideal he lent books open-handedly, that were not always easy to return. We admired the luxurious chairs in his rooms. 'Yes, they are a motor-car. A millionaire for whom I had done a service, saving him some thousands, wanted to give me a car: but what could I do with a car?'

He talked sparingly of his experiences in Arabia. He told me gleefully of his device of dropping by air, in the villages behind the Turkish lines, forged certificates of medical exemption. On one occasion he spoke to the University branch of the Fabian Society (without, of course, a single note); he said afterwards that he had been disappointed to find the audience a mixed one, for he had intended to deal faithfully with the tradition that the Turk is a gentleman.

After he left Oxford I did not see him again.

What little I have written here of Lawrence seems to show him as always the devoted antiquary: in Oxford or beyond it. Perhaps even Arabia should be seen as a triumph of archaeology: the piecing together with heroic skill and patience of the scattered fragments of an ancient people which, as a completed work, he had planned to set up on a noble, damascene base.

As I look back (with perhaps the natural conceit of the Oxford-born) I think of Lawrence as the perfect Oxonian. His upbringing in the old Oxford before petrol fed his love of ancient beauty, and both city and school taught a certain austerity. The town was then more manageable, had its history written more plainly across it, could be walked out of. To grow up in that Oxford was a sufficient education.

Through the University he followed — in externals — the perfect academic pattern: exhibitioner, senior demy, fellow. It is true that he escaped the cramping schoolmastery of a tutorship: but even the don, as Belloc has shown him, is characteristically an authority on some subject quite other than his professed study. Lawrence loved learning and the past, fine writing finely produced. He took the whole of life, not excluding science and invention, for his province. Like Oxford itself, he had that quiescence that is not lethargy, but poise and preparation: to his contemporaries and posterity a man of action, to himself a dreamer.

Archdeacon E. F. HALL. Born 1888. Oxford High School, 1900-07, and Jesus College, Oxford, 1907-11 (with T. E. L.); schoolmaster, vicar; now Archdeacon of Totnes and Canon Residentiary of Exeter.

MY earliest recollection of Lawrence is that of sitting by his side in the Lower Fourth at school, establishing to my satisfaction that I was exactly one day his senior in age, to be met by the retort that this was unfortunate, since it prevented me from being born, as he was, on Napoleon's birthday. Thus early was the future taking shape.

My last is of a lazy afternoon off Plymouth towards the end of his service at Mount Batten Air Station. We were in his motor boat — a strange-looking craft with its two motor-car headlamps mounted on the bows. He explained that it had been a speedboat, built for an American, which had developed an interesting habit of catching fire, but he had redesigned it; it was his sole luxury, and its appetite for petrol had made it necessary to supplement an aircraftman's pay by such trifles as translating the *Odyssey* for an American firm. He proceeded to show its paces by 'hops' of a mile or two at a time, till we moored on the Tamar. He was in a discursive, ruminative mood and for a couple of hours roamed over the past, present and future. He spoke of early days at school and college, of Kitchener and the Palestine exploration, of Foch (with criticism), of Winston Churchill (with gratitude), of Allenby (with something approaching veneration), of G. B. Shaw and D. H. Lawrence, of sex and sexlessness, of success and failure. He was his old self, impish, whimsical, flippant and serious by turn. Regrets? Yes, one — that the diminutive bicycle, specially built for him by Lord Nuffield's own hands for his first wanderings across France, had been stolen outside All Souls. I remembered the packing of its toolbag and the search for a shirt which could be folded into matchbox size to accompany his toothbrush — his sole baggage for the fortnight's journey. I remembered too the glee with which he related the peasants' crossing of themselves against the evil-eye as this strange, hatless and dusty apparition flashed through their villages.

In a serious interlude I ventured on the straight question: 'Why this ten years' self-banishment in the Air Force?' He replied: 'To forget and to be forgotten.' I could not hope to fathom all that those words implied but I understood at least a part — the need of recuperation after so great a mental strain, and the lingering hope, if only a curious Press and Public would agree to forget, that he might have once again returned to the 'digging' which had been his first love. But hope no longer lingered. I suggested that even now there must be some quiet spot where he could dig unhampered and unobserved, but he shook his head. The legend of the 'secret spy' was too well established and no country would grant him a passport, unless, he added with a smile, it might be America or Switzerland, and he had no wish to become a tourist.

He spoke of the cottage in Dorset and the books and translations that would fill his days — and then, with an abrupt transition to the past, there came from him the startling question, 'I wonder which of us all has become most famous?' He persisted, recalling one and another who had been the companions of those early days, and analysing their measure of success and fame. All were Lilliputians, measured by his stature. He seemed to be deliberately outraging that natural modesty and self-effacement which had always been his charm, and yet I felt that once again, as of old, he was drawing the mask over the face of his real self — watching the reaction of his words upon myself. Or was it his own reaction to his own criticism: 'The craving to be famous and the horror of being known to like being known . . . I was a standing court martial on myself'?

That self-analysis in the *Seven Pillars* is too severe, too one-sidedly introspective. It leaves out entirely the generosity and magnanimity of the man. Yet it throws light on the great enigma that Lawrence always was, even at school and college. Perhaps those of us who knew him best in those early days would have added, 'an enigma also to himself'. It was the only explanation we could give of a caprice so whimsical as to baffle all analysis. Of his powers and his ability we had no doubt, but it is safe to say that none of us then recognized in him a future leader of men. His eccentricity seemed too pronounced. Or was it that he always wore a mask, the outer covering of which was at school irreverently termed by us his 'grin'? How often a group of us, absorbed in some discussion of cricket or football, would gradually become conscious of a silent addition to our number, contemplating us with that provocative smile of his, till one of us would seize him and close in friendly wrestling, to feel even then the strength of those iron wrists. One such occasion resulted for him in the accident of a broken leg.

'There was my craving to be liked — so strong and nervous that never could I open myself friendly to another.' Yet, though he took no part in the organized games of school life, he was never unpopular. Any conception of a solitary, moody schoolboy shunning the company of his fellows is wide of the mark. He was far too whimsical in his leg-pulling, too trite in his comments (yet always without malice), too interesting in his hobbies, ever to be unpopular. He had always in his pockets a bit of pottery, or part of a bicycle 3-speed gear (at that time a new invention of which, among us, he was the first and proud possessor), or a brass-rubbing from some country church. I remember the fascination of that rubbing of a man 'eaten of worms' which rumour said that he kept by his bedside while he slept.

As I call to memory the Lawrence of those early days (Augustus John's pencil portrait of later years is striking in its faithfulness), three things remain outstanding — the intensity of those piercing blue eyes, the curiously nervous smile, and the voice of singular charm. There were times when his eyes appeared to burn with the intensity of a soul in pain — they could be positively terrifying after overstrain of work. He came one evening into my rooms in College — he used them freely, as, except for one term only, he lived at home — and began to fire a revolver, blank cartridge fortunately, out of the windows into the Turl. I was left in doubt whether he was play-acting; but one glance at his eyes left no doubt at all that he told the truth when he said that he had been working for forty-five hours at a stretch without food, to test his powers of endurance. I did not realize that he was, in his own later words, 'hardening for a great endeavour'. I thought it was that other side of him — the consuming power of the 'desire to know' — in this case, how much the human frame could stand.

The same blindness of perception left us astonished when he joined the Officers' Training Corps and camped at Tidworth Pennings. We put it down to his idiosyncrasy that when orders were issued forbidding 'sleeping out', he kept the letter of the law by sleeping with his legs inside the tent, and his head among the guy-ropes; and if I remember rightly it was a copy of the *Odyssey* carried inside his tunic pocket that was his constant companion.

It is only now, when memories of half-forgotten incidents come crowding back, that I realize how stern a training he had imposed upon himself, not only, as he says, the body 'for years made trim by constant carelessness', but the brain again and again ruthlessly fast driven. At such times he would find relief in still more impish and wanton problems of conduct, in nocturnal ramblings and quixotic expeditions — yet never purposeless. There was always the governing motive 'to see for myself'. The episode of the Trill Mill stream at Oxford was no madcap adventure. On the contrary, it was planned in every detail. He had been probing into the history of old Oxford and had read in *Wood* of the existence of this stream. He had established its identity at the mouth of a sewer at Hythe Bridge and desired to know if the other outlet was at Folly Bridge. He had brought a candle to stick in the bows of the canoe, and an acetylene cycle-lamp at the stern. As we drifted down the darkness of the sewer, he remarked casually that it would be interesting to notice, as the foulness of the air increased, which light would be extinguished first, also what the attitude of rats might be. 'At any rate', he added, as we lay prone in the canoe, touching the walls of the sewer as we guided it in the darkness, 'there is no room to turn back'. [He had wondered, says another school friend, what would happen if they came to a grating; it is impossible to paddle in some parts of the tunnel, but the draught keeps the air pure. — Ed.]. But Folly Bridge was reached in under twenty minutes — in fact, the trip became quite popular, until it was stopped by authority.

And those impish, inexplicable vagaries that also brought relief! I have known him to lie in wait, day after day, at the college porch while some of us came out, changed for the river or the football field, and then to follow us through the streets, solemnly walking a few paces in the rear, and afterwards to explain to us our merits or deficiencies judged by the Greek standard of physical excellence. I was never certain if this was sheer affectation — designed as a sop to the inquisitive curiosity of others which his own solitariness had brought upon him — or if it originated in leg-pulling, of which we could never tell where it began or ended.

At first we thought him a wanderer for wandering's sake, with no settled purpose that could bring real achievement; later, perhaps, oppressed with a sense of destiny, wandering for duty — the Arab cause that impelled him. Yet to leave it there would be to miss his joy of life — both the joy of fulfilment was his, achieved by his iron will, and the joy in beauty of form and colour, the safety-valve of a mighty brain, so often overtaxed beyond the limits of human endurance.

E. T. LEEDS, f.s.a. Born 1877. Keeper of the Ashmolean
Museum, Oxford, 1928-45; Fellow of Brasenose College,
1938-45; Hon. Fellow, 1946; Gold Medallist, Society of
Antiquaries.

THERE is always one trait in the personality of a friend
that stamps itself upon one's memory more ineffaceably
than another. To others it may have been of lesser
import, but to the writer from the time when first he came to
know Lawrence in 1908, it has always seemed that the trait
that paradoxically struck most directly by its very force was
his quietude. No hammering on the door, no sudden appearance startling out of concentration, but a silent, unassertive
presence slipping into one's consciousness, to ask a question,
to bring in some new-gathered relic of Oxford's past, or to
further towards fulfilment some self-appointed task. That is
as I knew him before the War, whether relabelling a large
collection of brass-rubbings, discussing and assessing the
date and sequence of medieval pottery, or in the later four
years bringing home from the Near East a packet of seal-
stones, or devising ingenious methods of shipping out of
Turkish territory antiquities of larger bulk.

The beginnings in Syria were in no measure a mere adventure, though they did not lack for such: they were part of a
deliberate, long cherished plan of work, in which dissatisfaction with statements of an academic kind urged him to submit
them to the test of his own severely critical judgment. By the
summer of 1909 when he set out for Syria to study crusading
castles, he went already well equipped with a first-hand
knowledge of the special features of English and French
castellar architecture acquired by constant tours on his bicycle.
He had also gathered a working acquaintance with Arabic
from a teacher in Oxford: his practical mind rejected his
teacher's assurance that 'Go on, donkey', was adequate for its
purpose, and returned fully justified by enlightenment. Only

with severe self-preparation would he approach the debated question of the influence of the Crusades upon the fortress-building of the West.

After taking his degree in 1910 he determined to examine the origins and history of medieval pottery in England on similar lines, and, though time and after-events gave a check to that undertaking, within a few months he had scoured the country and northern France, as before on his bicycle, returning at intervals with fresh ideas. Here again came to the fore the problem of the Crusades and their bearing upon a Western world, especially England, that ceramically lagged far behind the East: in the chance offered him to join the British Museum Expedition to Carchemish he saw a happy opportunity to explore new avenues of study.

That bicycle — I can see it now: no petrol-driven fury, it was nevertheless surely sped with wings. Vanishing swiftly and silently down the road, it seemed, almost before one had turned one's back, to come to rest again: Bristol, Hanley, York, Lincoln, Northampton, with an eighty-mile detour thrown in to collect a fragment of information jokingly suggested by a friend. Another time off to Southampton; a bad crossing to Le Havre, when the storm pitched him down from an upper berth upon the already ejected occupant of the lower, a *commis-voyageur*. Lawrence rose from and tried to thank his providential buffer, to be met with '*Mon Dieu, mon Dieu*', and regained his bunk convulsed with inward laughter. From Le Havre to Rouen, and then two days later at 3.30 p.m. the usual unheralded appearance. He had crossed to Newhaven the previous night and countered an inquiry whether he had even had time for breakfast with 'It's a great mistake to ride on a full stomach'. The same physical endurance and self-denial that had enabled him in the sweltering heat of a Syrian July and August to march on foot close on a thousand miles, sparing his meagre funds simply to enlarge the store of knowledge which he had already been collecting towards the writing of a thesis for his final schools. Few since then, the first time that it was permitted to submit a written thesis in the Final History School, can have been more arduously prepared.

In archaeology his natural bent leaned towards the medieval side: he could not, perhaps cared not, to throw himself wholly into the problems of a more ancient world. But that he could appreciate them is past all gainsaying. Quietly he would store away a questioning against the chance that the answer or a clue thereto might come his way. So comes the last memory of him three weeks before his death, when driven from Clouds Hill a third time by the gadfly torment of an insatiable and inconsiderate Press, he escaped to Oxford. There he made one of his never omitted, however short, calls, loyal to a favourite haunt of other days, to learn how the Ashmolean still fared. A restatement of certain facts surrounding an archaeological conundrum for which he himself had been largely responsible over twenty years before, a brief discussion of the ways and means to solve it, the smile and jest of farewell, and quietly he was gone as ever.

C. F. C. BEESON, c.i.e. Born 1889. Oxford High School (with T. E. L.), 1902-07; Non-Coll. and St. John's College, Oxford, 1907-10; Captain R.A.M.C. in Mesopotamian Campaign; Indian Forest Service, 1911-42; Director, Imperial Forestry Bureau, Oxford, 1945-47; Foundation Fellow, National Institute of Sciences of India.

ALTHOUGH at school for some terms with the Lawrence brothers it was not until about 1903, at the age of fourteen, that I began to do much in the company of Lawrence II. During the following four years the enduring bond of our friendship was archaeological research, undertaken by Lawrence with a passionate absorption beside which my urge was more akin to the curiosity of a magpie in a Baghdad bazaar. It was a dominant factor in the environment of his adolescence, and those who knew the man may assess its influence, for my contact does not warrant an analysis of personality. These memories merely restore some fragments of the background to his youth, as seen through the eyes of youth.

Our acquaintance ripened under his desire to share with others an already masterly appreciation of the treasures of Oxford. He disclosed to me the hidden lore of the city's museums and libraries, and revealed unsuspected principles in her architecture with a cogency that official teachers and elders had never attempted. In covering again, for my benefit, ground previously trodden, he left no impression of unusual erudition. A happy faculty of perceiving and ingenuously acclaiming new features in the already familiar made him appear rather as novice than mentor. We seemed to walk abreast.

At the age of fifteen he was well versed in monumental brasses and had acquired a fine series of rubbings from churches in the eastern and southern counties. Cut out and pasted on the walls of his bedroom were life-size figures of knights and priests with Sir John d'Abernon and Roger de Trumpington, a Crusader, in pride of place. Under his tuition my first brass was rubbed at Wytham in October 1904; and from that date onwards throughout the following school years we made excursions by cycle to nearly every village in the three counties and to many places farther afield.

It was no collector's hobby. There were experiments in the technique of rubbing with different grades of heelball and paper, assisted by friendly advice from shoemakers and paper-hangers whose shops supplied our raw materials. There was much searching in libraries for the histories of those priests and knights and ladies, which narrowed into a study of armour and costume. The Wallace Collection and the Tower Armouries became familiar, and the manufacture of camail and jointed plate armour was gravely projected as a means of interpreting the conventions of early illustrators: ffoulkes kept the project within practical bounds. Heraldry displayed an alluring field that resulted in the compilation of rolls of arms, painted in their proper tinctures, until the habit became philatelic and was condemned. Nevertheless a herald's jargon was permanently acquired, which, with many another special terminology, eventually enriched the vocabulary of the *Seven Pillars*. We ranged from palaeography to the Kelmscott Press and thence to ideal book making: a new Froissart's Chronicles illustrated only by contemporary art, a school history cleansed of anachronisms. Illuminated manuscripts, tooled leather work and enamels competed with the craftsmanship of Minoan Crete in the coloration of many hours. Until, jaded with overmuch variety, we found it good to take to the open country and explore another church or navigate some impassable reach of the Windrush and the Cher.

Many a trespass was committed in Lawrence's company. The artistry of his tact in convincing irate guardians of the honesty of our purpose was often put to test; it extricated us from such compromising positions as the middle of a rhodo-dendron covered tumulus, suspected of rabbit snaring, and the crypt of St. Cross in possession of human bones.

Brasses and the bypaths they opened into medieval history confirmed the gradual concentration of Lawrence's interest in the development of Gothic architecture and the design of military buildings in particular. Towards the end of 1905 most of the accessible British examples had been exhausted; a winter's reading in the Radcliffe and Ashmolean libraries prepared the way for an investigation of the ruins and restorations of France.

A bicycle tour of the country north of the Loire was planned for the summer vacation of 1906. In August of that year I was able to join him in the exploration of parts of Brittany. We met at St. Malo, each equipped for the venture with a small American-cloth covered basket (handiwork of our respective mothers) on the rear carrier, a waterproof cape and spare boots on the handlebars, and, wherever handiest, a volume of Viollet-le-Duc's *Dictionnaire Raisonnée*. The Côtes du Nord and Finisterre were covered closely in search of cathedrals and the less known fortifications. To those twelfth- and thirteenth-century castles with pleasant sounding names — Léhon, Montafilant, Tonquedec — were due many pleasant hours spent in constructing ground-plans and diagrams of peculiarities of style. Lawrence's main preoccupation was with the minds of the designers of these defensive works and the extent to which history had tested their intentions. He talked little of campaigns and military art in general. It was left to me to sketch architectural features, for he was not using a camera much at this period and relied on picture postcards, purchased in dozens. There was little time spared for megaliths or the *pêcheurs* of Pierre Loti or other Breton attractions; these were out of date with our mood. Search on the seacoast discovered a long flat beach of hard sand that satisfied Lawrence as a site for speed trials on his latest bicycle, a model with dropped racing handles and an unusually high ratio to the top gear. With the full force of a Channel gale behind (and Sir Malcolm Campbell's standards being then unknown) the results were mightily pleasing.

For the following month Lawrence continued the tour alone,

eager to set his own pace and estimate the prospects of completing the French survey. He returned to England with such glowing descriptions of what was to be seen in Normandy and the Loire valley, that A. J. Horniblow and I were stimulated to another bicycle tour in the summer of 1907. In August he was farther south but joined us for a short time by long forced rides that apparently were no effort to him.

The summer of 1908 was devoted to the most ambitious of his itineraries, a grand tour of France that took him down to Aigues Mortes and Carcassonne — weeks of frugal living and strenuous riding. He wrote me from Chalus on his way north . . . 'I hope to be in Saintes by Tuesday, Loches ten days later (unless you're coming), and Dinard in another six. This would be apparently about 100 miles a day: but I've ridden nearly 2,000 to date, am as brown as a Jap, and as thin as paper.' His letters on this tour were long chains of tabloid impressions of buildings, broken occasionally by an expanded description of some spot of wider appeal. Cordes was such a one . . . 'a paradise for a painter, albeit the man with the muck-rake would find his hands full . . . An artist might (barring fevers) paint here for a year without a repeat, and all his pictures would be lovely: it is a dream-city, with a little night-mare added as well.' Nevertheless the main objective was not aesthetic delights like Cordes or the discovery that 'the Tarasconnaises are hideous, exactly like grey horses, whereas the women of Arles are glorious'; but the evolution of medieval military architecture. At Agde on the Golfe du Lion he found a superb fortified church and regarded it as a stumbling-block to his thesis, but at Chalusset was more welcome evidence . . . 'a *most wonderful* thing of the thirteenth century, fine castle with donjon of twelfth century *and a large beak on the front of it*. Eureka. I've got it at last for the thesis: the transition from the square keep form: really it is too great for words: it was impossible to photo but I *can* plan, and have a SKETCH which it shall be your duty to render presentable.'

In between the French tours of these three years (1906-8) there had been in Oxford other archaeological diversions. We searched for evidence of Rome away from the Akeman and Dorchester roads, following the plough over presumed sites of villas and scratching into mounds that yielded naught but encaustic tiles of younger times. Lawrence produced a dictum that freed local legend of Rome or Cromwell and substituted Saxon. Egyptology, a museum-subject, claimed little attention and Greek sculpture had been an early love. But lectures by Flinders Petrie to the Ashmolean Society renewed an interest in Oriental antiquities. School friends were not particularly responsive to these phases and propaganda in the form of a collection of ushabtiu passed round during geometry class resulted in confiscation and lines. Misfortune also followed a study of the effect of repeated copying on primitive design, displayed in the art of Pacific islanders in the Pitt-Rivers collections, and in the frog-pattern of clay-lamps. The theory was tested experimentally on the school population by a sort of chain-letter-system, but its scientific value was soon submerged under the sniggering indecencies of adolescence.

In the autumn of 1906 a good deal of rebuilding took place in the heart of the city. There were excavations in progress in the Cornmarket, where the Leopold Arms and the Civet Cat were demolished, in the High for the construction of the New Masonic Hall, and in Balliol and Jesus Colleges. Lawrence soon discovered that the excavations were bringing to light quantities of early pottery and glass. To ensure that the specimens were carefully dug out and preserved the workmen were bribed with a few pence a piece. We made our rounds almost daily and were often rewarded by the recovery of a missing fragment of a greybeard or bottle months after the first portions were turned up. This organization was extended to other sites and lasted for two or three years. It yielded a fine series of vessels of pottery, glazed ware, blown and moulded bottles, pipes, coins and tokens, etc., mostly fifteenth- to seventeenth-century work. The cream of the collections was eventually presented to the Ashmolean Museum.

We matriculated in Michaelmas term, 1907, but to different colleges. A decision that I should read geology and forestry put an abrupt end to my aspirations for an archaeological career and marked the decline of my association with T. E. Lawrence. He had never possessed the average boy's interest in natural history and our rambles in the countryside of Oxford had ignored it. Small wonder that my budding enthusiasm for biology and new-won ability to interpret the familiar haunts in terms of botany or physiography could not prevail against his singleness of purpose. Acquiescent in a trial of beginnings he inspected my quarries and Jurassics but their cliffs and crags spoke no sermon in stones; they were fit material only for scaling. The plantations of St. John's in Bagley and Tubney woods remained just trees; and equally good subjects for climbing. Only the water-ways offered a common path; so long as there were weirs and lashers to surmount and mills or shallows to enforce a portage, it mattered little what forces entrenched the meanders or braided the channels. Yet with this indifference to the laws of natural science Lawrence had an almost involuntary power of assimilating its technical terms and storing them in memory to be used in the fullness of time in correct context.

In the subsequent terms we met less and less frequently, and in the vacations the forests of France and Germany claimed me. The last full day in Lawrence's company was in Christmas week of 1908. Oxford lay under many inches of snow. We set out to explore its unfamiliarity and, by a route as devious as our conversation, reached the top of Cumnor Hurst in a snowstorm. On the heights the wind blew keenly, sweeping the snow from the domed hill as fast as it fell, piling it in the gloom of the pine-clump or whirling over the cliffs of the brick-pit beyond. The drifts we failed to fathom; their shapes were wind fretted and grooved into cold white dunes. The pure monochrome of solitude around us grew duller in the distance, dissolving into low-lying fog that hid the city and the whole Hinksey plain.

Such a staging could scarcely have failed to provoke Lawrence's decision to return across country by a compass-bearing. We held to our compass-bearing, ploughed through snow-banks, climbed hedges and fences, waded icy streams shallow and deep, and were spared the Thames only by the intersection of Folly Bridge and the imminence of night.

So finished five years that had reflected one facet of the personality of T. E. Lawrence.

SIR ERNEST BARKER, F.B.A. Born 1874. Fellow of
Merton College, Oxford, 1898-1905; of St. John's College, 1909-
13; of New College, 1913-20; Principal of King's College,
London, 1920-27; Professor of Political Science and Fellow of
Peterhouse, Cambridge, 1928-39; Professor of Political Science,
University of Cologne, 1947-48.

I THINK it was over thirty years ago, some time before 1905,
that my wife and I became acquainted with Mr. and Mrs.
Lawrence and their sons. They were living in Polstead
Road, not far from our house in North Oxford; and we saw
one another from time to time for many years, down to the
year 1920, when I left Oxford for London.

I was a tutor in modern history; and over and above my
knowledge of the Lawrences as friends, I taught, at one time or
another, three of the sons. T.E. was sent to me by Dr. Lane
Poole (his tutor at Jesus College, where he was an undergraduate) for some work in medieval history. So far as I
remember he came to me in the academic year 1909-10, just
before he took his Final Schools.

His younger brother, W.G., was my pupil between 1911 and
1913. His youngest brother, A.W., did some work with me
just after the end of the War. These were the three Lawrences
I knew best; and they were all, in some respects alike. They
would go their own way and they were ready, and eager, to
find it for themselves. They had an instinct for wandering.
They had their own particular interests — in literature or art
or history or archaeology — and each cultivated his own interest
on his own lines. They all did the same sort of thing very
differently and quite independently.

I cannot refrain from some words about W. G. Lawrence,
partly because my memories of T.E. are so closely connected
with my memories of him, and partly because I felt so deep an
admiration, and indeed affection, for what he was in himself.

He came up to St. John's College as an Exhibitioner in 1909, and after taking his degree in 1913 went out at once to St. Stephen's College, Delhi. He had such gifts of sympathy that in a brief space he made himself the friend of many Indians and learned their minds; but when the War broke out he returned, and entering the Flying Corps was shot down in an aeroplane near St. Quentin at the end of October 1915. He had beauty of mind knit to beauty of body, and a fine generosity and grace of temper. He was a great lover of the classics, though an indifferent performer in classical examinations: his contemporaries said that he always carried a Pindar in his pocket. He had also a passion for Provençal poetry; and I think it was this which carried him into an admiration of the poetry of Mr. Ezra Pound. At any rate I remember his once asking Mr. Pound down to read a paper to a society in the College; and I remember too that I had the honour of entertaining Mr. Pound to dinner on his behalf before he read his paper.

One of W. G. Lawrence's friends in the College was an Egyptian who was also my pupil and of whom I have pleasant memories. On one occasion it happened that T.E., then digging in Carchemish, had brought back with him, on a visit to England, two Arabs from the diggings. He lodged them in the summer-house at the bottom of the garden in Polstead Road and charged his brother that the Egyptian should on no account be allowed to meet them. One day, however, the Egyptian came walking up the road (perhaps to see W.G.) and met the two Arabs. He said something which, as I heard it reported afterwards, was understood by them to mean 'Please God the time may soon come when we can cut the throats of these infidels'. They ran back into the house to T.E. exclaiming 'A gun, a gun — there is an Egyptian in the road and we want to shoot him'. There was no shooting.

But that happened in later days, about 1913; and I must go back to my earliest memories of T.E.

He spent his school days at the Oxford High School, under Mr. Cave, whom I honoured sincerely. All the Lawrences were under him and he was a good friend to them all. While he was still at school, T.E. used to haunt the sites of building operations at Oxford, on the chance of finding any old pottery or glass or metal that might be turned up in the course of excavation. I still cherish an old glass bottle, of a medieval shape, which he had found somewhere during some digging in the centre of Oxford, and which he gave to me.

He was always a generous giver, in my experience, sitting lightly to property and acquisitions, and always ready to fling out a hand and say 'Would you like it? It's yours.' Once he offered me a choice of two rugs which he had brought back from the East. I said that I found it very difficult to choose. 'Take both', he said; and I still have both. It is a story to my discredit; but I can only plead that I had to obey. For him the thing was over and done with when once he had spoken; and I had to digest the results — happy enough for me — of my own indecision and his rapidity.

One of the most vivid of my early memories must belong to the beginning of the October term of 1909. I was lecturing, in a lecture room at St. John's, on the original authorities for a special subject which was then prescribed for the History School — the history of the first three crusades. At the end of the lecture a man came up to me whom I did not recognize — a man with a very fine face, which seemed thinned to the bone by privation. When he spoke to me in his low, quick voice, I found that it was Lawrence. He told me what he had been doing. At that time, at the instance of Professor Firth, the Regius Professor of History, candidates for the History School had recently been given permission to submit a dissertation in their final examination on some topic connected with their special subject. Lawrence, intending to offer the Crusades as his special subject, had resolved to submit a dissertation on the castles built by the Crusaders in the Latin kingdom of Jerusalem. He had then determined, as a good scholar would, that he must go to see the castles for himself; and during the vacation he had quietly carried his determination into effect. With a small sum in his pocket, he had gone to Palestine; and living simply, on the food of the countryside, he had made his way from one castle ruin to another. He had climbed the old walls barefoot: he had had his troubles with Bedouin, and once (I think he told me) been assaulted and left unconscious: but he had seen for himself what he intended to write about, and he had brought back his own plans and photographs to illustrate what he wrote [*Crusader Castles*, published 1936].

I read the dissertation, which he submitted in the examination of 1910. It proved conclusively, so far as I could judge, that the old theory of the influence of the castles of Palestine on western military architecture must be abandoned, and that instead of the East affecting the West, it was the West that affected the East.

I do not remember any essays which he brought to me. I think that he went his own way in what he wrote, and though he would listen quietly to what I said about his essays, I do not suppose that I had an atom of influence upon him. He 'coached' with a remarkable man, L. C. Jane, afterwards a lecturer in the department of international politics at Aberystwyth; and he had always a deep regard for Jane. So far as he was influenced at all in the work which he did in history, I imagine that it was by Jane. The last time he ever came to see me (it was when I was living in London about 1922) he came to ask me to help in getting a post for him. Jane had an originality, and an individuality, which appealed to Lawrence. [*Editor's Note:* A letter in which L. C. Jane recorded memories of his pupil is printed in Robert Graves's *Lawrence and the Arabs*, p. 16.]

I should doubt if Lawrence ever was, or ever wished to be, an 'historical scholar' in the ordinary sense of the word. He was not interested in historic fact just for its own sake. He took the Oxford History School because it came in his way, and because it was a hurdle to be jumped on the road that led to action: he made it interesting to himself by doing something of his own free choice, and by doing it on the spot: but when the History School was past — well, it was past, and history had served its turn.

In the same way I should say that he took to archaeological work, and to digging at Carchemish, not as an end or a career, but as a phase and an experience. He wanted to taste experience — the more out of the way and the more far away in strange parts of the world, the better. He was more of the artist than the scholar — but an artist who found greater scope for art in the world of action than in the world of art itself. He wanted to try things out, and to put them into his own original pattern — in war, if there was war; in the pursuits of peace, if there was peace. But he had from the first, like his brother W.G., his own peculiar interests in poetry and the arts. I remember his saying that he liked the Arabs because they wrote good revolutionary poetry. (I also remember his telling me that he followed what he had read of the campaigns of Saladin in his fighting — keeping, like Saladin, a permanent nucleus, but collecting a new general body of troops in each vicinity in which he happened to be.)

After the War, his artistic interests seemed to grow in strength. He had a zest for fine printing; and he was beginning to come across architects, painters, poets and writers.

I was anxious, after the end of the War, that my college should make him a Research Fellow, in the field of archaeology. As it happened, he was elected a Fellow of All Souls College. That gave him encouragement and honour; but I can now see that whether or no he might have accepted a research fellow-ship in the subject, he would never have been allowed by his own temper and its development to go back to work in archaeology. His spirit had to work out its own way in its own direction. I remember him last, except for one visit in London which I have already mentioned, as I saw him in his rooms at All Souls about the middle of 1920. He told me, with acute relish, of his success in reducing Lord Curzon to tears.

During the ten years after he took his degree, in 1910, I had only seen him occasionally, when he was at home on visits — though he was more in Oxford, and I saw more of him, towards the end of 1919 and in 1920 than before. There followed fifteen years of his life of which I know nothing except from hearsay. From what I saw and can remember at first hand I should say that he was a man who liked to do curious things, and that he burned quickly through to the other side of whatever he took in hand. I do not mean for a minute that he was a dilettante, or that he was superficial in anything that he did. I only mean that he seemed to me like lightning, zig-zag and instantaneous. He liked the curious; he studied and did curious things. He had no taste for organized life and its conventions and institutions; it was his instinct to be against them, and he readily indulged his instinct.

He was always, in my experience, perfectly polite; but I always felt that my judgment of anything was likely to seem to him wrong. I might babble in conversation with him: he said few things, and they were often at an abrupt tangent. I think he liked to shock, perhaps to wound: but I do not remember that I was ever even scratched by anything he did or said.

How far he posed, and how far he simply indulged his genius, I cannot say; but the curiosity of the world about him, after the end of the War, was enough to drive any man into the self-defence of posing. Perhaps his genius was Irish, quintessentially Irish. At any rate he had far more fire than is usually carried by Englishmen; and he was fretted by the fire within him. Fine face, low memorable voice, and supple slight figure — he is still a vivid memory. When I think of him and his brother Will — who in a longer span might have shown himself a great power for good in India — I have two memories which are unique. One had a daemonic and wilful energy, which burned its way like a meteor; the other had the great gift of wise and gentle understanding. A proud thing, for their father and their mother, to have had such sons. T.E. was the eagle among them. But they were all far-flying.

THE EAST: ANCIENT AND MODERN

H. PIRIE-GORDON
FAREEDEH EL AKLE
LEONARD WOOLLEY
SHEIKH HAMOUDI
W. G. LAWRENCE

H . P I R I E - G O R D O N, D.S.C., F.S.A. Oxford, 1902-05; British School of Archaeology, Athens; visited Cyprus and Palestine, 1908, 1910 and subsequently, to study the military architecture of the Crusades. Member of Arab Bureau, Cairo, 1917 (with T.E.L.); Political Mission in Palestine, 1918-19.

IT was at the end of May 1909 (I think) while I was lunching at the Holborn Restaurant that I first met T. E. Lawrence. He came with a letter of introduction from my kinsman David Hogarth, and had followed me from where I was staying, as he was, he explained, in a hurry, and wanted to talk to me about Syria and Palestine, through which I had ridden for five months in the earlier part of the previous year while visiting some of the castles of the Crusaders.

We had finished lunch, but he sat with us over coffee and asked questions about the country and the castles. In those days travellers still welcomed information about the condition of roads, the position of bridges and the disposition of the local authorities, for the guide books were less helpful than at present when dealing with places off the main routes frequented by pilgrims and tourists, and even the German maps were rather vague and not always accurate so far as parts of the country were concerned.

Lawrence told me nothing about his plans, except that he proposed to visit the country of the Crusaders during the coming long vacation, and he must have been bored with much of the information imparted to him, as it concerned travel in comfort on horseback with a caravan, provided with an Iradé from Sultan Abdul Hamid II who, at the time of my visit, had still been an absolute autocrat and had decreed that my party was to enjoy quite unusual facilities and privileges.

For nearly two hours we talked about the castles of the Crusaders, and how they might best be reached, and from where they might best be seen, and finally Lawrence left, after having accepted my offer to lend him an annotated map of

Syria which I had used, and to give him copies of the photographs of castles which had been taken during my journey.

Some months later the map was returned to me with a letter from Lawrence, who apologized for blood-stains on it. Later I learned that he had been attacked by Kurds who had beaten him and left him for dead in indignation at finding that the 'treasure' which he had been reported to be carrying consisted of no more than his clothes, shabby after his remarkable tramp through Syria in the heat of summer, some Hittite cylinder seals which he had bought in Aleppo, and a few beshliks. They had taken most of his clothes and all the money, but had left the seals and the map as being valueless. He had worked his way to Marseilles, so I was told, and landed with enough money to pay his fare back to Oxford.

The map is still in my possession, and its case showed where T.E.L. had washed and rubbed the label in trying to clean away the stain made by his blood. It was appropriate that it should have been used again in 1936 in the course of verifying some of the names used on the maps which illustrate his recently published book, dealing with the castles about which he talked with me at our first meeting.

On several subsequent occasions we discussed those castles, and, while he was at Carchemish, he sent me some photographs of the castle at Urfa (Edessa) which I had never visited, to support a theory which he had evolved about the influence of Byzantine-Armenian military architecture and mason work upon that of some of the northern Crusader castles, notably on that at Saone (Sahyun).

He was interested in the existence of a pool with sacred fish in it at Urfa, similar to that near Tripolis, in Syria. The latter is traditionally supposed to be some sort of a survival of the worship of Derceto by the Phoenicians, but there was nothing, except the pool of sacred fish, to suggest that Derceto or the Phoenicians had ever had anything to do with Urfa.

During the War we met in Cairo, where T.E.L. was in the Map Department and provided the maps required by the Navy for preparing for the defence of the Suez Canal; and later at

Bir Salem, the G.H.Q. of the Egyptian Expeditionary Force, where on one occasion I was able to rescue T.E.L. from the attentions of a zealous military policeman who had instructions that no civilians were to be allowed into the camp, and could not understand how an Arab in desert robes came to be there. The more so, as T.E.L. was being impish and was offering explanations in Arabic only. The policeman was much relieved when an officer took charge of the wandering Sheikh and conducted him to the mess-tent in Brigadier-General Clayton's political camp.

FAREEDEH EL AKLE, Syrian Schoolmistress. Born 1882, at Beirut; educated in Girls' High School of Society of Friends, in the Lebanon; has taught in Syria in schools of the Society of Friends and the American Presbyterian Mission as well as at the American Mission School in Jebail (1911-14) where she first met T.E.L. Represented Syrian Protestant Women at Regional Conference, 1924; Syrian delegate to International Women's Congress, Paris, 1926; delegate to International Missionary Conference, Jerusalem, 1928.

ONE hot day in the summer of 1909 a weary young traveller stood knocking at the door of a school belonging to an American lady missionary, in the quaint old town of Jebail (the ancient Byblus). The maid who opened the door, seeing the dusty, tired-looking traveller with the bundle tied on his back, thought him one of the German tramps that were going about the town at that time; she rushed upstairs to inform the Principal of the School. The young traveller did not wait to be asked in; he followed the maid. At the top of the stairs he met the Principal, and after a few words had been exchanged between them he was immediately welcomed.

It was Lawrence's first visit to Syria, studying the remains of the Crusader castles. He walked through the length and breadth of the country, in three long months, taking nothing with him save his camera into which he tucked a few articles of underwear. It was on his way back that he went through Jebail to see the last of these castles.

The stories of his adventures and the hardships he endured on that trip, as he related them to us later, would make the most thrilling reading; they would sound like the Arabian Nights. Yet Lawrence made very light of all his sufferings and would joke over them. Many were his narrow escapes from death at the hands of cruel Kurds and Turks. I recall one which is the least horrible, but which might throw a little light on his character.

He was crossing one of the wild mountains up north when

he was met by a huge cruel-looking Turk. Instantly the Turk took up his gun, aimed and shot at Lawrence, but missed him. This made the giant furious and Lawrence, in order to frighten the man also took his revolver, aimed at the little finger of the giant — for he never intended to kill him — and shot so accurately that the bullet passed close to the hand wounding slightly the little finger. The giant stood spell-bound, quick to see that one who could handle a revolver so cleverly was not to be despised. Meanwhile, Lawrence had come up to him, and taking his handkerchief out of his pocket bandaged the wounded finger, and patted his adversary on the back to show his goodwill, for neither could speak the language of the other. Then Lawrence shared the little money he had with him, and the two went down the mountains together as friends.

It is the story of David and Goliath over again with the difference that David conquered his enemy with the sword whilst the weapon that won the day for Lawrence was that of friendliness, in which he so firmly believed.

A year after his return to England Lawrence set out on a second visit to Syria, to work on the excavations at Carchemish. He saw that it was necessary, before going, to acquire a certain knowledge of the Arabic language, so his thoughts turned to the school at Jebail, where he had been a few months before. He arrived on Christmas Eve, and was received very enthusiastically by those who knew him from his first short visit

From that day Lawrence made the school at Jebail his second home. He had not been long with us before we all realized that amongst us was a unique personality, a man with high ideals and aims, with keen intellect, and great ability — he possessed such a wide knowledge on so many subjects that the staff rightly named him the Encyclopaedia.

He was of a very shy, quiet nature and loved to dress very simply, giving little attention to outward appearance.

The material things of life had no attraction for him, and money he only valued for its convenience.

He had a wonderful charm about him; and his kindheartedness easily won him a way into the hearts of those with whom he came in contact. Even the little schoolchildren were drawn to him as by a magnet, and would come up to him with confidence carrying their broken dolls and toys, which he would spend hours mending, and perfect work he made of it. Lawrence's stay meant a great deal to us; he entered into the very life of the school. His advice was often sought and he always proved to be a wise adviser and a man of sound judgment.

Any form of injustice or unfair dealings Lawrence could not tolerate, and it pained him to see anything that was not straightforward. His youngest brother had asked him to bring him a tail of a jackal and when he failed to find one we suggested that he should shoot one himself — so one bright moonlight night, awakened by the howling of a jackal under his bedroom window, he jumped out of bed, climbed on to a roof under his window, and fired, but evidently missed, for the beast went merrily howling home. The next day he was teased about it. 'You see it would not have been *fair* to shoot the poor beast without giving him the chance to escape.'

Although Lawrence was of a shy, reserved nature yet he enjoyed the company of people. He went in and out with us, visiting the homes of our different friends and making their acquaintance. He was interested in everything he saw and heard. It was easy for him to adapt himself to the customs and ways of the people with whom he came in contact.

Once a big luncheon was given to us by a Moslem friend of ours. The lunch was served in the old Syrian fashion, the guests being seated on low cushions round a large brass tray; and as we sat partaking of the delicious food set before us, a discussion arose round the subject of old Syrian customs and civilization. It was a delicate question to handle; some were of the opinion that Syria was still in the background, and that its customs had not kept pace with modern civilization. Our hostess, who was a very intelligent woman, and who loved Lawrence as a son, turned to him and asked, 'What do you think about it?' Lawrence, who had sat listening intently, answered in his quiet impressive way — 'Why, you in Syria have very fine customs, some of them are better than ours — for instance, we in Europe, when we wash our hands, we first pour the water into a basin, then we wash in the same water; not so here; you pour the water over the hands, which is a cleaner way. This I call civilization.' This tactful and kind answer made its right impression on the people present and caused great pleasure.

It was always his way to see and acknowledge the good in others. He had a keen insight into the minds of people, and a power to understand other people's point of view. Perhaps that was one of the things that helped him to be the great success he was.

Lawrence studied Arabic for only three months and notwithstanding the difficulty of the language he made rapid progress; he was able to read, write and speak very simple Arabic in this short time. Lawrence never studied beyond that, although later on when he lived with the Arabs, he could speak their different dialects with ease. He was most delightful to teach, so quick to learn, and so full of humour that the hard Arabic lessons became the most enjoyable time for both student and teacher. I count it one of the greatest privileges of my life to have been his teacher even for this very short time and to have got to know him as a good friend.

When the time came for Lawrence to leave us he set his face towards Jerablus, where he was expected for the digging on a certain date. But how was he to get there when the snow lay metres deep on the mountains and even reached as far down as the sea coast? It was a winter such as Syria had not experienced for over seventy-five years — all communications were cut, no trains were able to run — in fact to most people travelling was impossible. But this did not make any difference to Lawrence. In vain we tried to persuade him to give it up. He would only reply, 'I must go, even if I have to cross the snow on sledges or walk in wooden shoes'. How he got there will ever remain a mystery to us: Lawrence was the kind of man who could accomplish the apparently impossible, through that unconquerable spirit of his.

Lawrence's interest in the Jebail school never ceased. He continued to write most interestingly about his work in Jerablus, and would visit us from time to time. Thus we kept in touch with him until the World War broke out.

On one of his visits to us an Arab accompanied him, a young fellow of about eighteen years of age, named Dahoum. This young man was greatly attached to Lawrence, and from him I learnt a great deal of what the Arabs thought of Lawrence.

To a question I put, Dahoum gave an answer in some such words as these:

'You ask why we love Lawrence? and who can help loving him? He is our brother, our friend and leader. He is one of us, there is nothing we do he cannot do, and he even excels us in doing it. He takes such an interest in us and cares for our welfare. We respect him and greatly admire his courage and bravery: we love him, because he loves us and we would lay down our lives for him.'

This boy in fact saved Lawrence's life three times.

Lawrence's war experiences were very painful to him and its consequences fell very heavily on him. He wrote to me in 1927, 'My war experience was horrible. I hated every moment of it and still hate it so much that I refuse to profit in any way by the reputation or position that I gained'. And many more such expressions as this, that he wrote at different times indicate what Lawrence must have gone through. There is no doubt that his sensitive soul suffered deeply and no one will ever know how deep were the waters that he crossed. But he bore it all so bravely. His life was a life of victory all through.

SIR C. LEONARD WOOLLEY. Born 1880. First met
T. E. L. while Assistant Keeper, Ashmolean Museum, Oxford,
1905-07. Excavated in England, Italy, Nubia, 1906-12; with
T. E. L. as Director, British Museum excavations at Carchemish, 1912-14; on survey of Sinai, 1914, and as Staff Officer,
Cairo, 1914-16; prisoner in Turkey, 1916-18; political department, N. Syria, 1919; directed excavations at Carchemish, 1919,
in Egypt, 1921-22, at Ur, 'Iraq, 1922-34, at Al Mina, near
Antioch, Syria, 1936-37, at Atchana, Hatay, 1937-39 and
1946-49. Author of *Dead Towns and Living Men* (partly
describing Carchemish), *The Wilderness of Zin* (with T. E. L.),
and many archaeological books.

WHEN Hogarth undertook a season's experimental work
at Carchemish in the winter of 1911-12 he called upon
Lawrence, who had been travelling in Syria and working on the Crusading castles, to join him. In the following
year I took Hogarth's place and gladly fell in with his suggestion that I should keep Lawrence, whom I had known
slightly since he was a boy at the Oxford High School; at
Carchemish then he and I worked together until the summer
of 1914.

In the actual work he was curiously erratic. It all depended
on how far he was interested, and not everything in field
archaeology did interest him or appeal to his sense of values.
He could take very full and careful notes, not always in a form
easy for others to follow, but giving all the gist of the matter,
and at other times he would take no notes at all. Once I asked
him to write a detailed description of a row of sculptured slabs
and he duly handed in a notebook which he said contained all
that was wanted; long afterwards when I came to look at it I
found that each slab was dismissed with a sentence or two
which merely made fun of it. Probably he thought that a
description was a waste of time — he would himself have much
preferred a good photograph; anyhow it could just as well be
written later, and the instruction to do a distasteful job gave
an opening for the impish humour that was so prominent in

him. His impatience of the written record might have been due in part to his prodigious memory. He would look at a small fragment of a Hittite inscription which had just come to light and remark that it fitted on to an equally small piece found twelve months before, and although there were many hundreds of such in our store-room he was always right; or he would quote from memory a particular potsherd that had been found in a former season and could describe its stratum and associations, although I and not he had excavated the piece and written the notes about it. His mind was indeed entirely set on the work he was doing, but he did it in his own way. He would make brilliant suggestions but would seldom argue in support of them; they were based on sound enough arguments, but he expected you to see those for yourself, and if you did not agree he would relapse into silence and smile.

In time, by tacit agreement, I did all the note-taking while Lawrence did the photography, on which he was very keen, and of course helped to run the work. From the outset he was excellent with the Arab workmen. In a way he was rather like them, for the fun of the thing appealed to him as much as did its scientific interest. It was he who invented the system whereby a discovery was saluted by revolver-shots carefully proportioned to its importance; the men competed together as to who should have the greatest number of shots to his credit in the course of a season, and the hope of a few more cartridges was the chief incitement to hard work. Or Lawrence and Hamoudi would suddenly turn the whole work into a game, the pick-men pitted against the basket-men or the entire gang against the wagon-boys, until with two hundred men running and yelling half a day's output would be accomplished in an hour; and Lawrence would lead the yells. But another time I might come along from another part of the field and find practically no work being done at all, because Lawrence was sitting with the men round him discussing some point of village custom or clearing up a question of local dialect; and if I groused at all he would grin and ask what anything mattered.

He already spoke Arabic well and after a summer spent at Byblos (Jebeil) in serious study of the language was always trying to improve his knowledge of the different dialects. Here too he had his strong likes and dislikes. The 'real' Arabic was that of the Bedouin, the best was the Hejazi; other dialects were good in so far as they approximated to that, and while he had no use for the corrupt Beiruti he resolutely refused ever to speak a word of Egyptian. Of course his ability to talk freely with them helped him very much with the men, as did his interest in them and his memory. Not only did he know all the workmen by name, but he knew a good deal about their family relations also; I have often heard him punish a slack worker by some remark unintelligible to me which raised a general laugh at his expense and obviously went very deeply home, and I would find that it was an allusion to some scandal in which a grandfather or a second cousin had been involved. His uncanny knowledge of their family history gave Lawrence a peculiar prestige amongst the local Arabs.

Yet for all his keenness on things Arab he had no great liking for the individual inhabitants of Jerablus and the Carchemish neighbourhood. There were only two whom he regarded as friends, but of those two he was very fond. Hamoudi, our foreman, he admired intensely and was bound to him by real gratitude, for Hamoudi had saved his life at no small risk to himself. After one of his tramps (I think in the summer of 1911) Lawrence had dragged himself into Jerablus in the throes of typhoid and Hamoudi had taken him in and nursed him. It was touch-and-go whether he would pull through, and just as the illness was at its worst the Turkish authorities, perhaps nervous about possible complications if an Englishman should die in their province, ordered Hamoudi to turn the dying man out; when Hamoudi expostulated he was told that if he disobeyed and Lawrence died he would be accused of having poisoned him for the sake of his money. It was a serious threat, and the village was all in favour of avoiding trouble and doing as the Turks bade; but Hamoudi stood firm, nursed Lawrence back to something like health and carried him off to Aleppo. It was in return for this that Lawrence brought Hamoudi and Dahoum to England in 1913 for a holiday in Oxford.

Dahoum was his other friend. He was then a boy of about fifteen, not particularly intelligent (though Lawrence taught him to take photographs quite well) but beautifully built and remarkably handsome. Lawrence was devoted to him. The Arabs were tolerantly scandalized by the friendship, especially when in 1913 Lawrence, stopping in the house after the dig was over, had Dahoum to live with him and got him to pose as model for a queer crouching figure which he carved in the soft local limestone and set up on the edge of the house roof; to make an image was bad enough in its way, but to portray a naked figure was proof to them of evil of another sort. The scandal about Lawrence was widely spread and firmly believed.

The charge was quite unfounded. Lawrence had in his make-up a very strong vein of sentiment, but he was in no sense a pervert; in fact, he had a remarkably clean mind. He was tolerant, thanks to his classical reading, and Greek homosexuality interested him, but in a detached way, and the interest was not morbid but perfectly serious; I never heard him make a smutty remark and am sure that he would have objected to one if it had been made for his benefit: but he would describe Arab abnormalities baldly and with a certain sardonic humour. He knew quite well what the Arabs said about himself and Dahoum and so far from resenting it was amused, and I think that he courted misunderstanding rather than tried to avoid it; it appealed to his sense of humour, which was broad and schoolboyish. He liked to shock. Similarly he liked practical jokes, not least those which might annoy, but his pleasure in them was so ingenuous that it was hard to take offence. On a wet and stormy night, when I had retired early with a bout of fever, Lawrence cut a wind-vane from a biscuit-tin and fixed it with a rusty nail to my tent-pole; its grinding screech kept me awake and on the search for the wretched thing all through the night, but when he told me about it in the morning he did so with such infectious amusement that I was constrained to enter

into the joke. When Hogarth came once to visit us at Carchemish Lawrence made most elaborate preparations; he produced, from somewhere or other, quantities of cheap pink satin
ribbon and some bits of lace; Hogarth's Spartan mud-walled
room was given lace curtains with big pink bows, there was a
coquettish pink bow on the looking-glass, and on the 'dressing-
table' a pincushion and a tray of hair-pins 'to make him feel at
home', while in the bath-room, a bare cell with a round tin
bath on the cement floor, there was a shelf crowded with small
bottles of cheap scent and, by way of contrast, a very good
Romano-Greek bronze strigil to take the place of a sponge.
Hogarth shouted with rage and flung scents and ribbons out
into the courtyard (the strigil he carried off for the Ashmolean
Museum), but Lawrence, who never laughed out loud, grinned
over the jest for weeks.

At the same time he hated being made ridiculous himself;
if you laughed at him he would at once retire into his shell and
very likely withdraw altogether from your company. Walking
back one day from the Tell Ahmar district, on the west bank
of the Euphrates, he came to a village where a number of
Kurdish girls were drawing water from the well, and asked for
a drink. They gave it to him, crowding round to look at a
white man — a creature they had perhaps never seen before —
and one bold hussy pulled open his shirt to see if his skin was
white all over; and soon, with shrieks of laughter, they were
all about him determined to see more, until he escaped almost
stripped. He could not take it as a joke, and would never go
that way again; and though he did tell me the story it was only
some time afterwards, and then with cold indignation.

That sensitiveness to ridicule was probably due in part to
his knowing that other people found it hard to take him
seriously. It was hard. Physically small, with a head disproportionately large, very unobtrusive with his quiet voice
and tendency to long silences and his slow and quiet movements
and a smile which if it was not entirely concerned with his own
thoughts seemed to be rather deprecating and apologetic, he
was not on the surface of things impressive; and however one

might learn to appreciate something of what lay behind there remained a feeling of his essential immaturity. Certainly he made that impression on me, and it was not due merely to his impish humour and to a few other very youthful traits, such as the fondness for 'dressing up' which he had then and perhaps never got over. At Carchemish he always wore a blazer of French grey trimmed with pink, white shorts held up by a gaudy Arab belt with swinging tassels (it was a belt worn only by bachelors, and Lawrence had his tassels made bigger than anyone else's), grey stockings, red Arab slippers and no hat; his hair was always very long and in wild disorder — he used to say that it was too long when it got into his mouth at meal-times. In the evening he would put on over his white shirt and shorts a white and gold embroidered Arab waistcoat and a magnificent cloak of gold and silver thread, a sixty-pound garment which he had picked up cheaply from a thief in the Aleppo market; in the evening too his hair was very carefully brushed: sitting in front of the winter fire reading — generally Homer, or Doughty's poems or Blake — he would look with his sleek head and air of luxury extraordinarily unlike the Lawrence of the daytime.

For while he frankly enjoyed his ability to live more roughly than most people could or would consent to do, and when tramping in Syria would put up with the plainest of fare and very little of it, deliberately training himself to do without things, he quite appreciated comfort. He did not smoke, he took wine seldom and spirits never, but he liked good food and had a very critical taste in the Arab dishes which we had at Carchemish, and in Arab coffee he had the judgment of an expert. In our living-room, which boasted a Roman mosaic pavement, there were some good rugs, the best of which Lawrence had bought. He had had made in Aleppo two arm-chairs of black wood and white leather of whose design he was very proud; he had brought out from home a piece of Morris tapestry to hang on the wall, he had some nice Kutachia pots, and of course books. The workmen knew well that he could always be placated by a gift of flowers — in fact the only garden near, that of Ahmed Effendi of Zormara, was regularly ransacked for his benefit during the rose season — and he would often come back from a bathing excursion with a great bunch of wild flowers for the house.

He was fond of bathing and spent much time in and on the Euphrates; he brought out from Oxford a Canadian canoe with a motor attachment and would make long excursions in it. The engine itself gave him great pleasure, as did most things mechanical. At Carchemish there was not much scope for such interests, but his keenness on photography was partly experimental, and in keeping with it was his keenness on revolver-shooting, which he practised constantly; he was a very fine shot. His shooting had already been of good service to him. Once on one of his wanderings, near Latakia, he had just had a sea bathe and was dressing on the beach when a bullet came past him and he looked round to see a man about fifty yards away taking aim at him for the second time; before he could fire Lawrence had picked up his own revolver and shot the fellow through his right hand; after which he tied up his wound, kicked him and sent him about his business. He had indeed a cool indomitable courage which showed itself clearly in such troubles as we had with Turks and Germans, its earnestness nearly always disguised by an impudent enjoyment of the humour of the situation; he did not mind the risk, and the bluff appealed to him immensely.

I had not the insight to see then the genius that was in him, though I could recognize that he was unusually gifted and remarkably lovable; but I was quite conscious that closely as we lived together I did not know him really well. The best of companions, he was frightfully reserved about himself and in all our long talks seemed detached from what he said; if he showed signs of sentiment, as very occasionally he did, he would at once turn them to ridicule. I do not remember his ever admitting to any affection for anybody, though I knew perfectly well that in the case of certain people the affection was there and was deeply felt; in all matters of the emotions he seemed to have a peculiar distrust of himself. Similarly he never discussed religion, at least in its personal aspects, but he gave to Hamoudi an Arabic version of the synoptic gospels and was very pleased to find that it impressed him; but he hated missionary activities and was vitriolic in his abuse of missions, though one of his best friends in Syria was Miss Holmes of the American mission at Jebeil. He was fond of talking to the men about the Moslem faith, but had no admiration for it except for its insistence on the virtue of charity.

Though he had an actual liking for few Arabs he was already an enthusiast for the Arabs as a whole; the one thing he condemned in Doughty was his lack of appreciation for and his constant suspicion of the Arab. But it would perhaps be truer to say that he was an enthusiast for Syria; the country appealed to him more than did its inhabitants and, while he really disliked the Syrian townsman, for Syria he had a passion. This went far to explain his attitude to the Germans and the French. For the Germans who were working close to us on the Baghdad Railway he had nothing but contempt because they did not know how to treat Arabs; he thought them idle and incompetent and corrupt, and loved to score off them and hold them up to ridicule, but it was their behaviour to the men that made him despise them. I think that he disliked Germans in general because his own type of scholarly mind was so essentially different from theirs, and he would rail at their meticulous scholarship and lack of imagination. The only German for whom I remember his speaking a good word was the librarian of the royal library at Munich who visited us at Jerablus and enthused over our bookshelf, declaring that of the six books he loved best in the world Lawrence had five. With the French it was quite otherwise. He liked France and often talked of the pleasant times he had had there, and I think he was even fond of the French people. But especially after a long stay in the Lebanon, he felt a profound jealousy of the part they played or wished to play in Syria. That French politicians should aim at a control of the country he had come to love infuriated him. He hated the Turks because they were masters of Syria and treated the Arabs as inferiors; that their place should be taken by another non-Arab power was monstrous. Long before the Sykes-Picot agreement drove him into a deliberate policy of frustration Lawrence was an enemy of France in the Levant, and that sentiment was the key to many of his later acts. He once said to me, after the War, that the stroke of humour which had pleased him most was that when he refused other decorations he accepted the Legion of Honour.

SHEIKH HAMOUDI, Moslem Arab. Born at Jerablus (Carchemish) about 1880. Chief local foreman, British Museum excavations at Carchemish, 1911-14; visited Oxford, 1913. Chief foreman, British Museum and University of Pennsylvania Museum excavations at Ur, 'Iraq, 1922-34; chief foreman, Sir L. Woolley's excavations at Soueidia, N. Syria, 1936.

AN INTERVIEW WITH E. H. R. ALTOUNYAN

SHEIKH HAMOUDI IBN SHEIKH IBRAHIM EL AWASSI of the tribe of the Damarkhan (4000 tents) is now about 55. He was a very suitable person to initiate Lawrence into the Arab world of action. 'My father was rich, and having no need to work it seemed to me good that I should arm and mount and seek freedom. When therefore I heard of some youth remarked for manliness, I sought him out; and if he said, "No. I am no better than you", I let him go. But if not, then we fought. So it is that this day I have round my neck the lives of six or seven men.' I was very impressed by this modest figure of six or seven. How much more likely to have said 'Twenty', more especially as his activities had caused sufficient stir to get him outlawed; for it was not until 1910, after seven years of swashbuckling, that he was pardoned by the new regime and could once more enter Jerablus undisguised. By 1911 he was thoroughly bored and jumped at the chance of working with pick and shovel for the newly opened dig. (Jerablus village adjoins the site of Carchemish where the British Museum expedition worked till 1913.) Then the three excavators, Hogarth, Thompson and Lawrence, selected him unanimously as foreman and he became T.E.'s tutor.

I don't think he really believed in Lawrence's death until that day when I showed him Howard Coster's superb portrait-photograph. As the flood of brilliant recollections swept over his fine-wrought features, and those delicate hands enhanced

77

the meaning of his words, it was impossible to believe that more than twenty years had passed since they had last met. 'Oh, if only he had died in battle' expressed quite simply the heart of his grief. For death itself had never meant much to either of them. 'I have lost my son,' he said, 'but I do not grieve for him as I do for Lawrence. My son can be replaced.' And again, 'I am counted brave, the bravest of my tribe; my heart is iron but his was steel. A man whose hand was never closed but open; as this' (and he held out his hand, arching it back, till the skin whitened). 'As I wake I think of him and as I fall asleep he is my last thought. Tell them,' he said, striding up and down the Aleppo stone-paved hall, 'tell them in England what I say. Of manhood the man, in freedom free; a mind without equal; I can see no flaw in him.' Biblical all this, out of date — for the moment, yet I can only set down the words I heard and try to convey the harsh impress of their deep sincerity.

Hamoudi's account of Lawrence is necessarily confined almost entirely to action. These two highly intelligent vivacious warriors understood each other from the first and each appreciated instinctively, even if he did not always understand, the other's activity. As to Lawrence's understanding of Arab character, Hamoudi leaves one in no doubt at all. Not by prowess of race or character, but by simple penetration and assimilation did he win and maintain his easy ascendancy. 'While we would twist and turn with our object far away, almost out of sight, he would smile and point out to us what we were after, and make us laugh, ashamed.' But the tale he told me that day was one of ceaseless moving. A new land, an unknown people, a youth unstrained, and a setting where scholarship was paramount, and yet where the body could measure itself against river and desert, cold night wind and a persistent sun — here lay in abundance the material for apprenticeship. Even while the dig was on, he seldom slept in his bed, preferring often to lie at the bottom of some newly opened trench or on the mound beside the river. 'Wherever there was discomfort or hardship there he would thrust himself.' As soon as the season was over he set about to explore the country. His first excursion comprised Jerablus, Nisib, Kardoush and back. He disguised himself as Hamoudi's servant, and as he knew no Turkish and little Arabic, Hamoudi passed him off as a Turk among the Arabs and as an Arab among the Turks. His next journey was on foot and alone, equipped with a box camera and a revolver: Jerablus — Tel Ahmar — Urfa — Mardin — Diarbekir — Samsat — Roumkallah — Marash — Aintab — Tel Beshir. When nearly home he was attacked by six Arabs of Hamoudi's own tribe and robbed of his revolver. Hamoudi, when he heard, was furious and started up at once to recover it, but Lawrence forbade him, and rested well content for a week in Hamoudi's own house. Another time they started down stream in the canoe taking Dahoum with them. At dusk, opposite Hammam they upset and had to swim for their lives, managing somehow to bring the canoe with them ashore. Hamoudi's eyes lit up as at a pleasant recollection. 'There we were on the bank, stripped and cold, wringing out each others' clothes and with a good chance of being attacked, as it was dark, but Lawrence was very joyful.' They got down this trip as far as Kalaat el Nijm, returned the canoe by some Arabs going up, and walked back, travelling only by night. They passed on the way the garden oasis of Abou Galgal. Twenty years later he still talked of this place with delight, and told how Feisal had promised it to him as booty when he came into his own. Between Mumbuj and Jerablus lies a particularly waterless tract, and here it was that Lawrence for the first time, and the last, lost his temper with Hamoudi. Though it was night they were all three parched with thirst. As hour after hour passed, Hamoudi, as yet unused to his charge, tried to improve matters by repeating that well-known formula, 'Just a little further and we'll get water', though he had not the slightest grounds for saying so. At last T.E. let fly at him, 'Just a little, just a little . . . I think nothing at all of your littles'. And at that moment they found a streamlet. They drank in silence, apart, and in dudgeon. But even from the first Hamoudi says he could outride, outwalk, outshoot and outlast the best of them. It is the recollection of his endurance that makes it so difficult for the village of Jerablus to believe in his death. 'One day,' continued Hamoudi, 'he decided to call on the district governor, who had failed to keep some promise. It was several hours' journey, and as we went he asked me to teach him the two foulest words in the Turkish language. I thought and told him; and all the way I could hear him repeating them, and asking me now and then if that was the right accent. When we arrived at the government house and were ceremoniously shown into the governor's presence, he walked straight up to him and pointing with his finger repeated over and over again, "You——, You——". Then the governor in great fear called out to me, "O Hamoudi, my brother, in the name of God, remove this danger from before me and I will do whatever he wants," and it was so.' The nearest British Consul was in Aleppo, a two days' journey.

'But once I was angry with him. When Dahoum and I went to Oxford many wished to photograph us as we sat with him in our customary clothes. And after they took a picture they would come and speak to him and always he said "No, No." One day I asked him why he was always saying "No, No," and he laughed and said, "I will tell you. These people wish to give you money. But for me you would now be rich." And he smiled again. Then I grew angry. Indeed I could not believe I heard right. "Do you call yourself my friend," I cried to him, "and say thus calmly that you keep me from riches?" And the angrier I grew the more he laughed and I was very wrath at this treachery. At last he said when I had turned away and would no longer look at him, "Yes, you might have been rich, richer than any in Jerablus. And I — what should I have been?" and he paused watching my face with his eyes. "I should have been the showman of two monkeys." And suddenly all my anger died down within me.

'Once he fell sick in my house and when it appeared that he would be very ill, the neighbours came round and advised me to put him out, lest he should die and his family should suspect me and the government put me in prison. I refused to listen; but before he lost consciousness he called me and said, "Don't

be afraid, Hamoudi. See, here on this paper I have written to
my father to say that if I die you are not the cause." So I fed
him with milk and nursed him till he was well.' But always as
he talked his eyes returned to the portrait and at times he would
get up and set it in another light trying to reconcile himself
with the impossible.

W. G. ('Will') L A W R E N C E, younger brother of T.E.L.
Born 1889; killed in action, 1915. St. John's College, Oxford,
1909-13; professor, St. Stephen's College, Delhi, 1913-15.
Visited T.E.L. ('Ned') at Carchemish on his way to India.

From a letter to his mother, written at Jerablus (Carchemish),
September 19th, 1913

'ALEPPO was chiefly good for its bazaars, full of beautiful
silk stuffs and all sorts of things in a huge stone-roofed
and paved market. On the roofs are the playing-fields
of the town where the goats browse on the grass and occasionally
fall down through the skylights.

'Ned gave me a particularly interesting time in Aleppo, not
only showing me over the bazaars pretty thoroughly, but also
paying visits with me to various houses of friends of his,
Christian and Moslem, in the town. They are very fine places,
with courtyards and fountains, and wonderful lacquer roofs.
Also it was jolly seeing how glad everyone was to entertain Ned.
Old Busrawi of the Milli Kurds was in Aleppo seeing his son who
was at the hospital there, and he has asked us out to his tents
next week. We are going for two nights, which will be great fun.

'So far Ned has not heard from you since he left home. That
means your letter of Aug. 16 has gone astray, and no doubt
others, which is usual but very annoying. Ned was very anxious
for news when I saw him.

'Carchemish comes as a surprise after the train has run over
flat dried up country, very much as though the Cambridge
fields were turned into thin plough-land and sand. The station
shows no mound in sight and no river. There we were met by
swarms of Ned's men, head of them the Hoja [Hamoudi].
And a walk of ten minutes or so over rocky slopes without,
really, any climbing into the Kalaat of Jerablus, which is thus
low on one side. It is a very wide circle full of old stones, and
trial pits of the digs dotted about it. The house is a long low
building as in the photographs. And the best part of the digs
lies between the house and the high bank of the river, quite
low down. The Mount is thus impressive only from the river

82

bank. There very much so. The river is at present extraordinarily low, but for all that it is several hundreds of yards across, shallow just now but running very fast. Swimming against the current in most places is impossible. As to the finds, the thing that most impresses me is the company of the captains. But I will talk about them another time. Just at this moment I am being devoured by sandflies, little white beasts, sitting alone in the big room. Ned is on the roof in bed, whither he went about 8.30 p.m., to try and sleep off a touch of fever. He's been as usual all day, but it makes him feel low.'

Added on the following day:

'Ned is better, but is going to take it easy. An old Kurdish gentleman has just sent him a magnificent carpet as a present, which has elated him. The weather here is perfectly fine, but not too hot. The pens for Ned were all right. Also the musical box appealed to the Hoja. I wish we could hear from you. Ned is grumbling continually at the post. You have no idea how hard it is to write here; we go to bed about 8.30, and in the day time there are too many flies for any sitting down.'

From a letter to his mother, written September 27th, 1913:

'You can get a very fair idea of the appearance of the Kalaat from photographs, but of course since they were not digging, its quiet, which struck me, is usually absent. It is just a huge circle of hilly land covered with stones, natural and hewn. The digs show all over it in trial pits, but the chief stones are all together in one corner, and set up in a fair order. One can get an idea of the place as it was when Nebuchadnezzar left it all smashed up.

'There are always two men on duty as site-guards, to prevent visitors taking photographs or damaging the stones. People seem to be frequently about, mostly Germans who are very much in evidence at Aleppo. And down on the right, less than a quarter of a mile from the main digs, is the railway bridge, with swarms of workmen carrying stones for the building material of the permanent bridge just above the temporary one.

'I didn't have much time alone with Ned. The day I wrote to you we had quite a lot of guests, a Lieutenant Young, making his way out to India via Bagdad, an American missionary Dr. Usher, going back to Lake Van, and the people from Aleppo the Altounyans. These people all stopped two days (one night) which were spent examining the digs and bathing. Then they went away, all except Lieut. Young, who is still at Jerablus. He is an interesting fellow, speaking Arabic and Persian very well, and he went with me in Ned's place to visit Busrawi Agha, in answer to the old Kurd's invitation. Ned had fever rather, and was glad to escape the ride and yet leave me in the hands of someone with the gift of tongues. We had great fun with Busrawi. He sent his son and some retainers for us, with horses, which we got after walking across the bridge. Then we had a ride of about six hours through steppes, perfectly barren stony country rolling up and down and with only a very occasional well surrounded always by great herds of large black goats in charge of boys with guns. Our horses were good and our escort very wild, riding singing and shouting most of the time and continually challenging each other to gallop. The result was the horses were deadbeat and it was dark before we got in to the tents. On the way we passed several camps of Kurds, guarded by large hounds. (At Busrawi's a man followed us always to keep us safe from them.)

'On arrival Busrawi came to greet us, ceremonially, and we were conducted to his tent, a great open-sided sort of marquee of forty poles. He was very proud of its size. We took off our boots, and sat down on a thick soft mat arranged in this shape ⊔ with our places where the two marks are. I sat on the right and Young on the left, and they served dinner immediately. Behind us was a thick curtain, right across the middle of the tent, which shut off the private apartments, but in the tent round us there were, I suppose, more than a hundred men. They laid down a long mat, thirty feet or so, upon the carpets in front of our mat, placed bread all along the edges of it, and then more than forty dishes. The old Agha sat between us and gave the signal to start by taking a

piece of meat in his hand and putting it in my spoon. Then
everyone fell to with eagerness, saying nothing but eating at
a great pace simply shovelling the stuff into their mouths.
Servants moved behind with mugs of water. The food was
very good, mostly highly seasoned hashes, some things like
mince-pies, boiled wheat, leben, tomatoes and, for fruit,
melons. After we had eaten we washed our hands where we
sat, in a basin like that in Ned's house, and drank coffee. All
the while we had been eating a man had been beating a drum,
and another blowing on a pipe which sounded at times like
the real pipes, but had no bag. After dinner there was a lot
of this music, and some dancing, just of men, who capered
about waving handkerchiefs and singing, not very exciting.
We slept close to where we had eaten, touching the hareem
curtain, which was an honour, and with all the rest of the men
in front of us. Next day we did very little but watch more
dancing, and the playing of the 'jereed'. This was a horse
racing game in which men hunt each other and try to hit with
sticks. The general effect is rather like polo, and there are all
sorts of rules which we didn't understand. It was very
picturesque seeing men in dazzling robes galloping splendid
horses through clouds of sand. There was lots more feasting
and Khaleel, the successor of Ibrahim Pasha who was
dramatically murdered by the Young Turks, came to see us.
He's the greatest of all the Kurds, but very young, and rather
under Busrawi's thumb. It was very interesting listening to
Busrawi chat with Young. He's an old man, very dignified
yet kindly looking, giving the effect rather of Dr. Warren. He
insisted on feeding us with his own hands, while one of his
sons took off our boots. Yet this is a man responsible for some
of the biggest massacres of modern times.

'We left Busrawi's tents, in his company and with twelve
horsemen, next morning while it was still moonlight, and had
a great ride in the half-dark getting in to Ned's in time for the
chief and me to catch the train to Aleppo. The galloping was
grand, and we acquitted ourselves fairly well, though we had
no bridles, only ropes, saddles which had to be kept on by

careful balancing, and stirrups which came off if one pressed on them. It's queer that people with such good horses should have such bad gear. Ned was quite right again when I got back. His fever was bad for two days, yet not enough to make it be obvious. I wouldn't have known anything was wrong from the sight of him. And he has Young with him still, who is going to meet Dr. Usher on Monday at Biredjik and ride with him to Van.

'I left Ned very fit, Gregori [the Cypriote foreman of the excavations] had turned up, and Woolley is expected on the 31st. His house is being enlarged. It is a very comfortable place, with the mosaic floor making it cooler always than outside. And feeding arrangements are good. We always got dinners and lunches of several courses and omelettes for breakfast. Haj Wahid [the cook] is quite a character, famous throughout Aleppo for his old prowess as a fighting man, but now quiet. The house is long and flat as in the photos, with a bathroom and three good bedrooms, with English beds, washstands and furniture. You must not think of Ned as leading an uncivilized existence. When I saw him last as the train left the station he was wearing white flannels, socks and red slippers, with a white Magdalen blazer, and was talking to the governor of Biredjik in lordly fashion. Altogether Jerablus is a very fine place.'

To T.E.L.

February 18*th*, 1914

I've talked with counsellors and lords
Whose words were as no blunted swords,
Watched two Emperors and five Kings
And three who had men's worshippings,
Ridden with horsemen of the East
And sat with scholars at their feast,
Known some the masters of their hours,
Some to whom years were as pressed flowers:
Still as I go this thought endures
No place too great to be made yours.

MANHOOD

E. H. R. ALTOUNYAN
HUBERT YOUNG

E. H. R. ALTOUNYAN, M.C., M.D. Born 1889 — father
Armenian, mother Irish; educated in England. First met
T.E.L. at Carchemish, 1911, while home from Cambridge.
Author of poems, *Ornament of Honour*, relating to T.E.L.

IF to a superlative intelligence be added courage, and both
are contained in a healthy body, we may reasonably expect
something like this man. The courage to which I refer is
of the kind that, passing swiftly through the gamut of the
living, is to be found as the solitary companion of the remarkable. The expanding consciousness of a mind self-freed is
hourly dogged by panic to which must be opposed an hourly
defence. Further, when the breaking strain is reached — as it
must be sometime if anything of sufficient magnitude is being
attempted — the recoil has, in the past, often proved disastrous
to the individual. It can only be met by a deep self-knowledge
and the courage that must follow on it if the intellect is to
remain in control. Though many have found it comparatively
easy to tauten towards some great desire, very few have dared
to begin again in a manner worthy of their own immediate
past. This courage he pre-eminently had. Let it be clear that
we are not contemplating mere endurance. He had no Faith
to lend a logic to continuity. His intellect, stripped of achievement (no longer intellect's concern) and of a quality unable to
lean easily on the future, was compelled to move on, deprived
of all ascertainable momentum. Compelled by what precisely?
Some endocrine? Gravity? The malignancy, or, if you prefer
it, the love, of the Creator? These fascinating but rather silly
questions did not detain him. It sufficed, as it must each one
of us, that this compulsion matched the texture of his being,
accorded with himself. It is here that we strike those springs
of his humour, feeding that stream of wit which was to flow,
with an occasional breath-catching plunge, so pleasantly
through his life. For what if all this intellectual fuss, this
spiritual hubbub should mean — nothing? Well — not that
perhaps — but mean something so different from its surface-
seeming as to make laughter the only intelligent comment?

It must not be supposed that all this knowledge came as a gift. Students of his life cannot but be impressed by his persistence as a learner. Nothing could master him, but he proved a brilliant pupil in each successive school, until once more driven to truancy by his unique sense of proportion. This quality has seldom met with its due regard in human history. Its exponents, however able, either have been hopelessly obscure, or have never quite convinced posterity that the potential scope of their power was as great as they, or their admirers, imagined. It is fortunate that the men of this generation have the opportunity of studying, with the intimacy of near vision, one who made it his business to expound it, through fame and obscurity.

The higher the mind soars the more necessary is it to attend to the lines of communication, unless one seeks disembodiment — in contravention of our present contract. The realization and practice of this truism undoubtedly kept him sane. Lop-sidedness could never appeal to so practised an aesthete. Though threatened with a bulge that took on the aspect of an empire he proved adequate, and was accordingly accused of wilfulness and waste. Yet no one can convict him of refusing to shoulder responsibility when it claimed his mind; it is equally impossible to assume that, after putting the Revolt in his country's pocket, he merely sulked. I believe that the historian of the fifteen years that followed his retirement will be unable to find any particular front line in that period which could specifically have claimed him. That at any rate was his own conviction, and in the evil days that followed, when the current set away from personalities and what life remained seemed to stir uneasily among the masses, he felt able to attend to those lines of communication, under his control, which had suffered severe damage. Only an accident has prevented us from seeing the results of that timely toil.

Nowhere more than in art and learning is our sense of proportion so imperilled. Poets have been known to accept haloes while still hearty, and the devotees of learning (archaeologists in particular) succumb to petty jealousies after a short struggle. He was a devoted scholar but never blind or prickly. As to art he held that no matter how passionately lived it could never stand up to mere living. Although endowed by his own hard work with a superlative sense of words, he could never give himself to letters unless he felt that it was the only way of saving something vital from oblivion. This condition was fulfilled for him only twice; and when we remember his boundless ambitions as a writer, his discrimination becomes all the more remarkable.

If we consider the manner of his living, we find that his technique was simple. Driven to take cover from an almost lecherous public curiosity he used, and liked, solitude, but was often open to intimacy. His choice, apparently so fastidious, was in fact as broad as a publican's. He was definitely good company. The conventional who approached him as a hero, he endeavoured to enlighten with his wit. For the unwary — some of the heaviest calibre — who attempted patronage, he had a cache of practically noiseless bombs. The man who had the instinct or the courage to meet him on equal terms, suddenly found himself travelling over familiar country at an illuminating speed, all barriers down. This insistence on equality, running all up and down the human scale, is his finest flower; and sprang direct from that sense of proportion which he had made his own. It is the secret of his power with men; for it entails a supreme reasonableness that does no violence except to the violent, and taking everything possible into consideration, applies the right remedy in the correct dosage. Taken in conjunction with an exquisite realization of self, it could hardly fail to be effective and place great power in the hands of the user. How great this power actually was we shall never know. He early realized its possibilities and resolutely refused to make full use of it except during two years of war. It is possible that at no epoch would he have felt justified in its continuous employment; for the love of speed was the only lust he ever allowed himself.

Women were to him persons, and as such to be appraised on their own merits. Preoccupation with sex is (except in the defective) due either to a sense of personal insufficiency and its resultant groping for fulfilment, or to a real sympathy with its biological purpose. Neither could hold much weight with him. He was justifiably self sufficient, and up to the time of his death no woman had convinced him of the necessity to secure his own succession. He was never married because he never happened to meet the right person; and nothing short of that would do: a bald statement of fact which cannot hope to convince the perverse intricacy of the public mind. It is true that possessiveness is perhaps more frequent among women (men having had up to date the more numerous possessions), and possessiveness in any form was a quality which caused him peculiar discomfort; but anyone who had traversed or hoped to traverse the same country as himself always aroused his sympathy. It is natural that the majority of his friends should have been men, but those women who were able to meet him on some common ground, found no lack of fellow feeling or respect.

He has been called a romantic. The term is out of use, it might be well if it were revived. Certainly, if the epithet applies, he must puzzle its critics; for he built solidly and made use of the latest improvements. There is no flimsiness in his streets, no yearning spire to atone for the smoking hovel; detractors of romance can find no fault with the lighting, the lifts, or the sanitation; scientifically inforced concrete has been used throughout, and there's a fire extinguisher on every floor. What more can they want? They must excuse the splendour of his façade. His almost pathological insistence on freedom was not only an instinct but the result of the profoundest study; the realization of what it meant, not only for himself but everyone. The unit of life is the self and it must at all costs remain intact. We can only know ourselves; and nothing of beauty, joy or use, but is the outcome of unfettered action based on this knowledge. All attachments contracted with the aim of improving or strengthening that self are not only bound to fail, but if persisted in, must damage another as well. 'I know how to protect myself,' he said, adding by implication, 'and others at the same time.' Most of us have not the stamina to face the loneliness which freedom thus pursued entails. The rarity of this capacity among his generation made him all the more determined to preserve his own freedom — 'for want of something better'. For the Self — could we but grasp it — is the only perfectible sphere, the only thing in our existence capable of effective illumination: and size, for once, does not count. If there is to be any human expansion in this Universe it must come from the spread of this knowledge ... Yes, almost pathological was his passion for freedom, but not quite, for, notwithstanding the dazzling magnitude of his discovery, he was able by sheer grit to remain companionable. As to achievement and his boyish pose of contempt, he displayed the merest common sense. If life is endless, as in some queer way it must eventually appear to each one of us (and as he himself long felt), what is the sense in pawing over what's been done when the greatest victory must be followed by the morrow's defeat unless we get on with our business? And this, surely, is what he did.

The by-products of this industry were altogether lovely — but not at first. At Carchemish in 1911 the casual visitor to the dig met a frail, pallid, silent youth. The shut-up Oxford face, the down-cast eyes, the soft reluctant speech, courteous, impersonal, were impressive, disturbing and disagreeable. For here obviously was someone cleaving through life propelled by an almost noiseless engine. A *poseur* certainly, but could anyone disturb that poise? And yet — and yet — however great the power, would it not have been still greater, more constructive, had it acknowledged less grudgingly the possibilities of others? Twenty years later we both confessed to having found each other rather impossible. Refined capacity must learn to clothe itself in a raw world. By 1911 he had spun his cocoon but had not yet the assurance that enables the full-grown man to leave it when required. Aesthetically he was mature. Under the shadow of a robust and pagan Hogarth, he and Woolley set up an exquisite temple of culture where learning but slyly intruded and the hobbledehoy from without, not too abashed, could enjoy leisure as he sipped his coffee from cups of thin unglazed clay, off the museum shelf. There

I experienced the sane and delicate mingling of living and dead which one misses so completely in the exhausted atmosphere of our great museums. In the unobtrusive courtyard of mud-brick with its low headquarter building, mud-walled but mosaic-paved, its rough but adequate shelves loaded with finds, and its smooth impeccable service recalling a first-class hotel, life at Carchemish during those years represented a highly stylized, conscious, but perfect composition; and the two men who ran the show were merged in their own creation. My aesthetic sense was ravished by the beauty of their 'building', but it was a beauty that aroused envy and left one too deeply dissatisfied with oneself to be a true perfection. T.E. at heart never meant to produce this effect, but he had not the skill at the time to be able to avoid it; although by 1911 he had already traced out his deep foundations. The stories of this period — his encounters with the German engineers, his complete ascendancy over a fine and difficult type of Arab, his comic and efficient management of the officials — all showed that he was already in possession of his phenomenal capacity for dealing with men and things. The power welling up from his youth did not indeed drive him to trample on others, but as he felt its irresistible workings he could not help watching, without much hope, waiting, almost wistfully, for someone to challenge him. He found none and justified to himself that disdainful curl of the lips, so useful in dissipating the fool, but which defeated also so many of the wise.

When in 1919 I determined to meet him in Paris, the years had somehow eroded all the irrelevancies and left me with the irreducible truth. I knew, before I saw him, that here was something dazzling, apparently much greater than oneself but yet, if one could overcome one's terror, something to be met, and waiting to be met, on terms of perfect equality. I found no longer the Oxford exquisite but a man whose wildest imaginings had been fulfilled; a hero shaken by his vision, not of past accomplishment, but of incredible possibilities which unless he was very careful would become, were becoming, actualities leading to regions where he instinctively felt it would be terribly dangerous to remain. His eyes no longer drooped but met you and appraised; and as they turned from my father to my sister and then to me at our bizarre reunion in Feisal's Paris house, I saw them light up with sheer pleasure in the romance of living and succeeding. He was still naughty and inconsiderate, and the subsequent dinner party where he pretended a complete ignorance of French was uncomfortable for others beside the unfortunate French attaché. As we sat at the table I was reminded again of Carchemish, as I watched him manipulating into some semblance of shape the very incongruous elements of the party. Indeed he was astonishingly unchanged as to physique, and I could see no outward marks of his campaign. Still the manipulator, still never giving himself away, playing one person against, or with the other, always towards some end. But I left him this time with an eagerness to come again, and a certainty that I need no longer screw up my courage to approach him on any matter of moment. With Feisal himself he was wholly delightful and their co-operation hardly required the intervention of speech. A day or two later as we were lunching in the vast dining-room that contained most of the British Peace Delegation, he came in to speak to my father. As he stood by our table the room stopped eating and under the impact of that silence, as his eye swept over the heads, I could almost hear him say 'How-jolly-and-how-foolish'. I only once saw him really moved by a personality. Waiting to see him in his bedroom at the Carlton (Feisal's London headquarters), he arrived in uniform and flinging his cap on the bed exclaimed, flushing with pride, 'I've just had half an hour with Curzon'. I feel positively that though by this time he must have known that his Arab policy was going west he was never troubled by remorse. He had so obviously done his best, and there remained for him but to make the logical renunciations of an honourable bankruptcy in order to win his peace. Notoriety and the persecution of a sensation-loving public were more serious enemies; for a clear conscience could not save him from that distress; and when I ran him to earth one day in a refuge in Dover Street he was beginning to feel hunted and no longer the master of his circumstance. Everyone knows how he set about to regain that mastery. I did not see him again till 1932. 'Will you meet me?' I wrote; 'say if you don't want to', I added unnecessarily, for it wasn't the first time I had written without result. 'Right', he answered; 'if you don't talk about the war'. This was not difficult to promise, and in December of that year we met for the first time on equal terms. A robust individual with a pronounced brogue and the indefinable mark of the ranker oozing through cultured speech. He gave me a hand the size of a loin chop. I felt dazed but willing calmly to wait developments. It was in an ignoble little pub in Wareham, deserted but for a pot boy who had been entertaining him with the life stories of plutocrats who had tipped him in bygone summers. Anyhow he vanished as soon as T.E. had assured himself that I really had no intention of saluting an uncrowned king. We commandeered a bleak drawing-room and things began to hum. 'A fire?' Yes, certainly a fire, and he was down and up with logs in a jiffy, and was ordering a stupendous dinner for two. Something happened while he gave that order. He suddenly let himself go, and the maid who had shuffled up listlessly enough flew down the passage with goggling eye. I had already of course seen the staff of the Carlton getting a move on, and here again was the authentic touch; the streaming galvanizing power which could move men, but had so little to move. We agreed that alcohol was not worth it. No, he was not a vegetarian — quite. We agreed that *Lady Chatterley* raised the lid on — nothing; that Lytton Strachey's explanation to the tribunal in 1917 was the goods; and he poured out stories of Winston, Hardy, Shaw, and Kipling until it was obvious that if I hadn't already met them I certainly should — the next day. And as he talked he changed. Transfiguration is the right word to use, if we could but once forget its sacred connotations. The more perfectly the body serves the spirit, the more swiftly and outwardly will it change as the spirit moves, while the mind expresses and enhances each alteration. I never met a man whose body was kept in such perfect discipline, transmitting naturally each movement of a steady flow of spirit. It was not surprising therefore that his friends found, in that almost perfect functioning, a beauty that thrilled and never staled: even as the eye can never tire of watching the wind at work on the level surface of a lake. He had strength without rigidity, but of a fluid quality whose power derived from his total mass. It is here that our intellectuals miss true achievement: lusting for the smooth ranging of the mind, they dare not allow the spirit to change levels; flying from boredom and possible ineffectualness, they maintain themselves by refining down efficiency to the narrowness and rigidity of a razor blade. That evening we turned and twisted, soared and sank, breaking off while there was yet much to say. Next morning the boy told me that 'the other young chap' had gone down to the river, so I strolled to Wareham bridge and met him coming up. As he approached I saw again that hunted look which I had last caught in Dover Street. He was afraid for a moment that I was going to ask him where he had been. It was as though he mistrusted the felicity of the evening and could not quite believe my respect and understanding of his need for absolute freedom. I never realized so keenly as I did at that moment the utter loneliness of his life. It was as though he had fallen into the habit (he who was so disdainful of all habits) of never expecting complete intimacy, however great the host of his devoted friends. 'I have never loved anyone,' he wrote to me once, 'or hardly ever; lands and peoples — yes'; meaning that he had never experienced an affection which he felt to be undamaging to his or the other's freedom. I said nothing, but after breakfast, getting up every particle of courage, I attacked, accusing him of cowardice in personal relationship. 'Don't retreat from me,' I said at last in despair. He looked at me dully and then asked me to come and see his motor bicycle. We never doubted each other again; but I saw now what he meant when he had said the night before, 'I haven't had much kick out of life; those days in Carchemish were the best'. By the merest accident of my own make-up I had stumbled upon the truth. No one has ever lived so much alone. However great the temptation he could never blind himself to stupidity, lust, or the faintest breath of heaviness in himself or others, and from first to last preferred nothingness to the second best. Six months later as I lay at Bart.'s recovering from an operation, the staff nurse announced, one dreary Sunday afternoon, that a Dr. Shaw had rung up from the porter's lodge and wished to see me. I thought of the various doctors I knew of that name, and grunted. He certainly must have required all the prestige of the prefix to have slipped past the guards, for he presently shot into my room dressed as a longshoreman, with the addition of the pale yellow of a pair of boots. He was always shy at first contact and would, disdaining greetings, launch forward at his accustomed pace as though unwilling to fall into step with you, afraid of losing speed, determined if possible not to break rhythm. So at each encounter I felt for a moment or two as though I listened to the hum of a high-speed engine until our gears engaged — usually on second. This time I remember we compared notes on the technique of dealing with supercilious nabobs on outward-bound P. & O.s.

Clouds Hill was like himself when he had no special job on hand; unobtrusive, undistinguished, unless chance led one inside. He was completely in love with it. This three-roomed cottage represented the slow creative evolution of ten years, the patient craft of an artist of limited means and still more limited time. He was right in thinking that his friends could there find, if they took the trouble, the salient points in his creed exposed in matter; self-revealed without the babble of words. Economy of effort — each stair of the steep flight had a pneumatic tread. Electric wiring throughout, but it was doubtful if the tiny turbine-plant he was devising would be able to run more than one bulb. This could be shifted as required from room to room. No kitchen; there was a pub within reach when a square meal became a necessity. No inside doors, but silent leather curtains. No bedrooms; were there not three whole rooms to sleep in and warm-lined bags neatly piled in store? Pictures? Only one, built into the wall (a mistake, he confessed), and the rest kept out of sight until one should choose to bring one out like a book. There was warmth and snugness in the thick pile on the floors; generosity in the fireplaces; luxury (the most modern) in the automatic hot water supply, and final grandeur in the close-packed waiting books. It was here that I was once more the astonished witness of his capacity for speed in movement. We had arrived on a cold Sunday in January after a nearly impossible cross-country journey from Southampton. A huge fire was burning, and I sat down contentedly to warm myself, but he was not satisfied. I half turned to protest but he had vanished, and I was spreading my hands to the blaze when with a slight rustle he was back dragging a huge dead branch that scraped past the doorway. On this branch he danced rapidly to the accompaniment of flying twigs. The fire roared, and I found myself, still half dazed, watching him sweep up the remaining leaves with a long-handled broom till he had swept himself and them out backwards from the room. I have seen no movement in ballet more magical. As we sat roasting by the blaze, we ate and discussed the pistachio. 'I lick the shell for the salt before cracking, and usually stop at the fourth, when you get the best of the flavour'. So simple. Doctors tell us we all overeat. He didn't, and that is all there is to it.

While we were waiting in Southampton for my train I protested against his celibacy. 'Don't you try,' I exclaimed, 'to buck people up? Don't you succeed in making them, for a time at least, think it worth while to be alive?' 'Yes,' he said very quietly, 'I try.' 'Well then,' I continued, 'and how many people do you think are living in this bloody world to-day who have that capacity? Can't you see that it is damnable of you not to leave something alive behind?' We were walking through the Sunday evening crowds and he was silent so long that I began to hope. 'Yes,' he murmured at last, 'but don't you think it's time to close down?' And I felt the whole human-laden globe reel by in smothering darkness. 'It can't be done,' I said in angry triumph, and he smiled, without reluctance, as the train moved out.

MAJOR SIR HUBERT W. YOUNG, K.C.M.G., D.S.O.
1885-1950. Indian Army, 1908; Political Officer, Mesopo-
tamia, 1915-17; Hejaz Operations, 1918 (see *Seven Pillars of
Wisdom*); Foreign Office, 1919-21; Middle East Department,
Colonial Office, 1921-27 (at first with T. E. L.); Counsellor to
High Commissioner, 'Iraq, 1929-32; Governor of Nyasaland,
1932-34; of Northern Rhodesia, 1934-38, and of Trinidad and
Tobago, 1938-42. Author of *The Independent Arab*, and articles
on Hejaz War in *Blackwood's Magazine*. See article by W. G.
Lawrence for first meeting.

W HEN I first met T.E., at Carchemish in 1913, we were
alone together for a few days, during which we talked
incessantly. For some reason he had stayed out there
when the 'digs' were closed for the hot weather, and was leading
a simple but fastidious life with no companions but Arabs and
Kurds. Even at that time he seems to have made up his mind
that regular soldiers were unworthy folk, for he told me many
years later that I had remained in his memory chiefly if not
solely because in the course of these talks I had confessed that
I was sometimes afraid, which he thought a strange and praise-
worthy confession from a regular soldier. I was surprised to
see in some account published during his lifetime that he had
always taken a great interest in strategy and the art of war,
since these were the subjects that were uppermost in my own
mind in those days, and we never even mentioned them. I
myself thought, when I read his references to Clausewitz and
others in the *Seven Pillars*, that he had only taken up the art
of war, as he did everything else, when it came his way, and
that he had mastered it in the same incredibly short time as he
mastered, for example, revolver-shooting, intelligence work,
the nature and use of explosives, and leadership, to mention
four of his accomplishments about which any regular soldier
should be qualified to speak. At all these four things he was
as good as any professional soldier and very much better than
most. Even more than his indomitable will and his personal

courage and endurance, it was this faculty of beating the professional at his own job that won the hearts of the primitive Bedouin, and compelled the admiration, if it did not win the hearts, of more sophisticated people such as Generals and other regular officers. I remember telling all my friends when I got back to India after our first meeting that there was a little man at Carchemish of whom more would be heard some day, and it was no surprise to me when he rose to the surface as he did. War or no war, he would have done it in any one of a dozen different lines.

I next met him in Mesopotamia, when he came out there with Aubrey Herbert, and was disappointed in him. He seemed to me thoroughly spoilt, and posing in a way that was quite unlike what I remembered of him at Carchemish. It was then that I first noticed his anti-regular soldier complex, and, perhaps not unnaturally, resented it hotly. We did not then recover our old friendship, and I was very much surprised two years later when I was unexpectedly sent for to join him in Arabia. This was at the beginning of 1918, when the Arab base had already been established for some months at Akaba, out of which the Turks had been driven by the most brilliant stroke of T.E.'s military genius. From this time on to the end of the war with Turkey in November, T.E. was more the political and military strategist than the tactician. He could not cope with the tactics of the strange little regular army that he had himself encouraged Feisal to create, and its very existence, as I have explained elsewhere, put out of the question the purely Bedouin operations of which he had made himself a master. More than once the Arabs failed to do what he rightly thought they should do, and he had on one occasion to import a battalion of the Imperial Camel Corps to get it done. The trained Arab officers were conscious of his impatience with their rusty text-book maxims, and determined to show that they knew as much about war as he did. Perhaps some of us British officers were just as bad. I do not know, but rightly or wrongly we were inclined to be critical and resentful of his omniscience. He recognized, much later, that he had not been quite fair to some of us in his account of the final raid, but he could not bring himself to alter what he had written. He and I went together to the first performance in London of an American film of his exploits, at one point in which a group of British officers was shown, with a caption saying that they had helped him at the base but had of course not gone up-country. I turned to him and said, 'Surely you are not going to have that?' He said that he would see that it was corrected, but I saw the thing again some weeks later and no change had been made.

Later on, he asked me to sit to a well-known artist for the *Seven Pillars*. He had already shown me some of the other portraits, chuckling at the skill with which the particular victim had been made to present the appearance required of him, and I wanted to know what he was going to do with mine, so I refused to sit unless he showed me the proofs first. This he declined to do, and I repeated that in that case I would not sit for him. We were both working in the Colonial Office at that time, and he used to come and lunch with me sometimes at my small house in North Street. One day he told me that a page was reserved in the *Seven Pillars* for my picture, and that if I persisted in my refusal to sit he would leave it blank, all but a footnote to say 'This page was for a portrait of Young, but he refused to sit because he was afraid of what I might have said about him'. 'All right,' I said, 'you can do that if you like. I don't know which of us will look the bigger fool.'

Nothing more happened for nearly two years, when, having married an artist, I agreed to sit to her, but only if he showed me the proofs. He gave way then, and sent them to me. There was one passage which I thought was unfair to myself, and I asked him either to alter it or to put me in under my own name instead of the name he had invented. 'No,' he said, 'I am not going to change it.' 'But the correct account may appear some day,' said I. 'Oh no, it won't,' said he. 'But it will,' I said, 'because I'm writing it, and it may perhaps be said that you put me in under a false name in these pages because you knew you were telling lies about me.' 'But that *is* why I have put you in under a false name,' he said, and cocked a metaphorical snook. Little monkey, I thought, and said no more. Am I the only writer in this book to call him a little monkey, I wonder? And am I the only one to criticize him? If so, I shall be the only one whose account will please him wherever he may be. I am afraid I always thought he was a mischievous little imp and this mischievousness was undoubtedly a flaw in his fine character. Another small failing was the vanity which led him to pose, and tortured the better side of his nature. He gloried in it and was ashamed of it by turns. His attitude towards publicity was that of Brer Rabbit to the briar-patch. 'Don't throw me into that briar-patch, Brer Fox,' he would protest, and all the time the briar-patch was where he longed to be. It was only when the blaze of limelight that he had himself turned on became embarrassing and even shameful to him that he made half-hearted efforts to turn it off, and by that time it was too late. It may seem ungracious to point out these comparatively small failings, but his great qualities so far transcended them that to mention them can do no harm to his reputation and may help to complete the picture of one of the most remarkable Englishmen of our generation.

As a statesman, T.E. possessed all the qualifications for success, including, it must be admitted, the faculty of calculated unscrupulousness in the interest of his main object. Whether he was in fact let down by the British Government, or whether he promised more to the Arabs than he had any right to promise will never be known, but he would certainly not have hesitated to exceed his instructions in what he regarded as true British interests, any more than did other successful makers of history in the past. As soon as it became clear to him that the British Government were not prepared to intervene further with the French Government, and that the clash between the French and King Feisal in Syria was final, he bent all his great brain and energy to securing for the Arabs in 'Iraq and Trans-Jordan the greatest possible measure of the independence promised to them, with qualifications, in the MacMahon letters. To this end he set himself to create a picture in the minds of the responsible authorities of himself as the best possible adviser on the Middle East and of King Feisal as the only possible candidate for the throne of 'Iraq. An instance of the lengths to which he was prepared to go to achieve this end was his creation of the phrase 'the first brown Dominion' for the Arab countries, and his fathering it upon Feisal himself. I was asked once by the authority concerned whether Feisal was loyal to the British Empire, and expressed the opinion that he was and would no doubt remain grateful to us for helping him to the throne of 'Iraq, but that his first and only aim was the re-establishment of an Arab Empire. 'But Lawrence says that his idea of the Arab countries is that they should form the first brown Dominion,' I was told. I could only reply that I wondered what Arabic terms His Majesty had employed to express this conception. On another occasion some critic of T.E.'s plans had urged that, while he might know a great deal about Syria and Western Arabia, he was completely ignorant of Mesopotamia. I said that so far as I knew this was correct, as I believed he had only visited the country once, for a few weeks, during the War. 'But he tells me that he lived there for two years before the War', was the puzzled reply. I hastened to explain that the blessed word Mesopotamia literally meant the whole tract of country lying between the Tigris and the Euphrates, including the basins of the two rivers, and that by this definition it was quite true to say that T.E. had lived there for two years. Instances could no doubt be multiplied of such calculated departures from the strict path of truth, but no one who knew T.E. would dream of imputing them to unworthy motives. He would have scorned to advance himself by either representation or misrepresentation. I shall never forget the night on which he came to tell me of his decision to join the Royal Air Force. We sat up till three o'clock in the morning, I pleading with him to reconsider his decision and he a monument of inflexible determination. 'But why not as an officer?' I asked. 'You know quite well that they would give you any rank you cared to ask for.' There was a flash of mischief as he said that he did not think much of the officers of the Royal Air Force. 'Then why not help to raise the standard?' I asked.

He said that he had given orders long enough: he wanted to see what it was like to have his life regulated for him and not to shoulder any more responsibility. But this was not his real difficulty. No amount of responsibility would have been too great for T.E. I never knew him hesitate to take a decision, and I would rather have served under him than under any regular soldier I have ever met, provided that he was not himself fettered by having to answer to higher authority for what he did. This is the true explanation both of his success and of his failure to achieve yet more than he did achieve. He could not reconcile responsibility with discipline. Given a free hand, as he was by General Allenby during the War, he was inimitable. Strong, resourceful, a born leader of men, and of matchless courage, when there was no restriction placed upon him he could and did make a success of anything and everything to which he turned his hand.

.

THE WAR: HIS COMMANDERS

ERNEST M. DOWSON
LORD ALLENBY
A. P. WAVELL

SIR ERNEST M. DOWSON, K.B.E. 1876-1950. Director-
General, Survey of Egypt, 1909; Under-Secretary of State for
Finance, Egypt, 1919; Financial Adviser to the Egyptian
Government, 1920-23; Adviser to Palestine and Transjordan
Governments on settlement of lands and land taxation, 1923-28,
and to the 'Iraq and Zanzibar and Kenya Governments on the
same problems, 1929-30 and 1935-40.

MAPWORK AND PRINTING IN THE NEAR EAST

THE course of events would no doubt have drawn Lawrence
somehow or other into the Near Eastern vortex of the
Great War in view of his earlier association with the countries so deeply affected thereby and of his knowledge of the
speech and ways of their peoples. It is of interest none the less
to trace back the impulse which actually brought him into
these troubled waters to a previous rumbling of the storm
which ultimately burst on Arab and Englishman, Turk and
German alike in these parts.

In 1906 Britain and Turkey stood on the brink of war about
the position of the eastern frontier of Egypt, which in theory
remained a line dividing one vilayet of the Ottoman Empire
from another. The Ottoman flag still flew and Ottoman
currency still circulated impartially on both sides of this line,
while a Khedive nominated by Ottoman firman reigned in
Cairo. Britain claimed the glacis of Sinai, whole and inviolate,
as Egypt's. Turkey asserted the glacis to be hers, or would
have sapped a permanent approach to the Suez Canal through
it. Faced with the still decisive naval threat to Constantinople,
Turkey yielded and Egypt held Sinai intact.

Sinai at that time was little known and the defensively
important northern portion was substantially unmapped.
Arrangements were therefore made a few years later for a survey to be made by the Survey of Egypt and the British War
Office in conjunction, the topographical field work being
carried out by a succession of military officers. The work pro-
gressed steadily until by the spring of 1913 an excellent series

of topographical maps covered the quadrilateral included between the Suez Canal and the Turko-Egyptian frontier. Newcombe, who was in charge of the field work at the time, wished to extend the survey across the frontier during the following season; but recognized that the Turkish authorities could not be expected to allow British military officers to carry out topographical mapping in Turkish territory. The survey itself was of a general topographical character, as valuable for peaceful as for defensive purposes; so that all parties were satisfied when it was agreed to give its extension into Palestine an archaeological character and entrust the conduct to two young and then little known archaeologists, Woolley and Lawrence.

There is imprinted on my mind an unforgettable picture of Lawrence's first appearance in the sunlit doorway of the Surveyor-General's Office in Egypt when he came on Newcombe's instructions at the beginning of the 1913-14 working season to report for duty and to collect field equipment and field staff. The room opened on to an outside balcony and I can see him now framed in the doorway against the trees and sky in clothes that were nondescript, if not khaki, with a half apologetic grin on his face and an introductory bend of his body, as he entered, the mischievousness of which I did not sense in that fleeting silhouette. This picture and the simultaneous thought 'Whoever can this extraordinary little pipsqueak be?' have remained embedded in my memory ever since. He almost danced in and sat down on the large leather-cushioned upright chair for visitors which always stood by the Surveyor-General's flat roll-top desk in that wide business-like room. In two words he said who he was and why he was there. The talk doubtless then turned to the topics usual on such occasions, to triangulation points and plane tables, tentage and water, chainmen and camels; although the details lie forgotten, buried beneath the strata of many later talks in the same surroundings on more far-reaching issues, my curiosity and surprise remained unquenched and it lingers tenaciously in my mind that I continued to wonder and to probe unsuccessfully throughout that first talk as to whether my visitor was real or pretended clown.

He passed on to other offices, took what he wanted in supplies and equipment and embarked on the season's desert topography, after which he returned like a string of predecessors to his customary occupations. Woolley and he had, however, completed in the nick of time the last of the six successive seasons' work, which provided a topographical map of Egypt's eastern approaches that was probably only rivalled in up-to-dateness, accuracy and informativeness throughout the whole range of territory battled for, outside of France at least, by the concurrent preparatory defensive survey of the Gallipoli peninsula carried out with corresponding foresight by the Turks.

The outbreak of the War in 1914 brought Lawrence back again to maps of Arabic-speaking lands and map-making therein. He began work in the Geographical Section of the General Staff at the War Office. His services were at once called upon to assist in the production of the maps of Sinai, on which he had worked in the field, and of Palestine and Syria. His transliteration of Arabic script and his rendering of local geographical terms so impressed those who worked with him that his decisions were accepted without demur, although his qualifications were unknown. On the one recorded occasion when his version was questioned, as it happened by a senior officer, a semi-explosion resulted. As a drawing office map-maker, however, he did not carry the same conviction. His treatment of generally accepted detail was very off-hand if it differed from what he thought it should be.

In December 1914 he was ordered in company with Newcombe and Woolley to Eygpt and quickly became the effective link between the Military Intelligence Service and in due course the Arab Bureau on the one side and the Survey of Egypt on the other. Both the Mediterranean Expeditionary Force and the Navy also dealt directly with the Survey, the latter establishing a Naval Officer at Survey Headquarters later on: but although the channels of communication from all quarters were kept completely mobile throughout the war, most threads passed to the Survey through Lawrence chiefly by virtue of the convenience and efficiency of this course.

Gradually a vast network was established to collect material for maps and ancillary records, in which the Military and Naval Intelligence Services, the Arab Bureau, the Air Forces, H.M. Ships, the Field Survey Companies, and many unknown people collaborated. When Lawrence left for the Hejaz, custom had produced mental and administrative ruts in which matters continued to run happily and effectively till the need ceased. To appreciate the nature of the service involved it is necessary to understand something of the character and functions of the organization worked with. The Survey of Egypt is an ordinary civil department of the Egyptian Government, built up primarily to carry out the cadastral, topographical and geological survey of Egypt, but including other scientific activities. As has already been illustrated in the conduct of the topographical survey of Northern Sinai, it had for some time been the practice for the Geographical Section of the General Staff and the Survey of Egypt to work together in matters of mutual cartographical interest, particularly those affecting the defence of Egypt. The necessities of the war naturally occasioned much heavier demands. In pursuance and extension of past practice the Survey was therefore asked in August 1914 to take over, so far as possible, the reproduction and supply of all maps required for the forces operating in the Near Eastern theatre of war. Outside of Egypt the territories chiefly affected were the Gallipoli Peninsula, Anatolia, Syria and Arabia. The available maps of these areas were both sketchy and undependable; so that at an early stage collaboration had to be extended from the office to the field. Field survey sections and field drawing and printing offices were formed initially in Gallipoli at Nugent's instance, and later in Palestine. These worked from the outset in conjunction with the Flying Services, and presented new information in provisional form from day to day on the spot and enabled this information to be as continuously embodied in the regular map series, the preparation and publication of which required the ampler resources available at Survey Headquarters. The capture on prisoners successively of all the sheets of the admirable Turkish map of Gallipoli already mentioned enabled this series to be promptly reproduced in Egypt and substituted for the defective maps with which the expedition was originally supplied. Material for progressive amendments of the current depictions of other neighbouring territory were, as stated, unceasingly furnished by many keen collaborators working from land, air or sea. Such material was commonly received through Lawrence and was digested and utilized under his direction. In addition to mapwork of all varieties, many curious demands were made for facsimiles or other special reproductions needed by the Intelligence or the Arab Bureau for this or that reason. In the absence of any field of technical assistance in the country to fall back upon, these demands often severely taxed the ingenuity of the staff and the resources of a service frequently quite unequipped to deal with them: but it quickly became a compact of craft pride and schoolboy fun never to be defeated on these occasions, a combination of incentives which Lawrence inspired or shared with equal rapture. The design and reproduction of a special set of arabesque postage stamps for the Sherif of Mecca was probably the most interesting of the improvisations undertaken in close collaboration with him.[1]

While the Survey was able to cope successfully in one way or another with all types of reproduction which could be executed by photo-metallic processes, it could not undertake letterpress printing and book-making of the quality and volume that the forces based in Egypt rapidly grew to require. So the well-found Egyptian Government Press was also soon linked with G.H.Q. through Lawrence in very much the same way. Let us now consider briefly some of the personal aspects of his manner of carrying out these two somewhat similar tasks.

The offices of the Survey are at Giza on the west bank of the Nile about two miles from the old Savoy Hotel in which G.H.Q. was located while in Cairo. Although Lawrence's relations with the Survey were not confined to the reproduction

---

[1] Described in 'A short notice on the design and issue of postage stamps for His Highness, Emir and Sherif of Mecca and King of the Hejaz', published by the Survey of Egypt in 1918.

of maps and other documents, his relations at Giza were mainly with officers connected with that branch of the work, more particularly with the Director of the Reproduction Office, and the Superintendents of the Map Compilation Office, the Photo-Process Office and the Printing Office. His relations with the Government Press were chiefly with the Director, but were similar in scope and character.

Although I had met Lawrence the previous year my knowledge of him had still to ripen, while he was quite unknown to the various officers of the Reproduction Office. It is instructive, therefore, to revive the first impressions of his impact on the minds of the two officers with whom his dealings at Giza from thenceforward chiefly lay. One of these was W. H. Crosthwaite, the Director of the Reproduction Office, who later on took over the duties of Map Officer at G.H.Q. when Lawrence joined the Sherif's Armies. The other was W. M. Logan, who was in charge of the Map Compilation Office in which all the cartographical material that streamed in during the next five years or so from the various fronts was examined, digested and absorbed.

At the outset must be pictured the extremely youthful and, to our unseeing eyes, insignificant figure with well-ruffled light hair, solitary pip on sleeve, minus belt and with peaked cap askew, who in these days and throughout his closest connection with the Survey used to be continuously at Giza, riding out on his motor cycle Boanerges with a care which was remarked both there and also later when he visited the Government Press at Bulaq.

Crosthwaite has a vivid recollection of my first introduction to him of a young Second Lieutenant who explained that he was going to have a good deal to do with the arrangements for the preparation and issue of the maps that would be required. In the course of this conversation Lawrence proceeded to criticize somewhat severely the system of transliteration of Arabic place names into Roman characters that the Survey of Egypt had adopted. As Crosthwaite had been closely concerned personally with the establishment of this system and had spent many months in studying the subject and in discussing it with recognized experts, his first impression of Lawrence was one of wonder as to who this young man was and of astonishment at his impudence. Logan's first contact was even less promising. His lifetime's experience of, and earnest devotion to, his work were deeply affronted when he was first presented to Lawrence and told that the latter had been charged with general control of the mapwork required by G.H.Q. Logan resented having to take orders from such a boy, and felt that the War Office had acted in accordance with the ineptitude traditionally pertaining to it in burlesque in putting such a youngster in charge of anything. The effect produced on other officers was equally unpromising. The stage, therefore, appeared to be set comfortably for friction and inefficiency in map production in the local theatre: but the Survey had a long established tradition of self-confident efficiency and no one was really perturbed. For Lawrence's quiet forcefulness had still to be realized.

Lawrence's opening gambit on the transliteration square, when he first met Crosthwaite, was characteristic of a move he frequently adopted to provoke the instinctive response of those he encountered to a sudden challenge to some established dogma, dignity or practice. The puckishness of the habit is evident. This was usually revealed to the onlooker at the time in an accompanying *moue* and glance or stood nakedly confessed in hilarious delight at any appropriate rejoinder. But although the speaker rejoiced in this puckishness and often displayed it in pure devilry the process served him to plumb a man's make-up in one unguarded moment. Pomposity was unquestionably apt to be pricked, inefficiency exposed, and pretension exploded in this way: and these were qualities which aroused Lawrence's worst incompatibilities. So for purposes of any useful collaboration with him the pompous, the ineffective and pretentious were best promptly recognized and, by hook or by crook, eliminated.

Realizing this, being determined to see good work produced, and not being of a passive temperament, he naturally sought from the outset, as later, to diagnose the minds and characters of the members of the team upon which he was to be dependent for the discharge of his responsibilities to the countries engaged in the War. It can be safely assumed that if he had found any important member of the Survey Reproduction Office Staff an unsatisfactory unit in that team, circumstances would have arisen which called for a transfer of that member's services elsewhere. We none of us realized the threat he then constituted to the pedestals upon which he found us. But for truthful balance it has of course to be recognized also that it was not only the pompous, the inefficient and the pretentious whose co-operation Lawrence's ways tended to alienate. Many men of sense and ability were repelled by the impudence, freakishness and frivolity he trailed so provocatively. Many sober and fair-minded men regarded his intrusions of Bedawi robes, accoutrements and bare feet into conventional gatherings as histrionic displays. And many of these regarded him in consequence at bottom as a posturing stage player whose tinsel exploits were the fruits of freely lavished gold.

During the two years in which Lawrence's association with the Survey and Government Press developed, no occasion for the fierce limelight that subsequently beat upon his actions had arisen: and in these smaller fields the weight of his real personality and wide knowledge rapidly effaced the initial impression of boyish irresponsibility and unseasonable trifling that he delighted to present. Throughout this time he visited the Survey two or three times a week at least, sometimes several times a day. No doubt formal orders were issued at the outset regulating his relations with the various offices with which he worked; but he seemed to us all to slide silently into the organization of the Department and to become embodied in it effortlessly. His slight figure, gentle step, quiet good morning and mischievous grin became of the familiar essence of things.

Although from the very first he had direct access to all offices and to individual craftsmen if he wished, and although he made the most exigent demands on everyone, I never received a grouse about him: and I never heard of an instance of misunderstanding or friction being created by him either through faulty human contact or owing to the many short-circuitings of official hierarchy that response to the kaleidoscopic situation demanded. Short-circuitings of authority and interventions with current procedures would no doubt have been constantly needed in those strenuous times, regardless of any personalities; but by a miracle of give and take Lawrence and the Survey Officers with whom he worked stereotyped them into a peaceful procedure without rupturing the normal conduct of the machine. For it must be remembered firstly that the machine was manned by a cosmopolitan crew and critically depended for its output upon its routine operation, and secondly that it had throughout concurrently to meet the heavier, if less spectacular, requirements of the civil administration of the country on which the local military effort was itself based. The elasticity of response to military requirements that was secured would not have been possible without the greatest good sense and good temper on the part of those departmentally responsible; but it was evoked and maintained by a remarkable combination of qualities in Lawrence, which foreshadowed those displayed in the wider and more exacting arena of Arabia later.

What then were those qualities? On reflection I think the foundation of all was a rare capacity to regard an operation of any sort objectively, and in the process to get inside the skin of the participants. This enabled him to look at his own part in any performance with an almost sardonic detachment, which in essentials led to sinking himself with complete self-abnegation in an enterprise, but might without any contradiction take the form of dressing the puppet up and letting it caper appropriately. It is idle to pretend he was not ambitious. He was vastly so: but, like all men of large calibre, ambitious for achievement rather than recognition, and for recognition of the worth of such achievement (large or small) rather than for approbation of his personal performance. Seeing himself under the microscope assisted him to sense how other actors in an enterprise were feeling and the character of the inspiration, encouragement or coercion that the cause or the occasion consequently demanded. He realized acutely that the satisfaction of achievement was not confined to large canvases or high places, and that the taste of achievement in any degree was ` the greatest stimulus to further effort in any man of worth. He therefore left men to the utmost extent possible to do their own work, even at the cost of quality and speed. Crosthwaite instances an experience of his own illustrating this, which is an interesting complement to the story of the original meeting of the two. In what were still the early days of their association, Lawrence one public holiday brought to Giza a captured Turkish map of which a reproduction was urgently needed. To save time Crosthwaite buckled to at once to transliterate the place names as well as he could. Lawrence watched him without comment, returning from time to time through a long afternoon. The map was reproduced and issued with the place names as thus rendered, without any emendation. Months later Crosthwaite learnt that Lawrence had a considerably better knowledge than himself both of the locality and of Turkish. He concluded that while Lawrence satisfied himself by his silent inspections that the results were adequate, he wished to avoid any belittlement of Crosthwaite's effort. It seems to me also probable that some genuine intolerance about the transliteration of place names from Arabic to Roman script originally imbibed by Lawrence in a more limited field, was even then being transmuted into an acceptance of the wide latitude, the need for which he sustained with such joyous exaggeration later.

Be this as it may it does not affect the justness of the deduction Crosthwaite drew from the episode. Throughout Lawrence treated the Survey and the Government Press, not as map producing and printing machines as he properly might have done; but as living organizations which had to be assisted in every way to respond not only effectively, but enthusiastically, to the insistent and heterogeneous demands made upon them by day and by night in these times. His tremendous keenness about anything to do with the work was remarkable and infectious, with the consequence that his frequent walks round the various offices and workshops had a most stimulating effect on the men. At times when they had been working very long hours, Crosthwaite noticed a brisking up and lifting of spirits after such visits. His impish jocosity contributed to secure this, no less than his unfailing appreciation of the work produced. In his dealings with us there was no limelight for Lawrence. It was all for the efficiency of the two services and of their officers and craftsmen.

The quality I am inclined to put next in value was his extra-ordinary capacity to get his own way quietly when this seemed of critical importance to a necessary end. The Director of the Government Press narrates how once a very competent and senior Military Officer, who was detailed for the purpose, Lawrence and himself carefully debated and agreed upon a procedure satisfactory to all three to govern certain necessarily delicate relations between the Arab Bureau and the Press. The latter, it will be appreciated, was an organ of Egyptian Government administration paid for by the Egyptian taxpayer. All three of them were then summoned to a Conference at G.H.Q. which was intended to regularize their conclusions. Lawrence, possibly suspecting what might occur, modestly remained in the corridor. The General who presided over-ruled the arrangement and decreed another and completely unworkable one, which the senior officer mentioned felt unable to question. On emerging from the Conference the result was communicated ruefully to Lawrence. He smiled and said it was of no consequence as the arrangement originally agreed upon would be adopted unmodified as it was.

His extraordinary resourcefulness and his versatile competence may be grouped as the third important component of his success. An instance of the former is also cited by the Director of the Government Press. The difficulty not only of keeping complicated technical operations going in Egypt during the War without any complementary industrial background, but also of meeting quite unanticipated demands, has been mentioned. One day an imperative need arose in the Government Press for an intricate spare part, which the Director happened to know existed in the depot of an enemy firm whose premises were under seal in charge of the official responsible for enemy property. G.H.Q. listened, considered and most politely regretted that nothing could be done without reference to London, which might very well fail and was certain to be slow. Lawrence was told of the incident the next day. He asked for the exact locality of the premises and for an exact description of the article, which he had never seen. The following morning he brought it along. No explanations were volunteered: no questions asked. He smiled as he produced it, merely saying that there had been 'no difficulty'.

The diversity of Lawrence's capacity was so remarkable that one only slowly and sceptically accepted its genuineness. It sprang I think from unusual clarity of mind working on an unusual catholicity of knowledge. This enabled him to seize and apply essentials even in technical processes with which he was quite unfamiliar. Both at the Survey and the Press he rapidly earned the respect of a very varied specialist staff, because of his quickness in understanding technical details and his appreciation of the difficulties and limitations of the different processes of map and book production. Those who dealt with him continuously are agreed that it stands out prominently in their memories that they were always encountering some new side to his knowledge and capacity. Thus one morning he came to the Press and asked if he could sit there for a couple of hours as he could not be quiet at the Arab Bureau. He explained that the forces operating against the Senussi in the Western Desert were using a code which was known to the Turks, and that he wanted to compile a new one. He completed this the same morning and the code he made appears to have continued in use until the end of these operations.

Many other instances of his many-sided competence could be given: but in view of the uses he put it to later, probably the most interesting expression of his personal capacity was the visualization and photographic memory of topographical features of any ground which he had traversed that he drew upon in the compilation of the new map series of the neighbouring territories that have been already mentioned. As explained, the preparation of maps of Anatolia, Syria, and Arabia presented great difficulties owing to the meagreness and inaccuracy of the material available. Lawrence, throughout the whole period of the War, devoted effort and time to correcting and adding to this detail personally whenever he had the opportunity. This he did with the greatest confidence entirely from memory if he had ever been over the ground himself. He seemed never to hesitate in such cases. His knowledge of other people's itineraries and observations was also wide, although his judgment of them was apt to be characteristically crisp and sweeping, if he had had some occasion to appraise the quality of the worker or his work in humdrum practice somewhere. He appreciated the value of faithful land survey and was capable of it, as his work in Sinai with Woolley shows; while he utilized compass and travelling time, or similar expedients himself when conditions permitted. But in the constant attempts of the Arab Bureau and the Survey to compile amendments of current representations of inaccessible territory the sparsity of material forced him as a rule to work with a bold brush to indicate primarily features of outstanding importance adequately for immediate burning needs. Work of this nature to be successful demands a power of topographical observation and memorization which is rare. Its performance of course merged in the general map compilation of which it formed part.

But here, as elsewhere, Puck was always breaking through: and it is Puck, not his abilities or achievements, that those of us who worked with him in the ways touched on keep in our hearts and memories. I will, therefore, close with an incident, trivial though it be, which by some chance pictures in several of our minds his irrepressible fooling. There being an irremediable lack of reliable material for the compilation of the hill features of the Cilicia Sheet of the quarter million map series, Logan asked him what should be done about the hills. He replied, 'Oh, do let us have some hills. It would be such fun to have hills.' The graphic creations, denudations and resurrections of those hills under Lawrence's wand and the draughtsman's brush were catastrophic. No one who shared in any way in the preparation of this wartime sheet will forget either Lawrence's refusal to treat the task seriously or his keenness to make the historic outlines of the Taurus at least rise from the paper plains and foothills more majestically and convincingly than any mountains in cartography had ever done before.

FIELD-MARSHAL VISCOUNT ALLENBY,

1861-1936. Commander-in-Chief, Egypt and Palestine, 1917-19; High Commissioner for Egypt, 1919-25.

T. E. LAWRENCE was perhaps the most interesting product of the Great War; yet, withal, a character difficult to know. Not that he was unsociable; the reason for his apparent aloofness was his way of reserving judgment on those he met until he had formed on them a mental diagnosis. But when Lawrence did give his friendship he gave it freely; and, in return, no man has had more faithful friends.

He depended little on others; he had his private reasons for all he did, and those reasons satisfied him. Loyal pursuance of his own ideals, and the habit of independent thought, brought about a sound self-education; practice in analysis of character resulted in a full understanding of other men. His exceptional intellectual gifts were developed by mental discipline; and the trained mind was quick to decide and to inspire instant action in any emergency.

Hence his brilliance as a leader in war.

Lawrence was under my command, but, after acquainting him with my strategical plan, I gave him a free hand. His co-operation was marked by the utmost loyalty, and I never had anything but praise for his work, which, indeed, was invaluable throughout the campaign.

Lawrence was, in manner, quiet and unassuming; his figure slight and unimposing; but a high forehead and a clear eye betokened a brain of unusual power, a mind dominant over the body.

Lawrence, by will power rather than by physical strength, could compete in endurance with the Arabs themselves. His fiery energy amazed and delighted them, and those children of the desert were drawn to him in almost fanatical devotion.

War ended, Lawrence renounced honours for which he had

no desire, and took up occupations more congenial to him than was the profession of arms.

But, even as Aircraftman Shaw, he could not escape from the fame which he had won as Lawrence.

On the occasion of his tragic death, the nation expressed with one voice the honour in which he was held.

FIELD-MARSHAL EARL WAVELL, P.C., G.C.B.,
G.C.S.I., C.M.G., M.C. 1883-1950. Served in South African War;
in France, 1914-16; in Egypt, 1917-20; Commander-in-Chief,
Middle East, 1939-41; Commander-in-Chief, India, 1941-43;
Viceroy and Governor-General of India, 1943-47. Author of
The Palestine Campaigns, Allenby, Other Men's Flowers
(Anthology), *Soldiers and Soldiering.*

My friendship with Lawrence was not deep nor intimate:
I never saw him at his heights of action nor in his
depths of disillusion. The man I write of in this short
tribute is an everyday Lawrence, a very charming acquaintance
and friend — wise, witty and sympathetic, with the unmistakable
stamp of greatness and goodness on him.

I met him first when he came to Allenby's headquarters in
December 1917, just as Jerusalem fell. At the official entry
into that city I walked beside him: he was gay that day, with
jests at his borrowed uniform and at the official appointment
that had been loaned him for the ceremony — staff officer to
Bertie Clayton. He said as usual little of himself, and barely
mentioned the great ride to, and unlucky failure at, the Yarmuk
Valley bridge, from which he had just returned.

During 1918 I saw him once or twice only, on his appear-
ances at Allenby's headquarters. Our next meeting — in
Egypt — had a certain dramatic quality. On a day in the
spring of 1919 Lord Allenby, then High Commissioner, sent
for me and showed me a Foreign Office telegram. Lawrence,
after leaving the Peace Conference at Paris, had been 'lost':
and the fiddle-stringed French were persuaded that he was on
his way to Damascus to aid Feisal in a revolt against them.
Lord Allenby was very straitly enjoined by the Foreign Office
that if Lawrence arrived in Egypt he was on no account to be
allowed to proceed to Syria. Allenby in turn made me answer-
able with my head to him that Lawrence did not pass through
Egypt without seeing him; I was to bring him to the Residency
as soon as he landed. I went back to my office and telephoned
the authorities at the various ports, telling them that their
military careers, if any, were at stake if Lawrence landed without

my knowledge. I also asked the Air Force to let me know at
once if he reached Egypt by air. I did not know T.E. very well
at that time, but I thought I knew him well enough to consider
it highly unlikely that he intended to start, or take any part in, a
war in Syria; and to be quite certain that if he did wish to pass
through Egypt in secret he would not arrive or depart by the
ordinary methods. Anyway it was probably only Foreign Office
'wind': I had dismissed the matter from my mind, when one
morning some weeks later I met a friend outside the headquarters
offices. In the course of casual conversation he remarked to me:
'By the way, isn't that Arab fellow Lawrence a friend of yours?
I saw him at Shepheard's Hotel this morning.' I sent a staff
officer to produce me Lawrence at once: he returned in half an
hour with a rather ruffled T.E., dressed in uniform but without
belt or cap — as a subaltern in something. He said that he had
come to Egypt merely to collect his papers, and was distinctly
aggrieved at the idea that he was suspected of any intention to
cause trouble in Syria. I explained that the apprehensions
were those of the French and Foreign Office only: he was soon
appeased, and we went off to see Allenby together.

Our meetings after the War were occasional and our correspondence irregular, but his friendship was one of my most
valued privileges and boasts; and it was always the greatest
pleasure to see his outsize motor cycle parked in the drive of
my father's house in Dorset — at the time when T.E. was a
storeman of the Tank Corps at Bovington — or, later, at our
house on Salisbury Plain or at Aldershot. His visits, usually
sudden and unheralded, were always too brief; one could never
have enough of his wise, kind and pungent talk, or cease to
admire the impression of steady enduring strength that the
stocky form, blue eyes and general air of decision conveyed.
One felt always when he departed that one had wasted one's
opportunities: with so keen and intelligent a mind one should
have discussed weighty and serious problems. And one had
spent the hours of his visits in talk of casual everyday matters,
amused and charmed by his fresh outlook and shrewd comments on people and things. He was witty and enlightening

on any subject that was raised, was always at his ease, simple, sympathetic and unaffected. He never spoke of himself or of his own experiences unless questioned, and then answered straightforwardly and without affectation. His self-consciousness, so marked in his writings — especially in *The Mint* — and in his letters, never intruded into his talk. He thought much, brooded even, on himself but never *for* himself, to gain any personal advancement. This self-consciousness, his anxiety of the impression he produced on others, was a curious thing in one so strong and independent. He had many fairy godmothers at his cradle, with gifts of fearlessness, of understanding, of a love of learning, of craftsmanship, of humour, of Spartan endurance, of frugality, of selflessness. But at last came the uninvited bad fairy, to spoil his enjoyment of the gifts of her sisters, so far as in her lay, with the curse of self-consciousness. In my experience, it showed little, if at all, in his talk or in his actions: but his letters and writings show how heavy the burden was on him.

As a professional soldier, I should say something of Lawrence's military achievements and qualities, though I saw them at long range only. The quickening of Sherif Hussein's family revolt into the movement that poured into Damascus was something that no one else could have achieved, even with unlimited gold: it was a spiritual even more than a physical exploit, the value of which to the Allied cause was great. The appreciation on which he based his campaign; the conduct of the campaign itself; and his one 'battle' — the engagement at Tafileh — were brilliancies of which any master might have been proud. But they are slender foundations on which to claim for him the title of a Great Captain. His name will live for his words and spirit more than for his wars. But had fate called him to the highest command, he would surely not have been found wanting. On the theoretical side, he had read more and thought more on military history and the military art than probably any great commander: physically he had courage and endurance beyond the ordinary: morally, he had the gift of inspiration and leadership, he had vision, determination in plenty, and an absence of the personal ambition that has marred the character of many great soldiers; he knew the common man; and, best of all, he had no hampering shackles of long professional training and prejudice. I discussed with him in talk and on paper his theory of irregular warfare, and of its antidotes; but on his ideas of regular warfare and the professional soldier we touched only once, and were interrupted: I had made notes on which to resume the subject with him when he had more leisure. But the date set for its discussion was a visit to him at his cottage early in June 1935.

How should he be judged in the end, this unwilling leader of a great adventure, this over-fastidious writer of one of the greatest masterpieces of the language, this cunning craftsman, this catholic scholar — as man of action or man of thought? I compared him once with Hamlet, a Hamlet who had slain his uncle neatly and efficiently at the beginning of Act II, had spent the remainder of the play in repenting his act and writing a long explanation of it to Horatio, and had then retired to a monastery. In the East, he might have been Emperor or Yogi, and, could he have controlled his impish sense of humour, would have earned veneration in either role.

He will always have his detractors, those who sneer at the 'Lawrence legend'; who ascribe his successes with the Arabs to gold; who view the man as a charlatan in search of notoriety by seeming to seek obscurity; who regard his descent from colonel to private as evidence of some morbid *nostalgie de la boue*. They knew not the man. Those who did, even casually and sporadically, like myself, can answer for his greatness. The complexity of his character, the 'mystery' of Lawrence, on which so much has been written, seems to me to lie mainly in the fact that he transcended the ordinary heights in so many qualities: in courage, in knowledge, in self-discipline, in skill with his hands, in artistry of words, in sympathy with the common working man and with the scholar, in demanding so little from life for his body and so much — too much perhaps — for his mind. But I am not competent to analyse the man: all I can say is that he was cast in heroic but very human mould, and that it was good to know him.

THE WAR: IN ACTION

JA'FAR PASHA
W. F. STIRLING
S. C. ROLLS

GENERAL JA' FAR PASHA EL ASKERI, g.c.v.o., c.m.g. Born 1885. Mesopotamian Arab; murdered 1936. Entered Turkish Army, 1902; commanded Senussi forces invading Egypt, 1915; captured by British; joined Hejaz Army, 1917; commanded Hejaz Northern Regulars; Military Governor of Aleppo, 1919; Minister of Defence, Baghdad, 1920-22; Prime Minister, 'Iraq, 1923; Prime Minister and Minister of Foreign Affairs, 'Iraq, 1926-28; Minister for 'Iraq in England, 1928-30; Minister of Foreign Affairs and Defence, 1930-36.

O F the numerous good and bright points in Lawrence's career during the War I especially admired one very good trait in him: he used to listen attentively to his colleagues' and comrades' suggestions without any superfluous remarks, and then take prompt action without any delay.

We had many *destructive* activities together, blowing up railway lines and bridges and firing at running trains, as well as fighting numerically very superior hostile forces, with success. I saw Lawrence on various occasions facing real dangers without the least hesitation. We all appreciated his courage and devotion to duty at all costs to his life and comfort. He gave us a good and concrete example of self sacrifice for the common cause and the benefit of others. He appeared very reserved, sometimes even cynical and sarcastic, but only against those who were not sincere and true in their dealings with him.

A simple man, he did like simplicity in almost everything. This is why he was so attractive to and attracted by the beduins of the desert.

I am sure that T. E. Lawrence will always be remembered by those who worked with him with admiration and sincere affection.

LIEUTENANT-COLONEL W. F. STIRLING,
D.S.O., M.C. Born 1880. Served in South African War; Egyptian
Army, 1906-12; Observer, Royal Flying Corps, 1914; infantry in
Gallipoli; General Staff, 1916-18 (see *Seven Pillars of Wisdom*);
Acting Governor of Sinai; Governor of Jaffa District; Adviser
to Albanian Government, 1923-31; Chief Telephone Censor
for the Continent, 1939, and since then has been in the Near
East on special service.

IT was my great good fortune to be appointed General Staff
Officer to the Arab Forces in the early part of 1918. From
then throughout the final phase of the Arab revolt on till
the capture of Damascus, I worked, travelled, and fought
alongside Lawrence. Night after night we lay wrapped in our
blankets under the cold stars of the desert.

At these times one learns much of a man. Lawrence took
the limelight from those of us professional soldiers who were
fortunate enough to serve with him, but never once have I
heard even a whisper of jealousy. We sensed that we were
serving with a man immeasurably our superior.

As I see it, his outstanding characteristic was his clarity of
vision and his power of shedding all unessentials from his
thoughts, added to his uncanny knowledge of what the other
man was thinking and doing.

Think of it! A young second lieutenant of the Egyptian
Expeditionary Force goes down the Arabian coast to where a
sporadic revolt of the Western Arabs had broken out against
their Turkish masters. Then, with the help of a few British
officers, all senior to himself and professional soldiers, who
willingly placed themselves under his general guidance, he
galvanizes the Arab revolt into a coherent whole. By his
daring courage, his strategy, his novel tactics, he welds the
turbulent Arab tribes into a fighting machine of such value that
he is able to immobilize two Turkish divisions and provide a
flank force for Lord Allenby's final advance through Palestine
and Syria, the value of which that great general acknowledged
again and again.

No one, looking at Lawrence, would have considered him strong physically. The fact remains that this man was to break all the records of Arabia for speed and endurance. The great sagas sung throughout the desert of phenomenal rides carried out by dispatch riders and dating back to the days of Caliph Haroun Al-Raschid have been completely eclipsed by Lawrence's achievements. On one occasion he averaged 100 miles a day for three consecutive days. Such endurance as this is almost incredible. I myself have ridden 50 miles in a night, but never do I want to do it again. The difficulty is to keep awake. After the bitter glow of the desert night when the sun begins to rise and a warm glow envelops everything, the urge to sleep becomes a veritable torture. If you sleep you are apt to fall, and it is a long way from the top of a camel to the ground.

What was it that enabled Lawrence to seize and hold the imagination of the Arabs? It is a difficult question to answer. The Arabs were noted individualists, intractable to a degree, and without any sense of discipline. Yet it was sufficient for almost any one of us to say that Lawrence wanted something done, and forthwith it was done.

How did he gain this power? The answer may partly be that he represented the heart of the Arab movement for freedom, and the Arabs realized that he had vitalized their cause; that he could do everything and endure everything just a little better than the Arabs themselves; that by his investment with the gold dagger of Mecca he ranked with the Ashraf or the descendants of the Prophet, and the Emir Feisal treated him as a brother and an equal.

But chiefly, I think, we must look for the answer in Lawrence's uncanny ability to sense the feelings of any group of men in whose company he found himself; his power to probe behind their minds and to uncover the well-springs of their actions.

Many stories have been told about Lawrence, most of them untrue. He was a good classical scholar, a military and political leader of world-wide renown, a writer of, perhaps, the greatest book of the century. After the peace he was offered a very high and responsible post under the British Government, and yet he cast everything aside and became a private in the Tank Corps and an aircraftman in the Air Force.

In that position he had been content to remain for fourteen years or so. Lawrence of his own choice immured himself in the shelter of the Air Force, much in the same way as, in an earlier age, he would have chosen the sanctuary of a monastery. No one has yet been able to provide a satisfactory reason for his action. I do not think that anyone ever will. The motives of his action came from within, and I doubt whether any of us living to-day would understand them even if he himself had cared to explain.

Lawrence was a man guided solely by his conscience. Had he accepted high office under the Government, he would never have carried out orders from Downing Street which conflicted in any way with what he thought was right. He knew this, and therefore refused. Further, he hated the petty trappings of officialdom, and the acceptance of any such post would have meant for him a life of continuous unease.

He could have retired to his University and lived the life of a don, but even there he could not get away from the fierce light of publicity.

His decision, therefore, to change his name and take the veil of the Air Force seemed to him his one way of escape. In the Air Force were no anxieties about money or food or clothing or lodging; his life would be an ordered routine, and his brain would have time to recover from the tremendous strain of the past few years.

'Ah, yes,' say some people, 'but what of the man himself? Wasn't Lawrence just a *poseur*?'

Was he? Who are we going to take as arbiters of such a question? Are we to take obscure writers who have given their opinions or men like Field-Marshal Lord Allenby, Admiral Lord Wemyss, Mr. Winston Churchill, and the British officers who served with Lawrence throughout the campaign? There is not one of these I have mentioned but has admitted the genius and compelling power of Lawrence.

Turning to Lawrence's great book, the *Seven Pillars of Wisdom*, which was published for private circulation, it is interesting to note the author's own feelings. He sent the book to me to review as to fact. I made certain comments upon it, and in particular said that I thought he had laid insufficient stress upon the climax of the book — that is, the capture of and entry into Damascus. I said I thought that this was the goal of the whole Arab movement, which had been aimed at from the start. I also added that people who read the book would so understand it and enjoy it the more.

Lawrence's answers to my criticisms were quite definite. He said: 'I don't want readers to "enjoy" the book. In girding at discipline and servitude, I seek mainly to condemn myself. My life has been service and I hate it . . . Service to an ideal of scholarship, to the nation-building demand of nationality, and now service in the Ranks. As you say, in such surrender lies a happiness . . . but this seems to me an immoral feeling, like an overdraft on our account of life. We should not be happy: and I think I've dodged that sin successfully! The Tank Corps is a hefty penance for too rich and full a youth!'

Later when discussing the *Seven Pillars of Wisdom* with Mr. H. G. Wells, who had also reviewed it, I asked him for his opinion. He said: 'It is a wonderful book. In my opinion it is the finest piece of prose that has been written in the English language for 150 years.' I do not think anyone will accuse Mr. Wells of being the sort of man to throw bouquets around unnecessarily.

During the latter part of Lawrence's service in the Air Force he devoted himself to the mechanical side of motor engineering. A very eminent engineer told me that Lawrence had written the last word on marine motor engines, and that, in fact, until there were fresh developments there was nothing more to be said. It is rare, and indeed almost incredible, for a fine scholar to be able to attain such eminence in a mechanical field.

In my considered opinion, Lawrence was the greatest genius whom England has produced in the last two centuries, and I do not believe that there is anyone who has known him who will not agree with me. If ever a genius, a scholar, an artist, and an imp of Shaitan were rolled into one personality, it was Lawrence.

S. C. ROLLS, Governing Director, Imperial Autocar Co., Northampton, and Proprietor, Rolls Motor Co., Northampton. Born 1893. Petty Officer, Armoured Car Section, Royal Naval Air Service, 1914; later transferred with cars to Army. Served against Senussi in Libyan Desert; sent to Akaba, 1917; Meritorious Service Medal. Author of *Steel Chariots in the Desert*.

I HAD volunteered for something of which I knew little or nothing. It had been vaguely explained by a Staff Officer in Alexandria; there was an air of — well — those who went would probably never come back — and one had the option of declining, but no hint was given regarding the destination we were bound for, or the type of war expected. Seven Rolls-Royce armoured cars, two Rolls tenders and transport were loaded at Suez and the ship sailed with a great air of mystery.

Outside a roughly improvised tent (made with tarpaulins drawn over petrol cases) crowds of Egyptian Labour Corps were getting ready for work, road making — that was our job. Huge boulders had to be blown out of the watercourse where once the stream worked its way down to the dried-up bed by which the Jordan had emptied itself into the Gulf of Akaba. We were ten miles in the Gorge of Itm and weeks of hard work brought us thus far. My job was ahead, marking one stone here and one stone there, destined for destruction, when Hassan, the Egyptian foreman, pointed with his long whip at a bunch of dirty-looking Arabs mounted on richly draped camels, about thirty in number, coming slowly down the pass. 'Arab no good, rob tobac, sell plenty money!' and he spat. 'Yalla! Emshi!' I yelled at the foremost, who was persuading his camel to kneel down with a series of hisses. Hassan was afraid of Arabs and backed away to leave me to deal with any possible trouble. I caught a glimpse of this Arab's eyes, steel grey eyes, and they seemed to glint with roguish impudence. From his white headdress there came a soft, almost girlish, 'Is your Captain with you?' I think I dropped my cigarette.

He patted me on the shoulder and reassured me: 'My name is Lawrence, I have come to join you.'

This new commander did not wax severe and military-like, indeed he was the very last person one would compare with the exalted ratings I had served with. Orders had been snapped out like the crack of musketry, salutes had been expected and duly received, commands had been obeyed to the letter, often grudgingly and unwillingly, but here was a power who seemed to command one's very soul, of charming persuasive manner, to seduce one's rebellion and counteract all obstinate ideas. He talked as he rode by my side in the Rolls-Royce tender, he explained the revolt, he discussed the great job which lay ahead, he spoke of his difficulties, of his hopes and fears, of his misgivings and good fortune.

We emerged from the Gorge of Itm, having covered some forty miles to the Tableland, the vast plain of Guweira, soft with sand dunes, hummocked with camel scrub. It was difficult finding a path for our four wheels, and the load (gold for bribery, guncotton, the machine gun on tripod in the centre) was jostled dangerously. Our column followed — all our armoured cars and light Ford transport with ammunition and water. Tents were stretched away in the distance and right around the rock which was Guweira, the present headquarters of the Emir Feisal. Our arrival was accorded great celebrations. We were met by expert horsemen who rode bare-backed, like fury, round and round, firing rifles in the air and yelling 'Aurans! Aurans!'

It pleased me greatly to learn that T.E. had chosen my Rolls tender for his future plans: his camel was not fast enough for the rapidly growing magnitude of our campaign. From that time we travelled together somewhere in the region of 20,000 miles.

Things were well on the way towards the assault of Maan, the key station of the railway to Medina, and the plan now was to harass the Turkish army corps which manned this line, not to demoralize them completely at the moment, but to check their supplies by blowing up culverts and bridges, until the time was ripe to cut them off from all directions.

T.E. took his seat by my side, to cut the line south of Maan at Mudawara. He pumped me as to the speed that could be obtained, given fair surface; I said I would show him at the first opportunity. This soon came; after traversing some forty miles we plunged between the tall rocks of Rum, crashed over soft sand dunes, then he shouted, 'Here we are!' For stretching away as far as I could see was the vast mud plain of Jefer, glinting white, looking like beach disappearing to the sea, but this was only mirage: forty miles of baked-hard, dead-level surface. T.E. had a craze for speed and with delight he watched our speedometer, 30-40-50-60-70 — there was nothing here to stop one travelling at any speed; other cars came along and T.E. shouted encouragement. We raced neck and neck, but the only danger was the strain on our tyres through the terrific heat. This made a pleasant break, for there was little relaxation for us in these days. We found our army under Ja'far some ten miles from the objective, and rumour ran that land mines had been laid to trap us. We decided to leave the armoured cars to deal with the main attack, after the Arabs had rushed in under cover of machine gun fire, while we went south to blow up a useful-looking railway bridge of about six arches; attention would be taken from our operations by the firing. We ran down, dumped our guncotton, inserted the explosive in the draining holes and set the detonators. T.E. shouted: 'Run back to the car, be ready to get out, when I have fired the mine!' Tremendous roar and up went the bridge, T.E. leapt in, and away we went to find out if the station had fallen. We found one camel had been blown to pieces on a land mine when the Arabs rushed in to loot; they had taken about twenty prisoners. A small garrison was left in case of any attack.

During the next months, Maan was taken, after we had dragged our cars up the Negab, a range of mountains 100 miles from Guweira. Thirteen hairpin bends were negotiated to enable us to get the cars up nothing more than camel tracks; the last rise was one in two and a half; one slip meant a sheer fall over the edge of a precipice to certain destruction. Another sixty miles brought us to Abu El Lissan, which was our advance base; and armoured cars were within easy reach of the Hejaz Railway. We were now on the Maan plateau some 300 ft. above sea-level and about 300 miles from Akaba.

It seemed we had three methods of progress, to bluff, to buy or to fight our way through. There were still hostile tracts of country which had to be crossed and re-crossed. T.E. had numerous consultations with the great chiefs. I remember on one occasion he squatted down to feast with an assembly of chiefs, the principal guest, bare feet tucked under him, swathed as the others, with gold dagger, girdle around his waist, gesticulating from one to the other, forcing his points home one by one; nods of satisfaction from the swarthy assembly. Slaves were ordered to prepare the feast, huge bowls of boiled rice were carried to the centre of the circle, the sizzling carcasses of two desert sheep, beautifully browned, were being constantly basted with hot liquid butter. Auda grabbed a handful of meat with his fingers and smiled a broad smile of satisfaction; this was a sign for the chief guest to do likewise. T.E. grabbed also, and he grinned at Auda, who grinned back, his face glistening with mutton fat.

On our long rides T.E. often confided his difficulties to me, his efforts to persuade Feisal who was continually losing heart and had to be coaxed and encouraged, the failure of various sections of the organization to do their job for the payment they were receiving. Often it would take months to arrange an attack and get the men there, but when we arrived on the day there would be grumblings and to save mutiny I have time and time again had to return, in some instances 500 miles or more, to get gold, the all-powerful persuader. I often thanked my natural sense of direction, for sometimes our tracks were invisible and one had only the sun or the stars as a guide. His encouragement and soothing humour eased my sufferings in apparently hopeless circumstances. I was countless times beaten by sheer fatigue, my hands bleeding and skinned by the wrenching of the steering wheel, trying to guide the Rolls tender across country strewn with rocks and boulders, unbelievable and seemingly impassable to anything other than a camel.

Azrak, the ancient oasis, was an objective coveted for a long time from a strategical point of view. After three days and nights running we had left Bair of the seven wells and struck north, soon we sighted the Three Sisters (Thlaithukhwat), a landmark looking like three thimbles, which could be seen on this stony desert of many undulations for nigh on 100 miles on days of good visibility. At Azrak T.E. told tales of the lava castle. There was another rebellion on foot, gold was running short again, our regulars were grousing seriously: T.E. asked me, although I was dead beat, to return to Abu El Lissan for gold. I said I would do the job. We left, two Rolls tenders, with myself in charge. T.E.'s last words were, 'Remember the Three Sisters — keep them in sight and whatever happens don't be taken prisoner.' I knew well what that advice meant. Having covered 100 miles, we drew up side by side for the night, when my companion began to fill his petrol tank by the light of a candle stump. Suddenly the whole tank burst into flames. I looked on momentarily in despair, both cars would be burnt to cinders and our bones would bleach in the sun. I seized my blankets as I was preparing a bed on the desert, slammed the lot on to his tank and managed to dout the flames. Four hundred miles out and four hundred return in two and a half days saw us back with the gold which again saved the situation.

T.E. loved his Arabs as they loved him, after his life with them for two years. We few Britishers seemed to be part of a family marooned and having mixed only with ourselves grew very attached to each other. All gave of their very best in the cause which he firmly believed was his chief mission in life, to give the Arab a sense of responsibility and self respect, for the well being of the world as a whole. Often after a gruelling day, T.E. weary himself, to give us a chance to snatch a little rest, would steal around our little camp with his revolver, ready to warn us if danger was near.

The enemy had fled wildly to the north, hoping to find shelter in Damascus where their headquarters staff were preparing to make a final stand. T.E. followed hotly in pursuit, we searched Deraa for petrol and found half a barrel which was hurriedly emptied into our tanks, and then began the most horrible drive over the coarse fields of Hauran, cultivated in parts. That gruesome journey will live long in my memory, dead and dying Turks lay about wholesale, villages looted and ravaged, the peasants cruelly murdered, women and children and even babies lay soaked in blood, atrocities beyond the imagination of human decency had been enacted. Our troops had no time to take prisoners, every one seemed for himself, we met with startling rumours concerning the fate of Damascus. 'Damascus was burning!' the refugees cried.

We drove into Damascus. The citizens thronged the streets, sang songs and shouted themselves hoarse as we drew the cars up in front of the Government buildings.

There were great rejoicings and carnival in the city. I heard the Arabs firing in the air at the rear of the Government Buildings, I heard the cry in a near minaret, calling them to prayer, I felt a hand grip mine. 'Good-bye, old fellow, I shall not be wanted any more. My job is done. We have had great fun together.'

THE WAR AND AFTER

RONALD STORRS
B. H. LIDDELL HART
WINSTON CHURCHILL

SIR RONALD STORRS, K.C.M.G., C.B.E. Born 1881. Egyptian Government, 1904; Oriental Secretary to British Agency, Egypt, 1909 (see *Seven Pillars of Wisdom*); Governor of Jerusalem, 1917-26; Governor of Cyprus, 1926-32; of Northern Rhodesia, 1932-34. Author of *Orientations*, etc.

From a speech

LAWRENCE was of lesser medium stature and, though slight, strongly built. His forehead was high; the face upright and, in proportion to the back of the head, long. His yellow hair was naturally-growing pre-War hair; that is parted and brushed sideways; not worn immensely long and plastered backwards under a pall of grease. He had a straight nose, piercing gentian-blue eyes, a firm and very full mouth, a strong square chin and fine, careful and accomplished hands. Augustus John's first drawing is perfect of his Arab period; Kennington's bronze gives the plastic and Homeric simplicity of his lines and rhythm, and Howard Coster's photograph besides being a good likeness hints somehow at the unhappiness latent behind the eyes.

As a Captain in the Intelligence Branch of the Egyptian Expeditionary Force Lawrence was elusive, and utterly careless of his dress. He would be found unexpectedly in my flat reading Latin or Greek, and these unexpected visits partly cancelled out his occasional failure to appear at dinner when expected. He was very fond of music and would sit listening to the piano with closed eyes. As a colleague his quickness and instantaneous grasp of essentials were astonishing. 'What does he want?' he would ask as we examined an Arab, or an Arabic document. For what he wanted usually proved to be something very different from the demand expressed.

Shortly after the Arab Revolution we found that its success was being denied or blanketed by the Enemy Press (which was of course quoted by neutrals) and we decided that the best proof that it had taken place could be provided by an issue of Hejaz stamps which would carry the Arab propaganda, self-paying and incontrovertible, to the four corners of the earth. We went round the Arab Museum in Cairo collecting suitable designs — when it became apparent that Lawrence already possessed or had immediately assimilated a complete working technique of philatelic and three-colour reproduction, so that he was able to supervise the issue from start to finish. And it seemed only a few weeks when this Hittite Archaeologist was on the most intimate terms with machine guns, with tulip bombs, even with the zealously forbidden subtleties of a Rolls-Royce engine. There exists at this moment the last motor-cycle he had had built, never ridden, never delivered, carrying ten improvements, all invented by Lawrence.

How instinctively from the beginning he played his cards when first presented to the Sherif Abdalla at Jeddah! We sat in a circle and the conversation was led up to the whereabouts of the various Turkish regiments — which was of course pooled and common knowledge of Lawrence's Department and for which King Hussein had his own contacts of accurate information. As Syrian, Circassian, Anatolian, Mesopotamian names came up, Lawrence at once stated exactly which unit was in each position, until Abdalla turned to me in amazement: 'Is this man God, to know everything?' So deeply impressed was he by Lawrence's personality that he induced his father, King Hussein, to write him the long desired letter of introduction to Feisal, the letter that made his dream come true; and I can still see Lawrence three days later on the shore at Rabegh waving grateful hands as we left him there to return ourselves to Egypt — left him to walk from that moment into the pages of history.

Early in January 1918, I was sitting in a snow-bound Jerusalem when an orderly announced a Beduin and Lawrence walked in and sat beside me. He remained for the rest of the day and left me temporarily the poorer by a Virgil and a Catullus. Later on, when in Jerusalem, he always stayed in my house, an amusing as well as an absorbing if sometimes disconcerting guest. He had Shelley's trick of noiselessly vanishing and reappearing. We would be sitting, reading on my only sofa: I would look up and Lawrence was not only not in the room, he was not in the house, he was not in Jerusalem. He was in the train on his way to Egypt.

In those days and (owing to the dead hand of an Ottoman concession) for years after, there was no electric light in Jerusalem, and in my bachelor household the hands of the Arab servants fell heavy upon the incandescent mantles of our paraffin lamps, from which a generous volcano of filthy smuts would nightly stream upon and cover the books, the carpets and everything in the room. Lawrence took the lamp situation daily in hand and so long as he was in the house all was bright on the Aladdin front. He said he liked the house because it contained the necessities and not the tiresomenesses of life; that is to say, there were a few Greek marbles, a good piano and a great many books — but (I fear) not enough towel horses, no huckabacks and a very irregular supply of cruets and dinner-napkins. Not all my guests agreed with Lawrence.

My wife and I found him later returning from India by the *Rajputana* where he spent his time lying in his berth translating the *Odyssey* into a version which has, for those who knew him well, the merit of representing Lawrence as well as Homer. In England we met (as might have been expected) always unexpectedly and never by appointment — in the street, on a bus or at a railway station. Once, when I was choosing gramophone records, a hand from behind descended firmly upon my shoulder. I had only just arrived in England and supposed for a moment that this must be an attempt on the part of an assistant at Brighter British Salesmanship. It was Lawrence, replenishing the immense collection of records which, arranged in volumes round a square of deep shelves, then took up almost half of the upper room in his cottage. On another occasion he led me to his publishers where, walking round the room, he picked out half a dozen expensive books and, as though he were the head of the firm, made me a present of them. He was a loyal, unchanging and affectionate friend and would charge down from London on the iron steed from which he met his death to visit me in a nursing-home, or run up 200 miles from the West of England to say good-bye before I returned to Cyprus. And we were seen off in 1934 for Canada from Southampton by a capless aircraftman in overalls who side-slipped the photographers by taking me for a joy ride in an R.A.F. Inspector's power-boat.

Lawrence hated society but loved company. He refused the post of Director of Archaeology in Cyprus because of what he chose to imagine the social obligations of an official there. But he liked to walk and talk with friends. The simplicity of his life was extreme. He smoked no tobacco, he drank no alcohol; but alas, he used a drug. His drug was speed, which cost him his life. He once raced along the open road against an aeroplane and led it for nearly a quarter of an hour.

He was a mass of contradictions; shy and retiring, yet he positively enjoyed sitting for, and criticizing, his portrait. None could have been more remote from the standard product of the public school, and I can as easily picture him in a frock coat or in hunting pink as an old school tie. In action he was an individual force of driving intelligence, with nothing of the administrator; having indeed about as much of the team spirit as Alexander the Great or Mr. Lloyd George.

Consider the variety of elements in his composition. It has been given to few to achieve and to enshrine their achievement in splendid prose; to which other of these few has been added the fastidious artistry to plan every detail of the setting up, the illustration, the printing and the binding of the material presentation of his genius. On any topic he was one of those who let fall, whether in speech or writing, the creative and illuminating idea or phrase — unmistakably his, signed all over, which held your memory and recharged your intellectual and spiritual batteries.

Lawrence suffered acutely from public exaggeration in all directions. And his reputation has been subjected by some to a steady dribble of depreciation. It must have irritated some other public servants to find a man without a handle before his name or letters after it, without a dress suit and with an income of less than a hundred a year, nevertheless pursued and chronicled by an eager limelight which seemed by comparison to black out their particular merits. There are two classes of public servant. Of one it is said, 'What is he doing now?' Of the other, 'Who is Minister of this or Governor of that?' The first category will interest and arrest and fascinate the world. Lawrence was of these first. The second, a far more numerous category — will be found occupying most of the best places.

Lawrence was throughout the last months of his life oppressed by gloomy forebodings. In one of his latest letters he spoke of 'an utterly blank wall' after leaving his beloved R.A.F.; his last to me ends with three words from the Greek Anthology of a man who wished he had not been born. Here is the second half of what was probably his very last letter, written on Jubilee Day to Kennington: 'You wonder what I am doing? Well, so do I, in truth. Days seem to dawn, suns to shine, evenings to follow, and then I sleep. What I have done, what I am doing, what I am going to do puzzle and bewilder me. Have you ever been a leaf fallen from your tree in autumn and been really puzzled about it? That's the feeling.' Some think that he would have created at least one more great work, for like Plato he felt deeply that what gives life its value is the sight, however revealed, of Eternal Beauty. In this he is with the great Elizabethans, Sir Philip Sidney; with the great Victorians, Charles Gordon, whose whole lives free from fear and gain — those old perverters of mankind — are a protest against the guaranteed, the pensioned, the standardized and the safety-first existence.

Lawrence, unaccountable, unpredictable, seemed to be a phantasm of the living as now he is of the dead; and it was somehow unreal to be watching beside him in his cerements, so strangely resembling the Abaya, the Kuffiya and the Aigal of an Arab Chief, as he lay in his last littlest room, very grave and strong and noble. Suddenly, in a flash, as by a bolt from the cloudless serene he has been rapt into Eternity; and we may well believe that his adventurous spirit leapt gladly to the call, as the trumpets sounded for him on the other side.

.

CAPTAIN B. H. LIDDELL HART. Born 1895.
Infantry, 1914-24; Military Editor, *Encyclopaedia Britannica*;
Military Correspondent of the *Daily Telegraph*, 1925-35, of
The Times, 1935-39. Author of the authorized biography of
T. E. L. and many books on Military History.

From a speech

AIRCRAFTMAN SHAW vanished on leaving the Air Force.
Mr. T. E. Shaw, after a brief holiday passed from us.
Lawrence of Arabia lives on. Rarely has a territorial
title, popularly conferred, made such an impression, not
perhaps since Scipio Africanus; despite his own protests it
stuck fast— because of its aptness. What was its justification?
Partly the nature of his achievement; but, more deeply, his
own nature. The desert was in his blood. And he was one with
the spirit of the desert.

I would briefly touch on the meaning of his achievement —
in the War. When opportunity came to him in 1916, his
purpose was two-fold — to relieve Britain's difficult situation
in the East by creating a new lever, an Arab lever, in her aid;
secondly, to free the Arabs from the Turkish yoke — and in
so doing to give them a *fair* chance of fulfilling their own
aspirations. To attain true freedom — to make of it what they
would.

That double purpose he more than fulfilled. The tide of the
Arab Revolt, carried a thousand miles from Mecca to
Damascus, was crowned by the establishment of an Arab state
in Syria. That state was overthrown by the French after the
War; but in 1921, Lawrence, emerging from his Oxford
retreat, guided policy to such effect that Feisal, robbed of one
kingdom, was given another in 'Iraq. An Arab state was also
created in Transjordan. Whether for good or ill, the Arabs
had again become, after a lapse of centuries, a factor with
which the world must reckon. In an historical sense, it is,
above all, because of this fresh impact of the Arab upon the

European peoples that the propelling agent is rightly styled Lawrence of Arabia.

How was it achieved? One might describe it as *born* of ambition, *founded* on knowledge, *executed* through personality.

He certainly had ambition, at the start. An ambition so immense as to dream of being supreme, both in the field of action and in the realm of thought. It was not a selfish ambition, however. Rather was it the *immersed* ambition of the artist — sinking himself in his purpose.

He was also, in the deeper sense, a 'Crusader'. It was begun as a Crusade in the modern form — a freeing of a race from bondage. It would become, as he developed his reflection, a philosophical crusade. While formal religion did not touch him, I have come to view him as a man driven by what one may describe as a religious urge, as intense as it was deeply buried. But his urge gained its way because it was based on *knowledge*. Such knowledge, in its width and depth, as no man of action has perhaps equalled. Here is an aspect of him which is least understood — especially by those who view him as a romantic figure.

His knowledge of the Arabs came by immersion as well as by study. His poverty, his freedom from any class sense, his instinctive independence — these helped him to understand the Arabs. They showed him, as he said, 'That no man could be their leader except he ate the ranks' food, wore their clothes, lived level with them, and yet appeared better in himself'. He got inside the Arab's skin first, and then transcended it.

So, too, his knowledge of the art of war came by touch as well as by thought.

When merely an undergraduate, he had, as a sideline in his wide range of reading, gone far into the history and theory of war. I have never known a general who had gone so far. Practical experience enabled him to check, to apply, to adapt, this knowledge. He became a supreme artist of war.

He fought only one battle, Tafileh. It was a miniature masterpiece. He made fun of it in his report, but his mockery did not hide the fact that it was in the best classical tradition.

The distilled experience of two thousand years was at his finger-tips.

But it was in *strategy* that he stands out; if his strategy had a classical foundation he gave it an original adaptation. He turned the weakness of the Arabs into an asset, and the very strength of the Turks into a debit — forcing them to spread as widely as possible, in vain attempt to check the flame of revolt — a flame which, like a will-o'-the-wisp, was always dancing in places where they were not. By this strategy, the Arabs inflicted the maximum damage with the minimum loss, and so with the maximum encouragement to themselves. With vain chase the Turks grew exhausted and depressed. For orthodox concentration, Lawrence substituted dispersion. For battle, he substituted a creeping paralysis — produced by intangibility and ubiquity. But he did more than paralyse the Turks. He foreshadowed what I believe will be the trend of the future — a super-guerrilla kind of warfare.

In my book, I compared him with the Great Captains. This startled some readers. Is it justified? they asked. It might be worth asking whether the names we commonly accept were themselves justified — by anything more than a dramatic success, born of accident or superior advantages. To be candid, as my study of war has gone deeper, I have come to question the assumptions of history. I have at any rate less doubt of his claims than of some of the others. Because I have more evidence that he foresaw, and understood, what he was doing. He is the only one of whom it can truly be said — that he evolved a theory, developed it, and grasped its bearing on the whole evolution of war. I do not think he saw it in perfect clearness at the outset, but he *came* to see it. This knowledge and insight, however, needed something more — a driving force. It was provided by *personality*. To this force all who came in close contact with him have borne testimony. There is no need for me to enlarge on it. But there are one or two aspects on which I would briefly dwell.

The criticism has often been made that he owed his success to the bags of gold that were at his disposal. The answer may well be given in the words of one who differed from him on many points — Sir Hubert Young. He has written: 'Lawrence could certainly not have done what he did without the gold, but no one else could have done it with ten times the amount.' That gold amounted in all to less than half a million distributed by him. The criticism is essentially a foolish one, for war cannot be waged without money. Only those ignorant of history imagine that Britain's subsidies have not played an essential part in her wars. But perhaps never before has so great a result been attained for so slight an outlay.

The money invested brought a great return. Greater still was the result of invested knowledge. And in this, Lawrence's understanding of human nature was perhaps the greatest factor. It has been aptly expressed by Colonel Stirling — 'How did he gain this power? . . . Chiefly, I think, we may look for the answer in Lawrence's uncanny ability to sense the feelings of any group of men in whose company he found himself; this power to probe behind their minds and to uncover the well-springs of their actions.'

It *was* uncanny. I have never known a man who seemed to have such power to read one's thoughts. He gave one the feeling that it was hopeless to indulge in any deception — and only the stupid attempted it. He saw all things clearly — perhaps too clearly. Here we may have a clue to his perplexing career. He knew others; himself he did not know. Perhaps because he saw too many facets. As he wrote me once — 'At an O.T.C. field day I was once told to disguise myself as a battalion in close order: and have done ever since!'

All motives are mixed. Lawrence saw it. Charitable to others he was hard on himself — too ready to exaggerate the less worthy elements in the mixture. This, maybe, explains his puzzling attitude to public acclaim — that he saw its worthlessness, then found himself being interested, then despised himself for being interested. A depressing circle.

His introspection was too sharp. 'Hearing other people praised made me despair jealously of myself, for I took it at its face value; whereas, had they spoken ten times as well of me,

I would have discounted it to nothing. I was a standing court-martial on myself, inevitably, because to me the inner springs of action were bare with the knowledge of exploited chance.'

But his dissatisfaction was, above all, the divine discontent of the artist. His highest admiration was reserved for the creative artist — and to be one was his highest ambition. For in this sphere achievement was least competitive. He saw competition as an unending source of evil — involving the frustration of others, and the deformation of the end. He competed only with a standard, that of the best. The standard may, to some extent, have been personified in the man he most admired in one particular line. To quote his own words, 'I had had one craving all my life, for the power of self-expression in some imaginative form — but had been too diffuse ever to acquire a technique'. Literature seemed to him the art least dependent on an acquired technique and his experiences in the Arab revolt offered a ready-made theme. The result was the *Seven Pillars of Wisdom*. Reflection *should* vie with description. In *style*, in *form*, and in *production* alike, he aimed at perfection. .

Despite its laudation by others, it left him dissatisfied. After some years, he made a fresh attempt on a large scale, an attempt at supreme realism — in a record of daily life in the Air Force which he christened *The Mint*. This he himself thought was his best writing — less 'mannered' and pretentious than the *Seven Pillars*. For my own part, I am not sure that he may not live longest in literature through his letters. They were works of art, unforced.

Between the *Seven Pillars* and *The Mint*, a decisive turn had come in his own career. Undue dissatisfaction with his literary attempt, was a factor. It was accentuated, first, by the strain of the 'excitement' generated in writing the *Seven Pillars*; secondly, by the effect of refusals.

Unwilling to draw help from his fame, and as a better test, he submitted a number of anonymous contributions to various editors, about 1921 or 1922. They came back, not unnaturally. Many great writers have suffered a similar fate in their earlier days and often with their best stuff. T.E. too readily jumped at the explanation that the fault lay with him. He deemed himself too imitative. He once remarked to me that he had the power of description and analysis, but not of synthesis. There may have been some truth in this judgment, but the greater truth was that he had too high a standard. Thus it was, I think, that he came to feel that the military art was the only one in which he had attained creativeness.

In 1922 came the great abandonment — when he enlisted in the ranks of the Air Force. It was prompted by several causes, of which I have indicated one. Another may be explained by saying that he went into the Air Force for the same reason that thoughtful men in the Middle Ages went into a monastery. Another, was that he knew that he had overstrained the delicate balance of his mind — even more, he told me, by the strain of writing the *Seven Pillars* than by the strain of the War.

The years of humdrum service in the Air Force were years of restoration — it was a healthier man, physically and mentally, who took his discharge in 1935. A man who looked much less than his forty-six years, and radiated an air of contentment, whatever the unease that might lie deeper in one who saw all things too clearly. During the later years of his service, he had played an important part in a new development which may affect sea warfare as greatly as his wartime career has potentially influenced the art of war on land.

In letters and conversation during the past year, he had repeatedly expressed the desire for 'a rest that should go on and on, till I wanted no more of it — or wanted nothing else. The last thing desirable is activity for the sake of activity. I hope I have enough mind for it to be quietly happy by itself.'

Again, in a letter written on New Year's Eve, 1934-35, after urging me to pursue certain paths of study which we had travelled together, he ended:

'For myself I am going to taste the flavour of true leisure. For 46 years have I worked and been worked. Remaineth 23 years (of expectancy). May they be like Flecker's "a great Sunday that goes on and on".'

Yet, there were moments in this last year when he hinted of a return, and that his greatest period might still lie ahead.

The opportunity has gone — with the man. But nothing that he might have done is equal to what he may do — as a legendary figure. Legends are more potent than emperors or dictators. Others who worked with him were outstanding men: he would have been the first to wish their merits due recognition. Legend has made his fame as 100 to 1. But magnification is the way of legend. And *for once* legend had a really substantial basis. There will be nothing but good in it, if this real message is remembered, and not merely the romance.

For he was a message to mankind in freedom from possessiveness. In freedom from competitiveness. In freeing oneself from ambition, especially from the lust of power. His power sprang from knowledge and understanding, not from position. His influence was free from domination. That influence is likely to grow — because it is a spiritual message transmitting a spiritual force.

The man was great; the message is greater.

THE RIGHT HON. SIR WINSTON S.
CHURCHILL, P.C., O.M., C.H., F.R.S. Born 1874.

I DID not meet Lawrence till after the War was over. It was
the spring of 1919, when the peace-makers, or, at any rate,
the Treaty-makers, were gathered in Paris, and all England
was in the ferment of the aftermath. So great had been the
pressure in the War, so vast its scale, so dominating the great
battles in France, that I had only been dimly conscious of the
part played in Allenby's campaigns by the Arab revolt in the
desert. But now someone said to me: 'You ought to meet this
wonderful young man. His exploits are an epic.' So Lawrence
came to luncheon.

Usually at this time in London or Paris he wore his Arab
dress, in order to identify himself with the interests of the
Emir Feisal, and with the Arabian claims then under harsh
debate. On this occasion, however, he wore plain clothes, and
looked at first sight like one of the many clean-cut young
officers who had gained high rank and distinction in the struggle.

We were men only, and the conversation was general; but
presently someone rather mischievously told the story of his
behaviour at the Investiture a few days before. Lawrence was to
be decorated a Commander of the Bath. The long queue of
recipients of honours was filing past the King. When Colonel
Lawrence's turn came and the King took the decoration from
the velvet cushion and prepared to hang it on the hook, which
officers in these circumstances have attached to their tunics,
Lawrence stopped him and in a low voice stated with the
utmost respect that it was impossible for him to receive any
honour from His Majesty while Britain was about to dishonour
the pledges which he had made in her name to the Arabs who
had fought so bravely. The scene and the incident were
unprecedented. The King was naturally surprised and dis-
pleased. The decoration, coveted by so many gallant men, was
replaced upon its cushion, Lawrence bowed and passed on,
and the ceremony proceeded.

[*Editor's Note:* In reality, it was in the preceding private audience with the King that he asked to be excused from receiving decorations; but I have printed the incorrect version of the incident because, in Mr. Churchill's words, 'I certainly understood at the time that this was what happened, and your brother himself discussed it with me on the basis that it had happened'. Compare R. H. Isham's article.]

I raised my eyebrows at this story; I had not heard of it before. I was Secretary of State for War, so I said at once that his conduct was most wrong and not fair to the King as a gentleman and grossly disrespectful to him as a Sovereign. Any man might refuse a title or a decoration, any man might in refusing state the reasons of principle which led to his action, but to choose the occasion when His Majesty in pursuance of his constitutional duty was actually about to perform the gracious act of personally investing him as the occasion for making a political demonstration was monstrous. As he was my guest I could not say more, but in my official position I could not say less.

He accepted the rebuke with good humour. This was the only way in his power, he said, of rousing the highest authorities in the State to a realization of the fact that the honour of Great Britain was at stake in the faithful treatment of the Arabs, and that their betrayal to the Syrian demands of France would be an indelible blot in our history. The King himself should be made aware of what was being done in his name, and he knew no other way. I said that this was no defence at all for the method adopted, and then turned the conversation into other and more agreeable channels.

But I must admit that this episode made me anxious to learn more about what had actually happened in the desert war and opened my eyes to the passions which were seething in Arab bosoms. I called for reports and pondered them. I talked to the Prime Minister about it. He said that the French meant to have Syria and rule it from Damascus, and that nothing would turn them from it. The Sykes-Picot agreement, which we had made during the War, had greatly confused the issue of principle and only the Peace Conference could decide conflicting claims and pledges. This was unanswerable.

I did not see Lawrence again for some weeks. It was, if my memory serves me right, in Paris. He wore his Arab robes, and the full magnificence of his countenance revealed itself. The gravity of his demeanour, the precision of his opinions, the range and quality of his conversation all seemed enhanced to a remarkable degree by the splendid Arab head-dress and garb. From amid the flowing draperies his noble features, his perfectly chiselled lips, and flashing eyes loaded with fire and comprehension shone forth. He looked what he was, one of nature's greatest princes.

We got on much better this time, and I began to form that impression of his strength and majesty which afterwards has never left me. Dressed in the prosaic clothes of English daily life, or afterwards in the uniform of an Air Force mechanic, I always saw him henceforward as he appears in Augustus John's brilliant pencil sketch. I began to hear much more about him from friends who had fought under his command, and, indeed, there was endless talk about him in every circle — military, diplomatic and academic.

It soon became evident that his cause was not going well in Paris. He accompanied Feisal everywhere as friend and interpreter. Well did he interpret him. He scorned his English connections and all question of his own career compared to what he regarded as his duty to the Arabs. He clashed with the French. He faced Clemenceau in long and repeated controversies. Here was foeman worthy of his steel. The old 'Tiger' had a face as fierce as that of Lawrence could become, an eye as unquailing, and a will-power well matched. Clemenceau had a deep feeling for the East; he loved a paladin; admired Lawrence's exploits and recognized his genius. But the French sentiment about Syria was a hundred years old. The idea that France, bled white in the trenches of Flanders, should emerge from the Great War without her share of conquered territories was insupportable to him, and would never have been tolerated by his countrymen.

Everyone knows what followed. After long and bitter controversies, both in Paris and in the East, the Peace Conference assigned the mandate for Syria to France. When the Arabs resisted this by force, the French troops threw the Emir Feisal out of Damascus after a fight in which some of the bravest of the Arab chiefs were killed. They settled down in the occupation of this splendid province, repressed the subsequent revolts with the utmost sternness, and rule there to this day by the aid of a very large army.

I did not see Lawrence while all this was going on, and, indeed, when so many things were crashing in the post-War world the treatment of the Arabs did not seem exceptional. But when from time to time my mind turned to the subject, I realized how intense his emotions must be. He simply did not know what to do. He turned this way and that in desperation and in disgust of life. In his public writings he has declared that all personal ambition had died within him before he entered Damascus in triumph in the closing phase of the War. But I am sure that the ordeal of watching the helplessness of his Arab friends to whom he had pledged his word, and, as he conceived it, the word of Britain, maltreated in this horrible manner, must have been the main cause which decided his eventual renunciation of all power in great affairs. His highly-wrought nature had been subjected to the most extraordinary strains during the War, but then his spirit had sustained it. Now it was the spirit that was injured.

In the spring of 1921 I was sent to the Colonial Office to take over our business in the Middle East and bring matters into some kind of order. At that time we had recently suppressed a most dangerous and bloody rebellion in 'Iraq, and upwards of 40,000 troops, at a cost of £30,000,000 a year, were required to preserve order. This could not go on. In Palestine the strife between the Arabs and the Jews threatened at any moment to take the form of actual violence. The Arab chieftains, driven out of Syria with many of their followers — all of them our late allies — lurked furious in the deserts beyond the Jordan. Egypt was in ferment. Thus the whole of the Middle East presented a most melancholy and alarming picture.

I formed a new department of the Colonial Office to discharge these new responsibilities. Half a dozen very able men from the India Office and from those who had served in 'Iraq and Palestine during the war formed the nucleus. I resolved to add Lawrence to their number, if he could be persuaded. They all knew him well, and several had served with or under him in the field. When I broached this project to them, they were frankly aghast — 'What! Wilt thou bridle the wild ass of the desert?' Such was the attitude, dictated by no small jealousy or undervaluing of Lawrence's qualities, but from a sincere conviction that in his mood and with his temperament he could never work at the routine of a public office. However, I persisted. An important post was offered to Lawrence, and to the surprise of most people, though not altogether to mine, he accepted at once.

This is not the place to enter upon the details of the tangled and thorny problems we had to settle. The barest outline will suffice.

It was necessary to handle the matter on the spot. I therefore convened a conference at Cairo, to which practically all the experts and authorities of the Middle East were summoned. Accompanied by Lawrence, Young, and Trenchard from the Air Ministry, I set out for Cairo. We stayed there and in Palestine for about a month. We submitted the following main proposals to the Cabinet. First, we would repair the injury done to the Arabs and to the House of the Sherifs of Mecca by placing the Emir Feisal upon the throne of 'Iraq as King, and by entrusting the Emir Abdulla with the government of Trans-Jordania. Secondly, we would remove practically all the troops from 'Iraq, and entrust its defence to the Royal Air Force. Thirdly, we made an adjustment of the immediate difficulties between the Jews and Arabs in Palestine, which served as a foundation for the future. Tremendous opposition was aroused against the first two proposals. The French Government deeply resented the favour shown to the Emir

Feisal, whom they regarded as a defeated rebel; the British War Office was shocked at the removal of the troops and predicted carnage and ruin. I had, however, already noticed that when Trenchard undertook to do anything particular, he usually carried it through.

It required a year of most difficult and anxious administration to give effect to what had been so speedily decided. This was the phase in Lawrence's life when he was a Civil Servant. Everyone was astonished by his calm and tactful demeanour. His patience and readiness to work with others amazed those who knew him best. Tremendous confabulations must have taken place among these experts, and tension at times must have been extreme. But so far as I was concerned I received always united advice from two or three of the very best men it has ever been my fortune to work with.

It would not be just to assign the whole credit for the great success which the new policy secured to Lawrence alone. The wonder was that he was able to sink his personality, to bend his imperious will, and pool his knowledge in the common stock. Here is one of the proofs of the greatness of his character and the versatility of his genius. He saw the hope of redeeming in a large measure the promises he had made to the Arab chiefs, and of re-establishing a tolerable measure of peace in those wide regions. In that cause he was capable of becoming — I hazard the word — a humdrum official. The effort was not in vain. His purposes prevailed.

Towards the end of the year things began to go better. All our measures were implemented one by one. The Army left 'Iraq; the Air Force was installed in a loop of the Euphrates; Baghdad acclaimed Feisal as king; Abdulla settled down loyally and comfortably in Trans-Jordania.

One day I said to Lawrence: 'What would you like to do when all this is smoothed out? The greatest employments are open to you if you care to pursue your new career in the Colonial service.' He smiled his bland, beaming, cryptic smile, and said: 'In a very few months my work here will be finished. The job is done, and it will last.'

'But what about you?'

'All you will see of me is a small cloud of dust on the horizon.'

He kept his word. At that time he was, I believe, almost without resources. His salary was £1200 a year, and governor-ships and great commands were then at my disposal. Nothing availed. As a last resort I sent him out to Trans-Jordania, where sudden difficulties had arisen. He had plenary powers. He used them with his old vigour. He removed officers. He used force. He restored complete tranquillity. Everyone was delighted with the success of his mission; but nothing would persuade him to continue. It was with sadness that I saw 'the small cloud of dust' vanishing on the horizon. It was several years before we met again.

I have dwelt upon this part of his activities because in a letter recently published he assigns to it an importance greater than his deeds in war. But this is not a true judgment.

His next episode in life was the writing, the printing, the binding, and the publication of his book, the *Seven Pillars*. We heard that he was engaged upon this work, and that a certain number of those whom he regarded as worthy of the honour were invited to subscribe £30 for a copy. I gladly did so. In the copy which eventually reached me he wrote an inscription which I greatly value. He refused to allow me to pay for the book. I had deserved it, he said.

As a narrative of war and adventure, as a presentation of all that the Arabs mean to the world, the *Seven Pillars* is un-surpassable. It ranks with the greatest books ever written in the English language.

In principle the structure of the story is simple. The Turkish armies operating against Egypt depended upon the desert railway. This slender steel track ran through hundreds of miles of blistering desert. If it were permanently cut, the Turkish armies must perish, the ruin of Turkey must follow, and with it the downfall of the mighty Teutonic power which hurled its hate from ten thousand cannons on the plains of Flanders. Here was the Achilles heel, and it was upon this that this man in his twenties directed his audacious, desperate, romantic assaults. We read of them in numerous succession, long, grim camel rides through sun-scorched, blasted lands. The extreme desolation of nature appals the traveller. With a motor-car or aeroplane we may inspect these forbidding solitudes, their endless sands, their hot savage wind-whipped rocks, the mountain gorges of a red hot moon! And yet, through these with infinite privation men on camels with shattering toil carried dynamite to destroy railway bridges, and win the War, and, as we then hoped, free the world.

There are no mass-effects. All is intense, individual, sentient — and yet cast in conditions which seemed to forbid human existence. Through all, one mind, one soul, one will-power. An epic, a prodigy, a tale of torment, and in the heart of it — a Man.

It is an interesting question what would have happened to Lawrence if the Great War had continued into another year. News in the East, where it is scarce, travels fast. The fame of this man was spreading throughout Asia. Nothing was impossible; he might have arrived at Constantinople in 1919 with most of the races and tribes of Asia Minor and Arabia at his back. He was already in close negotiation with Mustapha Kemal. Napoleon's young dream of conquering the East, stopped by British sea-power and Abercrombie at Acre — the 'grain of sand' — might well have been realized by one in whom one can hardly see lacking any of the qualities of which world conquerors are made. But the enemy collapsed. The bells of armistice rang out. The grand conclusions were withheld. The hideous deluge subsided. Lawrence was left like some prehistoric monster carried by a tidal wave from ocean depths far inland, and left strangely stranded when the waters fell.

The rest of his life may be epitomized. His pride and many of his virtues were superhuman. He was one of those beings whose pace of life was faster and more intense than what is normal. Just as an aeroplane only flies by its speed and pressure against the air, so he could only fly in a hurricane. He was out of harmony with the normal, and when the storm-wind stopped, he could with difficulty find a reason for existence. In a religious age, and if he had been a religious man, the monastery would have been his refuge. A harder task was reserved for him. He found it in the Royal Air Force.

In an honourable service, 'the simple round, the common task' furnished him with a way of living.

When Clemenceau came back from India in his old age the reporters asked him, 'What will you do now?' He replied, 'I am going to live till I die'. This was the case of Lawrence. For twelve years he served as an air mechanic. The gallant Service, the decent fellows, good-hearted British comrades, the mechanism of aeroplane engines, the design of flying-boats — he held on to these. On one of the very rare occasions when I saw him I taxed him with hiding his talent in a napkin while the Empire needed its best. He rejoined that he was setting an example, and that there was nothing in life better than to be a good aircraftman. He was certainly that. But how much more besides!

His grip upon the imagination of the modern world was due to his indifference to all the delights which nature offers to her multitudes of children. He could feel her pangs to the full. Her prizes did not stir him. Home, money, comfort, fame, power itself — meant little or nothing to him. The modern world had no means of exerting the slightest pull upon him. Solitary, austere, inexorable, he moved upon a plane apart from and above our common lot. Existence was no more than a duty, yet a duty faithfully to be discharged.

It was only at long intervals that we talked together. But I was under his spell, and deemed myself his friend. Sometimes he would stop on his motor bicycle at my house, and I would make haste to kill the fatted calf. Sometimes he would stop, and then hurry away for fear of intruding — where he was ever welcome.

The last time he came was a few weeks before his death. He was riding only a 'push-bike'! He was going, he told me, to get rid of his motor cycle. He could not afford such luxuries. I reminded him that he had the purse of Fortunatus. He had but to lift his hand. But he tossed his head disdainfully. Such a thing as a motor cycle was beyond his means. Alas, he did not stick to this opinion!

I deem him one of the greatest beings alive in our time. I do not see his like elsewhere. I fear whatever our need we shall never see his like again. King George V wrote to his brother, 'His name will live in history'. That is true. It will live in English letters; it will live in the annals of war; it will live in the traditions of the Royal Air Force, and in the legends of Arabia.

PUBLICITY

LOWELL THOMAS

L O W E L L T H O M A S. Author, Lecturer, Radio and News-
reel Commentator. Born 1892. Fellow of the American Geographical Society; Royal Geographical Society. Toured the
world for four years with his travelogue 'With Allenby in
Palestine and Lawrence in Arabia'. Has since led various
expeditions. Author of some thirty books of biography, exploration and adventure, including *With Lawrence in Arabia*, the first
book on T. E. L.

IN various places I have written and all over the world
I have related most of what I know about T. E. Lawrence.
Indeed, some have been good enough to proclaim that I
have said more than I know. On the contrary, I kept several
things to myself during his lifetime. In themselves they were
innocent enough. But they were of that fatally innocent kind
that might have shown him in a false light to people lacking in
sympathy and understanding. I admired the man beyond any
other human being I have ever met in a lifetime of travel
around the Seven Seas. Naturally, it was my constant desire
that the entire world share that admiration. That desire failed
of fulfilment for the human but rather unhandsome reason
that for every man who loves a hero there is another who
resents him. And the resentment is of a venomous and virulent
kind. But the more virulent it was the more it, too, failed of its
object. The more serpentine the tongues of Lawrence's
detractors the farther they thrust him, victim of twentieth-
century hydra-headed publicity, unwilling into the limelight.

Now Lawrence is dead, his reputation beyond assail and
there is no longer any need, real or fancied, to withhold any
truth, particularly if it may help to throw a brighter illumination into the sometimes labyrinthine depths of his unique
mind.

I had been sent to Europe on a propaganda mission. My
orders from Washington were to cover the Allied campaigns

on all fronts, obtain all the interesting material available, rush back to America, and tell what I had seen in as optimistic a vein as might be. The idea was, of course, to chant hallelujahs for the gallant pitch of belligerent frenzy and thus stimulate a popular demand by the voters and taxpayers that Uncle Sam throw his full weight into the war. The farther I went on the European fronts the lower sank my spirits.

What was a propaganda emissary to do? In that dark moment John Buchan came cheerfully to the rescue. It looked a bit dusty, he agreed in a matter-of-fact tone after I had described my plight. But Lloyd George was getting fed up with the deadlock in the West and was sending Allenby to Palestine, vice Sir Archibald Murray, who had taken two lickings from the Turks at Gaza. Allenby hadn't been happy in trench warfare, for he was a cavalry general. But at that he was first-rate in South Africa and he might repeat in the Palestine show. That might be just my pigeon. Perhaps I could be given a lift in that quarter, if I cared to take it on.

Later I learned that it was no light favour which Colonel Buchan of the London Foreign office had undertaken. 'Bull' Allenby looked upon every observer as Sinbad looked upon the Old Man of the Sea. Of them all, a ruddy American was just the last straw. However, in some fashion or other Buchan pulled it off for me. I was accredited to the Palestine Expeditionary Force. Thus I was enabled to meet Lawrence, not having the faintest idea that the meeting and its consequences were destined actually to change the entire course of my career and existence — and possibly his.

The circumstances of that meeting I have described elsewhere and oft. Long before I saw him I had heard about him. Hardly had I reached Cairo before I was regaled with wild rumours about the Arab revolt against the Turk. Yet it was remarkable that the name of Lawrence was known only to a bare handful of British officers, some of whom dismissed him with a shrug or openly denigrated his ideas, his tactics, his impatience with the hallowed routine of professional soldierdom. The farther I penetrated across the Sinai peninsula into

Palestine, the stranger grew the rumours. I did not actually encounter Lawrence until after the fall of Jerusalem.

Walking through the streets of the Holy City, I saw a man, slim and short of stature but of most magnetic and imposing presence. At first I took him for one of Sherifian rank. He was arrayed — the only word for it — in the magnificent white silk robes of an Arab prince, wearing in his sash the short, curved gold sword distinctive of the Ashraf, descendants of the Prophet. But it wasn't his regalia nor his Ashrafian insignia that made him a personage to stare at. It was the cool, bold, lofty bearing. When under his Sherifian headrobes I perceived the flashing blue eyes and Norman-English features he seemed indeed the reincarnation of a Crusader in the train of Richard — or, had he been endowed with a mighty frame, the Cœur de Lion himself.

Such was the appearance of the man to whom I was introduced by the Governor of Jerusalem. At this juncture there arises one of the first questions I hope to answer: 'Was Lawrence really as modest as I have painted him? If so, why the gaudy, princely panoply?' Now it can be told frankly that I have not hitherto been entirely frank about this. I was, perhaps, over-anxious to avoid putting him in a false light, so I leaned over backwards. In my book, *With Lawrence in Arabia*, I deliberately gave the impression that he garbed himself as an Arab because he had come across the desert through the Turkish lines and had no regular British uniform. Though the mis-explanation satisfied many people, actually it was pretty feeble. When he got to Jerusalem he could easily have borrowed a uniform.

Another circumstance made me the target for many awkward questions. When I joined Lawrence on the Arabian coast shortly before the march on Damascus, Mr. Harry Chase, the camera man who was with me, obtained many striking photographs of T.E. in his most glittering raiment. Years later when I was lecturing in Calcutta, Colonel Robert Lorraine looked me up. He told me he had listened to me several times, both in London and in India. And one thing puzzled him immeasurably. If the leader of the revolt in the desert was so painfully modest, why in the world did he ever permit those photographs? Surely a contradiction was there. Now Lawrence was still alive at the time, almost pathologically sensitive, desperately seeking privacy. So I gave Bob Lorraine the same cock-and-bull story I had put in my book. Harry Chase and I had tricked 'Aurans'. That was the figment. While I distracted T.E. with a conversation about Hittite archaeology, his pet subject, Chase sat near us, pretending to fiddle with a high-speed camera of the sort used by tabloid photographers in America. I could see no other explanation that would not place T.E. in a false light. Now that he is gone, no such rot is necessary. Its falsity should have been obvious in subsequent years when he posed for a portrait by Augustus John in that same Arab costume.

I told Bob Lorraine the truth later in America and here it is. Not only was it unnecessary to trick Lawrence but it was he who helped wangle permission from Lord Allenby for me to join him in the desert for the Damascus campaign. Furthermore, we never had the slightest difficulty persuading T.E. to pose for Harry Chase's camera. He posed himself and contrived to prevail upon his extremely camera-shy fellow-officers to do the same. What was more ticklish still, he induced scores of Beduin sheiks to let us 'shoot' them, when it was still a cardinal suspicion among the children of the desert that the camera was an invention of Eblis.

In the face of all this, was T. E. Lawrence really modest? Yes, in the finest sense of the term. Professional neurologists have told me that there isn't the slightest incompatibility between his modesty and his predilection for picturesque garment, his modesty and his willingness to let his photograph be taken. Lawrence loved the sensation of wearing his Sherifian regalia. He enjoyed posing for his photographs. He enjoyed to the hilt what he accomplished with Feisal in the desert, and, subconsciously, revelled in being the leader of an army, a strategist, a maker of history. And he got a real thrill out of the kudos that accrued out of his success.

The explanation of the apparent paradox of Lawrence really is excessively simple. It is human to enjoy fame, especially when you have reason to suspect that you have earned it. By the same token it is human to hide that enjoyment from the peering, sneering eyes of other and lesser men. Lawrence was, above all things, human. For instance:

While I was delivering my illustrated account of his campaign at Covent Garden, Queen's Hall, and the Albert Hall, Lawrence came at least five times. Invariably he slipped in alone. His presence would have passed unobserved but for the managerial staff who were always on the lookout for celebrated visitors. Usually it was my wife who espied T.E. Whenever he was spotted he would blush crimson, laugh in confusion, and hurry away with a stammered word of apology. As you can realize, he enjoyed it all, enjoyed the glamour and the honour. But he wanted to remain on the sidelines, he would run miles to avoid the spotlight. At the same time he wrote me a note saying: 'I saw your show last night and thank God the lights were out!' Percy Burton, the impresario responsible for the success of the show, received an even stronger communication. Lord Northcliffe had offered Burton and Lawrence any price they cared to name for an interview. Burton conveyed the offer to Lawrence, who declined most positively, adding the words: 'It is unpleasant to see one's name in print and — in spite of the nice way Lowell Thomas does it — I much wish he had left me out of his Palestine show.' And yet he had helped me to be an eye-witness of the indispensable part he had played in that show! Subsequently he notified us that if Burton published anything about him personally he never would speak to Burton again. His wish was respected.

All over the Empire I have encountered people, educated people, sometimes persons of a modicum of distinction who passionately resented Lawrence's fame. And holding me to blame for it and, having plenty of hatred in their systems to spare, poured part of it over me. Frankly, I have always been proud to be in such company as Lawrence's, if only as a target for venom.

In New York after the Armistice I found myself at loose ends so, just to occupy myself, decided to prepare a few talks. On every side I heard: 'Nobody wants to hear about the War. Look at the theatre — all the War plays have been taken off. The best thing you can do is to put your material on the shelf and forget it.' Having been away for the entire duration of the War I failed to appreciate what everybody thought they felt and, pig-headed, went ahead with my plans. After the material was in rough shape I began looking around for a theatre, an auditorium, a hall, any kind of a place in which to tell my story. Everybody gave me the cold shoulder, everybody save one New York editor. He was as mad as I was, so together we plunged and booked the largest theatre in all New York, the Century, a white elephant, a washout. Somehow or other, we managed to hold the fort not one but several weeks, after which we moved to Madison Square Garden, something like London's Olympia.

My programme was a series of shows describing the various Allied campaigns. On the nights when I jawed about the Western front, France and Flanders, or the Serbian business, the attendance was only fair. But whenever I put on the Arabian and Palestine campaigns we had huge mobs. So, on the very last night of the engagement at Madison Square Garden a stroke of luck came my way. It arrived in the person of Percy Burton, the famous English impresario. After the performance he came around to the back of the house and introduced himself. He expressed his astonishment that he, an Englishman, had had to come to New York to hear about a great British hero, whom he hitherto had not even known to exist. He was dumbfounded that Americans were learning all about Lawrence while Lawrence's countrymen didn't even know he was on earth. Then he gave me shock for shock, inviting me to go to London under his aegis.

Now I never even had dreamed of such a thing. Moreover, I couldn't take Burton seriously and thought he was pulling my leg. By way of retaliation I tried to pull his at luncheon on the following day, pretending I would go to London IF he would procure me an invitation from the King or from the British Government. I also stipulated that he should put me at either Drury Lane or Covent Garden, supposing that such a famous sanctum sanctorum of drama and opera would be out of the question. Burton grinned, said: 'You don't want much, do you?'; we parted and I forgot all about it. One month later came a cable from London, Burton had complied with both my impossible conditions, or close enough. So I sailed for England expecting to stay a couple of weeks and return home.

Evidently I didn't know the English people and I didn't know Burton. Almost literally he set old London town back on its ears in my behalf. In all candour, I claim no credit for what happened. That the English people liked the show so much astounded me at the time. Looking back upon it, I see no cause for astonishment. After all it *was* a story, a great story about two great Englishmen, one of the great stories in the annals of the British Empire, great because of the greatness of the principal actors in it. Furthermore, up to that time exceedingly little was generally known, even in London, about the Palestine campaign, the capture of Jerusalem and Damascus. As for Lawrence, they didn't know he was on earth.

We hired the famous band of the Welch Guards to play before and during the showing of my pictures and my talk. Using one of Sir Thomas Beecham's opera scenes, the 'Moonlight on the Nile' setting from *Joseph and His Brethren*, I created the first stage prologue ever employed with a film. Another element of novelty may have been the fact that an American was telling, for the first time, about a British achievement.

Nevertheless, the success that awaited my show in London simply amazed me and actually upset my plans. Candidly, when I opened at the Royal Opera House I didn't care a rap whether London liked me or not. I was prepared to stay only two weeks, since a tour of America had been booked for me and I took it for granted that there would be no profit on the banks of the Thames and that Burton would lose his shirt. So I was casual in manner, somewhat reflecting my indifference. Later on I was told that this was just the sort of manner that London audiences liked. I didn't alter my text by one iota for the English public except for an impromptu opening remark to the effect that: 'It never had occurred to me that the British people might be interested in hearing the story of their own campaigns told through the nose of a Yankee.' That went down rather well, and seemed to put the audience in a hospitable frame of mind. And — what an 'audience! Every theatrical wiseacre along the Strand had told Burton we hadn't an earthly. First of all, they said, all the Londoners who might be interested in anything so highbrow as our show probably was, would be out of town (it was August 1919), on their first vacation in five years. Secondly, it was a sacrilege to use the Royal Opera House, Covent Garden, for any performance that involved pictures. Thirdly — and most important — it never had been done before. In the face of these discouragements, Burton weakened a trifle and had sold half his interest while I was on the Atlantic. Nevertheless, by dint of his prestige and his incomparable, argute devices, he contrived to fill Covent Garden with the finest première audience London had seen since August 1914, the first full dress congregation in five years. To paraphrase Gilbert:

> 'On every side Field Marshals gleamed,
> Small beer were Lords-Lieutenant deemed,
> With Admirals the boxes teemed . . .'

In short, the story of Lawrence caught on. Instead of staying in London for a bare two weeks my engagement was prolonged for months and months. I had to cancel my American tour at a loss of six thousand pounds. When the opera could be held off no longer, we moved to the Albert Hall, which until then had never been booked for more than a single engagement. Still the crowds came, including the Prime Minister and the Cabinet, M.P.s and their lordships from the House of Peers. Lord and Lady Allenby, Emir

Feisal and his staff, all the distinguished officers who had taken part in the Arabian and Palestine campaigns attended the show, some of them several times. I was honoured with a Royal Command to appear before Their Majesties at Balmoral. Unfortunately the great railway strike cut me out of this distinction.

More than a million people in London alone came to hear me tell about Lawrence, while he, to escape the crowds, fled to the country. But apparently he enjoyed it for he returned to town and came to see us. I never told anybody where he was and said nothing about his visits. Since I was, in all *bona fides*, drawing a picture of him as the most modest man who ever lived, I wanted to avoid complicated explanations. I felt that many would have found it difficult to reconcile his modesty with the fact that he frequently came to hear me tell about his campaigns in Asia.

It was during this time that I decided to set down the story on paper. Magazine and book publishers had been constantly on my doorstep. I consulted T.E., who told me he did not intend to write a book although he was working on his notes. But he added that when he had finished those notes he probably would stick them away somewhere in a vault, to be published after his death. This is a fact of some importance, since my book has been the source of considerable controversy not only among Lawrence's enemies but also his partisans. I made a particular point of asking him whether he had any objection to my doing a bit of writing about him. 'Not the slightest', he replied, and specifically authorized me by all means to go ahead. What was more, he helped me. My physician had ordered me to move out of London to the edge of Richmond Park where I could get out into the open every morning. The physical strain of speaking to thousands of people twice a day for four solid months had rather knocked me up. From his own digs near Westminster Abbey T.E. walked out regularly, some twelve miles or more, and worked with me. In the course of these consultations I frequently asked him whether certain anecdotes I had gathered were true, anecdotes concerning his experiences before the War. He would laugh with glee and reply: 'History isn't made up of truth anyhow, so why worry?' I mention this because in recent years other writers have accused me of including a number of yarns in my book which were really apocryphal.

There is one bit of false witness against Lawrence that I particularly want to nail. That is the charge spread by certain of his enemies that he was a homosexual.

In answer to this stupid canard I can say in the first place that anybody who has met thousands of men of all sorts and conditions can recognize a homosexual. If one has any prolonged contact with pathologues they are bound to give themselves away sooner or later by a gesture, a phrase, an inflection, a peculiar fashion of enunciating the sibilants. I have met all sorts and conditions, including several whose endocrine imbalance afflicted them with a sexual inversion. Furthermore, my father is a physician. I passed many hours, weeks, months, in Lawrence's company and never discerned in him the slightest *indicia* of the homosexual. But you don't have to take my word for it.

Another question that people have asked me all over the world is: 'Why did Lawrence avoid or decline the honours that were offered to him?' This has been attributed to an Adullamite sulking: his chagrin at the treatment meted out to the Arabs since the War. That I know to be untrue, at least, only fractionally true. He told me in the desert that, no matter whether they were given what they wanted or not, they were incapable of pulling together and creating a great Arab state. I am confident that he declined honours because he was a genuinely modest man who looked upon titles and decorations as of no earthly importance. He loved his fame, but at the same time wanted to run from it.

Personally I feel that I made a great mistake in my relations with Lawrence. He would protest that he wanted to be left alone by the world. He would laughingly insist that he never wanted a word said about him. But at heart, he loved it all. The mistake I made was eventually to take him at his word.

After giving a number of years to spreading the story of his achievements, I left him severely alone. So he probably acquired the impression that I had lost interest in him.

In many years of going up and down and around the globe it has been my privilege to know many unusual men. But none to compare with Lawrence of Arabia.

There is an old Turkish saying which admirably illustrates the character of T.E. and which, being interpreted, signifies: 'He had a genius for backing into the limelight.'

EASTERN POLITICS

CHAIM WEIZMANN
L. B. NAMIER

CHAIM WEIZMANN, D.SC., SC.D., LL.D. 1874-1952.
Born at Motol, Province of Grodno, Russia. President of the
World Zionist Organization and Jewish Agency for Palestine,
1921-31 and 1935-46; President of the State of Israel from
1949 until his death.

M
Y acquaintance with Lawrence was mainly the result of
my interest in the future of Palestine and the particular
aspect which I represented, namely the establishment
of a Jewish national home in that country. I first met him
under unusual circumstances on a rather hot day in June in
1918 in Akaba. The journey from Jerusalem to the spot
where he encamped was very long and extremely trying, but I
was amply rewarded. I met the man who had become a
legendary figure. And in spite of rumours to the contrary
I found in him a sympathetic understanding of Jewish aspirations in Palestine.

The desirability of meeting Lawrence was suggested to me
by Lord Allenby with whom I was in close touch in my
capacity as head of the Zionist Commission, which proceeded
to Palestine shortly after the Balfour Declaration in 1917.
The function of that Commission was to organize the existing
Jewish community in Palestine and to prepare the way for a
Jewish immigration and for Jewish settlement on the land in
accordance with the policy foreshadowed by the British
Government. It had always been the wish of myself and of
those whom I had the privilege to represent, to co-operate
with the Arabs and I consequently sought an opportunity of
establishing direct contact with Arab spokesmen. The chief
representative of the Arabs.at the time, one of the few Arab
leaders who exercised influence with his own people and the
outside world, was the Emir Feisal; and Field-Marshal
Allenby, who was so helpful, first in his official position and in
later years, after seeing Jewish achievements in Palestine, in his
private capacity, advised me to see Lawrence, discuss with him
the situation and get him to introduce me to the Emir Feisal.

Travelling in those days was no easy matter. Military
operations were still in progress and the difficult and exhaustive

journey to Akaba throughout which I was kindly accompanied by British soldiers lasted seven days. On the following morning, we proceeded to a place near Amman where Lawrence was encamped. I was at once struck by the presence of this man under such incongruous surroundings. The slenderly built British officer, blue-eyed, with his spiritualized face and somewhat whimsical expression, was in marked contrast to the swarthy desert warriors, restless, unable to stand still, constantly shooting and indulging in all sorts of antics. It seemed unreal — almost an Arab 'phantasia'. Lawrence was busily engaged preparing an attack on the Hejaz railway and there was ceaseless movement and much shouting. Under such inauspicious conditions, amidst din and noise, I was introduced to him. Lawrence had of course been informed by Headquarters of the purpose of my visit, but in the light of experience I had had with other officers who neither knew nor cared about British policy in Palestine — a policy that had aroused the interest of the whole world — I was beset by misgivings. I knew of the tremendous influence he wielded, and though the British Government, with the approval of other Powers, was already committed to the policy of the Jewish National Home, I nevertheless feared that Lawrence might be hostile to it.

It was therefore a great relief to me to find him not only friendly to the ideals embodied in Zionism but fully conversant with the subject. Our first talk was, in view of the circumstances, a hurried one. In the short conversation Lawrence did not conceal a measure of scepticism with regard to the projected Jewish National Home. These doubts, however, were not on political grounds but were based on other considerations to which I shall refer later. It was obviously neither the time nor the place to discuss the various aspects and implications of Zionism and we therefore arranged to have further talks at a later stage, either at G.H.Q. in Palestine or in Egypt. Meanwhile he, there and then, arranged for me an appointment with the Emir Feisal and told me that I would meet with a cordial reception.

An opportunity for a longer and more thorough talk with Lawrence on Zionism presented itself shortly after my return from Akaba. I was informed by General Clayton, the political officer of the Expeditionary Force, that Lawrence was expected at the camp in Palestine and he asked me to come and see him. I immediately proceeded to Beersalem where on this occasion we had a full discussion on the position of Palestine in all its aspects. We talked of the country's future and of the possibilities for the development of the Jewish National Home. Throughout the talk Lawrence displayed great intellectual keenness and genuine interest. Unlike others with less knowledge of the subject, and contrary to some misleading statements that still seem to persist, Lawrence never regarded the policy of the Jewish National Home as in any way incompatible with assurances given to the Arabs. He did not think the aims and aspirations of the Jewish people in Palestine contrary to the interests of the Arabs.

Appreciating the mystical call which Palestine exercises on the Jews, Lawrence nevertheless had some doubts as to the practicability of the Zionist aspirations. With characteristic frankness he did not conceal them from me. Zionism, in his view, was morally justified, but would the Jewish people respond to the call? Did they possess the potentialities, the energy, the power of endurance and all the other qualities essential for the reconstruction of their historical home? He candidly doubted the possession by the Jews of such latent qualities. Lawrence probably knew many Jews, but like many other distinguished Westerners had no knowledge of the Jewish masses in Eastern and Central Europe. And in common with others, he feared that the Jews had become so Westernized and so completely estranged from the soil that they would not, perhaps could not, cope with the gigantic task of reviving the desolate land of their ancestors. He was sceptical too regarding the strength of the Zionist ideal in Jewry. He wondered whether scattered Jewry would take up the call and avail themselves of the opportunity which now presented itself. He personally was conscious of the historic significance of the Messianic trumpet-call; it appealed to his nature and was moreover sound politically. But would not this trumpet-call fall on deaf ears? He spoke with great earnestness though his talk frequently took a whimsical turn, straying into other paths. It was probably this characteristic whimsicality that sometimes gave a wholly erroneous impression of flippancy. It was a way of his to stray from earnest talk as if ashamed of excessive seriousness. Such deviation was momentary and it was not difficult to bring him back to the subject under discussion and to provoke the application of his sensitive mind and equally sensitive sympathies.

I endeavoured to dispel his doubts about the Jews, explaining that the quality and character of the Jewish people is unknown and frequently misunderstood in many quarters. People were apt to draw wrong inferences from individual Jews or even small Jewish communities in the Western countries. The Jewish people as a whole are far less sophisticated than is imagined by the outside world. I told him of the vast masses of Jews in Eastern and Central Europe whose inward spiritual life is totally unknown to the West. He listened to that with great mental curiosity. He was interested to hear that the Balfour Declaration was received by the Jewish people with such enthusiastic fervour; that Jewry regarded the British pledge both as a challenge and a promise. Whether I succeeded in dispelling his doubts, I am unable to say. The things I told him were new to him.

The world knows so little about the inwardness of Jewish life — and probably cares even less — that it is not in the least surprising that even men of distinction rarely take the trouble to familiarize themselves with the Jewish problem, which is also an international problem.

Lawrence, however, whether convinced by what I said or not, took note of my information. He said that he would wait and watch with the deepest interest the development of the Jewish National Home. If, he said, Jews succeeded in translating the policy embodied in the Balfour Declaration, it would certainly be a performance unique in the history of mankind. His words deeply impressed me and despite some of his doubts I felt greatly encouraged and grateful for his sympathetic understanding.

This long and memorable talk with Lawrence was the foundation of, if I may say so, a lasting friendship between us. I frequently had occasion to seek his advice in connection with my negotiations with Arab leaders. Lawrence readily gave not only his advice, but his personal help in furthering both the Zionist aspirations and an understanding with the Arabs. Actuated by the desire to bring about co-operation between the two peoples, he was instrumental in drawing up the Treaty between the Emir Feisal and myself in 1919, which appeared in the press in 1936. That, whatever the subsequent result, was a very great service on his part to the cause of Zionism.

Lawrence maintained his interest, as he said he would, in the work undertaken by the Zionists. In 1920 there was a flow of Jewish immigrants into Palestine. They came from Eastern Europe, from Russia, Poland, Lithuania, Rumania and other countries. They were Jews who had burnt behind them such bridges as still remained in their ruined world, they were men who had fought in the War on different fronts and frequently in hostile camps; people who had fled from pogroms, wholesale massacres, and people who wanted to escape for ever from a demoralized civilization and who were anxious to build a new world, to build it peacefully by their hard labour. All these Jewish immigrants were united by one aim, one common object, that of rebuilding the ancient home on a new basis, on foundations of social justice. They all threw themselves into the constructive work with unparalleled zeal and industry. Many who had doubted the pioneering spirit of the Jewish people looked on with amazement and admiration. And Lawrence was among them. During his visits to Palestine he had an opportunity of watching Jewish efforts and observing their rapid achievements. This release of Jewish zeal and energy appealed to his dramatic instincts, and, with his keen perception, he discerned the possibilities of this historic enterprise. If I failed to convince him in that intimate talk we had on that one memorable occasion, he later revised some of his views through personal observation of the potentialities of the Jewish people. His faith in the Jewish National Home grew correspondingly with the growth and development of Palestine as a result of Jewish efforts. In the winter of 1921 I had a long talk with him, our conversation turning mainly on Jewish-Arab co-operation. He regarded such co-operation as of the utmost importance, from the Jewish point of view, but equally in the interests of the Arabs. He thought that the Jews acted as a ferment and were likely to be instrumental in bringing out the latent energies of the Arab people. He thought that Arab redemption was likely to come about through Jewish redemption. Lawrence certainly understood both sides, if anyone can be said to have done so, and he did his utmost to interpret the spirit of one people, and to explain the aspirations of the other, believing that close co-operation between the two peoples was to their mutual advantage.

I cherish his memory on personal grounds and remember with gratitude his help in furthering the cause of the Jewish people.

SIR LEWIS NAMIER, F. B. A. Hon. Fellow, Balliol College, Oxford. Professor of Modern History, Manchester. Born 1888. Political Secretary of the Jewish Agency for Palestine, 1929-31; Ford's Lecturer in the University of Oxford, 1933-34; Raleigh Lecturer, British Academy, 1944; Waynflete Lecturer, Magdalen College, Oxford, 1946-47; Romanes Lecturer, Oxford, 1952; Creighton Lecturer, London, 1952. Author of *The Structure of Politics at the Accession of George III; England in the Age of the American Revolution;* and many other historical works.

I HAD a slight acquaintance with Lawrence in our undergraduate days but knew nothing about him. A day or two after war had been declared he took me to a rifle range constructed by his younger brother in a disused clay pit in North Oxford, to practise shooting. I do not remember how I fell in with him that day, nor where he got the rifle, and it strikes me only now that this cannot have been his first visit to the range. With what plans or dreams had he been practising there?

After that for several years I heard nothing of him, for only when I met him in the lounge of the Hôtel Majestic at the Paris Conference in a colonel's uniform did I realize that he was 'Lawrence of Arabia'. It was in 1920, when I was at Balliol and he at All Souls, that I came to know him. He was accessible and communicative, and there must be hundreds of men who have known him as well as I, or better. He was retiring and yet craved to be seen, he was sincerely shy and naively exhibitionist. He had to rise above others, and then humble himself, and in his self-inflicted humiliation demonstrate his superiority. It was a mysterious game which he had started long before he became a private. It amused or puzzled some, annoyed or put off others; he himself enjoyed it in a quaint, whimsical manner. A deep cleavage in his own life lay at the root of it. I wonder whether he himself ever knew why he did it, or rather had to do it.

One day in 1926 I met him at the gate of the British Museum in his private's uniform.

'Hullo, Lawrence.'

'Do you recognize me?'

'Of course.'

He said: 'The whole afternoon I have been walking about the Museum where every attendant used to know me, and not one recognized me, till I inquired about someone I missed. Then the man knew me.' Quite so — what was the good of disguising if no one recognized him?

As a private he once rang at the door of a field marshal and asked the butler whether his master was in. He was not. Would he lunch at home? Yes. 'Then tell his Lordship that Aircraftman Shaw will lunch with him.'

Like the figures in Rostand, T.E. would fasten on certain details — see, for instance, his remarks on hats in the *Seven Pillars of Wisdom*, p. 109. As I came out from the church, after Lionel Curtis's wedding in 1920, I saw Lawrence, lost in thought and observation. I went up to him but was told to wait: he was counting the number of top hats which emerged from the church (he and I alone were without them). After the last guest had apparently left, Lawrence suddenly noticed two more top hats in the porch, and eagerly registered their presence.

After that we went to the reception in St. James's Square. On the way he said: 'I do not want to have my name called out. What is the Christian name of Lenin?' — 'Vladimir.' — 'Will you be Lenin and I shall be Trotsky?' 'No,' I replied, 'Trotsky is a Jew, I shall be Trotsky and you will be Lenin.' Of course I took it for a joke. As we reached the door he pushed me in and said to the butler: 'This is Mr. Trotsky.' — 'Mr. Trotsky!' called out the butler. 'And I am Mr. Lenin.' — 'Mr. Lenin!' I was annoyed and embarrassed, and said: 'You are so shy that you always insist on creating a sensation.'

He was a man of genius, a great artist, and suffered as few men ever do, and he knew how much he suffered. 'Go into the desert for a few years,' he said, 'and you will return a prophet.

If you stay there too long, you will never speak again.' Had he been born on the fringe of a desert, he would have become a prophet; had he lived in the Christian Middle Ages, he would have become a saint. He had the instincts and negations of both, without their faith, and under modern conditions had to turn it all into an incomprehensible joke. When I saw him last, in 1930, I showed him a passage in my forthcoming book and asked whether he objected. He did not. Here it is:

'There are men who crave for mortification, "*la mia allegrezza è la malinconia*." But unless this desire assumes a standardized religious form — hair-shirt or hermit's hut — and can be represented as a profitable bargain for another world men dare not admit it, even to themselves. If proved beyond doubt it is described as madness. Educated men may become monks, but must not enlist as privates in the army.'

There was in him a deep neurotic negation of life; but he wished to believe that his mode of life was the result of his philosophy: 'Trees grew down by the river, till they rose above its bank and saw the ruins of Troy, and they withered away.' It was this deep negation of life which drew him to the desert, and next to the sterility of garrison life. Besides, there was the infinite capacity for suffering, and even the downright craving for it. He could bear any pain, outride the Arabs on a camel, do without sleep or food; at times it almost seemed as if he had no physical existence.

He was small, but so well proportioned that, except by comparison, one hardly realized how undersized he was. He had sad, piercing eyes; his greatness was in them. He spoke in a low, soft voice. When he talked seriously, people would listen spellbound. He had style in talking and style in every line he wrote.

One night when I was with him, he brought coal in a big sheet of brown paper and shoved it into the grate. The sheet caught fire. He was crouching by the fireplace and did not move an inch. He turned the blazing fringe upwards, looked at it for a moment, and then quietly blew it out, starting each time from the outer end, as if he were licking the flap of an envelope. He had first considered whether he needed the paper, and next, at one glance realized the strategical position: that the flame travels quickest along the edge and by gently blowing it out towards the top you can stop it completely. I said that if I survived him I would tell that story. 'You know too much Dostoievsky,' he replied.

He was a great novel reader: I am not. One night, however, when I was bored, I asked him for a novel, a good novel. 'But there must be no love story in it. Do you know such a novel?' He sat curled up in one of his big leather armchairs (he got them from a financier whom he had saved from a wrong invest- ment in the Middle East). He thought for a moment. Then his face lit up, and he pointed to a manuscript on the table. 'Yes, I know one. The Arab revolt. There is no love story in it, and that's why it succeeded. Take it.'

The thing which was wholly absent from Lawrence's mental make-up was a legal conception of fact or a mathematical idea of accuracy. He was fond of Cubist paintings, and his state- ments sometimes partook of a Cubist character. It was easy to arraign them on formal grounds, but if probed they would often be found to express the truth better than would a formally correct account. He never bothered or condescended to make his statements 'foolproof'. On one occasion he accused some- one of having 'packed a delegation'. When afterwards I repeated to him a passionate denunciation of what he had said, he replied, 'The man asked the delegation whether he might have some of his own friends present. He filled the room with them. There, people do not understand these nice distinctions. It was like a football match on an Irish village green; soon the entire village is playing. The room was packed, and that sufficed. In fact, the man afterwards boasted how clever he had been.'

There was a stillness of soul in him and a pain that was time- less; he seemed to dislike the precision of dates. He told me that in his History Finals at Oxford he spoke in centuries — 'in the beginning of the twelfth' or 'towards the end of the fifteenth century', etc. Only once he named a date — in brackets: 'about the middle of the eleventh century (1066)...' *Seven Pillars of Wisdom* starts in a timeless fashion, and it is only on p. 135, in the last days of 1916, that dating begins; until then the reader can merely guess that these things happened during the Great War, but neither year, nor month, nor day is mentioned.

Lawrence was not happy outside England. He loved the English countryside, and was miserable when in 1926 he had to go with his regiment to India. He said he had finished with the East. He made the army his monastery. He wanted to be 'like a brown paper parcel' and have no decisions to make. It was his penance. Some said that it was because the British Government had 'let down the Arabs'. This was nonsense. He never felt that way, and as adviser for Arab affairs to Mr. Churchill had full scope for working further on their behalf. His penance was like that of the medieval monks, cosmic rather than individual. 'For the sins of mankind' might have been the definition of a devout Roman Catholic, but he was neither a Catholic nor devout, and kept no accounts with Heaven. But the instincts behind the penance were the same.

In the summer of 1930, when I was Political Secretary to the Jewish Agency for Palestine, I wanted to see and consult him. To secure a reply, I goaded him, and asked why he continued to call on friends who were lords and generals, but not on 'ex-Private Namier'. He replied:

338,171 A/C Shaw, R.A.F., Mount Batten,
15/7/30

Dear Namier,

Lords and Generals! They were long ago, I think — unless you mean the Plymouth ones who see me (I am a local curio) when they come to Mount Batten.

I'm out of conceit with London this year. It costs too much to get there, and camp is home now. Outside the fences I feel exposed and lonely.

Yet if you must see me, so be it. Must I come up, or can you get travelling expenses in coming down here? Plymouth is a filthy hole, where man is vile, but the salt sea glorious.

Take warning that I am eight years in the ranks now, and by that much out of date in affairs. I read nothing, correspond with nobody, and meet no one concerned in the wide world. So I'm a blind man to ask a direction of. Yet, as I say, what I am is wholly at your disposal. I can get off any midday of a Saturday, and am free till midnight of the Sunday. Here or there. — Yours ever,

T. E. Shaw.

He widely differed from those who love the Arabs as a weapon against the Jews: and was therefore pro-Zionist. In the conversation which I had with him on July 19th, 1930, he said — I took down his words in shorthand and read them back to him afterwards:

'The problem of Zionism is the problem of the third generation. It is the grandsons of your immigrants who will make it succeed or fail, but the odds are so much in its favour that the experiment is worth backing, and I back it not because of the Jews, but because a regenerated Palestine is going to raise the whole moral and material status of its Middle East neighbours.'

He was prepared to testify on behalf of Zionism to the Cabinet. I repeated at the time the offer to Mr. Malcolm MacDonald, but nothing came of it.

Among other things, Lawrence told me that day the story of the Cairo Conference of 1921, and how Transjordan has come to be separated from Palestine. I put down in a minute what I heard from him, and a funny story it was — Lawrence had a great sense of humour. But the time has not yet come to publish it and I give here the bare gist of it:

'The decisions of the Cairo Conference were prepared by us in London, over dinner tables at the Ship Restaurant in Whitehall. It was decided to include Transjordan in Palestine, to make it indistinguishable from Palestine, and to open it to Jewish immigration. Every point was decided at Cairo, as originally settled in London, except the one about Transjordan. When the Conference met, Abdulla was marching from the

Hejaz to Transjordan with a view to attacking the French in Syria. To stop him would have required troops and money. It was decided to negotiate with him.

'There were three possibilities:

'1. To keep a British garrison in Transjordan.

'2. To establish there a native State under British direction.

'3. To let the French have it.

'As the Cabinet were absolutely opposed to British troops being sent across the Jordan and money being spent on operations, the first possibility was ruled out. Abdulla could therefore be stopped by persuasion only. Had he gone on against Syria, the French, after having dealt with him there, could not have been stopped from occupying Transjordan, which had been used as a base against them. Therefore the best solution was to have a "British Abdulla" in Transjordan. The situation which had arisen in the spring of 1921 left no other choice.'

'And we had to foot the bill,' I said.

'Yes,' he replied, 'you had to foot the bill. But you would have been no better off if the French had taken Transjordan.'

And here are a few other scraps from that conversation:

'If you had four hundred decent British policemen in Palestine, there would be no problem.' I asked whether that did not depend very much on who commanded them. He thought not. Policemen go about the country on their own and are not commanded.

About Ibn-Saud, he said that he was the last protest of the desert against Europe. He was a great man, but had no creative idea behind him. His work could not survive him. Such waves of reaction have come out of the interior of Arabia again and again.

Lawrence talked disparagingly about Pan-Islamism in politics. It is a fiction, and there is no more to it than there would be to a Pan-Christianity. There are at present at least nine Khalifs. Every Mohammedan ruler who has the power compels his people to believe in him as a Khalif. The bogy of

the Khalifate was merely a weapon against the British Government and a means of self-aggrandizement, and its managers had
to go lower and lower in that game. They started with the
Sultan, next they tried the Emir of Afghanistan, now they
might be capable of trying some Mufti, but it is a game which
leads nowhere.

The British Government know little. When he wanted
support for the Hejaz he made them believe that it was a great
thing to have the Sherif of Mecca on our side. But that was
mere bluff.

He told me a great deal about the future of the Jews in
Palestine and of British rule in the East. About the Mesopotamia rebellion he said that it was due to British administra-
tors having become accustomed during the war to numerous
battalions. Only when we learn again how to rule without
soldiers shall we be safe.

He said to me once about Semites: 'To the end of the world
will they go for loot but if an idea crosses their path they forget
the loot and follow the idea.'

I never saw him after 1930. When I once asked him why
he did not come to see me, he wrote on October 12, 1932:

'I came to London for a leave of a few days carrying your
letter of 6 ix. in my pocket. I hoped to . . . see you. But the
powers were unkind. I had many worries which took most of
my day energies, and when the nights came I walked up and
down the crowds, or looked at lights and listened to traffic as a
refuge against seeing people.'

And in a later letter, 'Sick of Plymouth . . . there is no place
like London'.

The last letter which I ever received from him he concluded
by saying about a common friend: 'It is sad to see a big man
in retirement and not knowing what to do. I wish we could
all die in harness.'

POST-WAR GENERAL VIEWS

BERNARD SHAW
HERBERT BAKER
LIONEL CURTIS
ERIC KENNINGTON
E.-M. FORSTER
WILLIAM ROTHENSTEIN
RALPH H. ISHAM

BERNARD SHAW, playwright &c. 1856-1950. Wrote play *Too True to be Good*, 1932, introducing T. E. L. in the character of Private Meek. For their first meeting see article by Sir Sydney Cockerell. The first half of what follows was written in 1926, the remainder in May 1935.

IN the War of 1914-18, all those of the belligerent Powers which were holding alien peoples in subjection for their own good or otherwise, had to face the risk of such peoples seeing in the War their opportunity to rise and strike for independence. The Germans banked on a rising in Ireland. What is more to the present point, they considered the possibility of a nationalist rising in Algeria against the French. If they could have brought that about, the consequences might have been serious. But the steps they took to provoke it were futile, ending in a merely literary propaganda, which was easily and effectively countered, not from France but from England. I myself was concerned in the affair in a comic opera manner as a reputed Prophet. Nevertheless the thing could have been done had there been a man of genius on the German side to do it.

The proof of this is that England, having a man of genius at her disposal, succeeded in effecting the parallel operation of stirring up a nationalist rebellion against the Turkish Empire in Arabia. The genius in question was a young archaeologist with a careless fancy for calling himself by any name that came into his head at the moment. His mission caught him when he was T. E. Lawrence, and immortalized him under that name, in spite of all his subsequent efforts to discard it, which included, by the way, an avatar as Shaw. As this caused him to be taken for my son one day by a clergyman at the house of Thomas Hardy, I had better, perhaps, explain that we are two different people, not related in the way of vulgar consanguinity.

Lawrence had a passion for digging up old civilizations, to gratify which he had to go to the East, where such excavations are not obstructed by precarious and extremely uninteresting new civilizations. He picked up some Arabic, and found out the sort of people the Arabs are. Knowing already only too well the sort of people we are, he saw that if he came to our rescue by making the Arabs revolt during the War he would have more trouble with us than with them; for British public opinion and official routine disapproves intensely of geniuses, even when they have been hallmarked at Oxford. As to the British Army, its feelings when, after having to make Lawrence a colonel rather than be ordered about by a nobody, it found him leading his hosts to battle on camel-back in a picturesque Arab costume, can be more easily imagined in messrooms than described by me. Even the camel did not get its regulation meals.

The limelight of history follows the authentic hero as the theatre limelight follows the *prima ballerina assoluta*. It soon concentrated in its whitest radiance on Colonel Lawrence, *alias* Luruns Bey, *alias* Prince of Damascus, the mystery man, the wonder man, the man who might have, if provoked, put on Arabia Felix and Arabia Deserta as a shepherd putteth on his garment, and who did, when all the lies and all the legends are subtracted, authentically and unquestionably in his own way and largely with his own hands explode and smash the Turkish dominion in Arabia and join up with Allenby in Damascus at the head of Arabia Liberata, Arabia Redenta, Arabia allied to Britannia just when Britannia wanted her.

This might have left Britannia in a difficulty when the War was over. It is said that in 1918 Marshal Foch was asked how Napoleon would have fought the Great War. 'Superbly', said the Marshal; 'but what the devil should we have done with him afterwards?' The Prince of Damascus solved the problem for Britannia. He simply walked away and became a nobody again under another name. Any country with a Valhalla or a spark of gratitude would have rewarded him with a munificent pension and built him another Blenheim. The British Government left him to pension himself by writing a book about it all and living on the proceeds. That is how fortunes are made nowadays by ex-Cabinet Ministers, and even by active ones.

Now it happened that Lawrence's genius included literary genius; and that his maddeningly intense conscientiousness obliged him to write a book in order that the truth might be disentangled from the legends and lies, and history enjoy another of her rare escapes from romance and partisan scurrility. But he had inexorably determined that he would not coin the blood of the Arabs or his own into drachmas. He wrote the history, and, when it got lost, rewrote it as Carlyle rewrote his *French Revolution* when Mill's housemaid lit the fire with it. It was a prodigious task; and the result was a masterpiece. Commercially it was worth to the author a handsome endowment for the rest of his natural life, a big advance on which was ready on the nail from eager publishers.

Lawrence made up his mind to lose money by it. He set able painters to work to make portraits of his Arab comrades-in-arms, and imaginative draughtsmen to let their fancy play on illustrations in black-and-white. He had the portraits reproduced in color. He had paper specially made, and directed the printing himself in the manner of Morris or Caxton. Finally he produced a private subscription edition after bringing the cost per copy up to £90 or so, the subscription price being £30. It was scarcely out when advertisements appeared in *The Times* offering £5 a week for the loan of a copy.

If you ask me, as you well may, how all these extravagances were financed, I can point only to the subscription, and to a mortgage on the popular abridgment of the book. An Oxford grant which Lawrence refused to exploit for his private ends, and some remnants of his own property, were sunk in the enterprise. As to Arabian booty, it seems to have consisted in a presentation camel which he shot under himself in the excitement of battle.

How then, did he live whilst all this expenditure was going on? Well, how does anybody live when he has made himself totally unintelligible to commercial civilization? The Government was not at first wholly ungrateful. It offered him all sorts of jobs that he did not want. It found him a handsome berth at the Colonial Office, which he held under Mr. Winston

Churchill until the settlement of the Arabian affair. When he threw up his Colonial Office berth he found himself destitute, and after a brief experience of actual hunger enlisted as a mechanic in the R.A.F., where he discovered that the lowest rank in His Majesty's Forces is the most advantageous for command of them and the most free from responsibility. But the resultant situation and his publicity were intolerable to the authorities. He was ejected from the Air Force, whereupon he re-enlisted in the Tanks. Finally he was allowed to re-enter the Air Force as aircraftman of the lowest rank, in which capacity he organized the Schneider Cup contests and took command of the shipbuilding and marine engineering operations into which the R.A.F. was driven by the obsolescence of its boats. He was formally admonished to confine himself strictly to the duties of his station, with as much effect as if the Thames had been admonished to confine its flow to Gloucestershire.

In the Middle Ages Lawrence would have gone into a monastery as a retired *condottiero*. Living as he was in the Dark Ages, he deliberately chose the lot of a common soldier as the next best thing. It was objected that this was not fair, as he would be a most embarrassingly uncommon soldier, and that Private-Colonel Lawrence would make the army ridiculous. He promptly took another name, and wore down the War Office as he had worn down headquarters in Egypt. As a tanker-ranker soldier living humbly with his comrades (though I must confess that when they invited me to tea he looked very like Colonel Lawrence with several aides-de-camp) he directed the manufacture of the *Seven Pillars* even to ordering a different binding for every copy, so that there might be no 'first edition' in the collector's sense, meanwhile refusing any position in which he would have to give an order, and making me wonder whether he ever did anything else.

*   *   *

With the single doubtful exception of myself, no man of our time has had such a power of tempting journalists and even diplomatists to tell lies about him as Lawrence. Look at the obituary notices! They are all headed 'Mystery Man'. Yet there has never been any mystery about Lawrence since the end of the War. He changed his name twice; but everybody knew it as well as when the King changed his name from Guelph to Windsor.

All the Powers of Europe would have it that he was spying in India, when a word of inquiry would have ascertained that he was routining prosaically in the ranks in Dorset, in Plymouth, in Lincolnshire, taking not the smallest interest in politics, dropping in on his friends whenever he was on leave at incredible distances on the famous bicycle that killed him in the end, and busy with books and boats and the Schneider Cup trials, and all sorts of immediate and homely jobs about which he talked freely to everybody.

The mysterious missions to Asia were really visits to Bumpus's bookshop in Oxford Street.

The books he wrote about himself, though he made them the talk of the town by withdrawing them at the height of their fame, were paraphrased by half a dozen popular writers. When he was in the middle of the stage with ten limelights blazing on him, everybody pointed to him and said: 'See! He is in hiding. He hates publicity.' He was so conspicuous that he was bothered by it and really did make some half-hearted efforts to hide himself; but it was no use: he was the most impish of comedians, and always did something that turned up the lights again.

Nobody has ever called Mr. Lloyd George a mystery man, nor Mr. Ramsay MacDonald. Well, I defy you to tell me about either of them one tenth of what everybody knows about Lawrence. Yet people persist in romancing about him. They will keep on at it until the end of history, probably.

He was a very notable military figure; but he had the limitations of a soldier. I have talked to him on every subject on which he could be induced to talk; and they were many and various; but they did not include politics or religion or any other branch of sociology. For instance, though the Russian Revolution, with its amazing new departures in political science and education, is so momentous that people of all political complexions question me eagerly about it because I have visited Russia, Lawrence never once mentioned it to me. Any little chieftain who was putting up a fight, whether in Morocco against Spain or in Syria against France, he would talk about with keen interest, laying down the law as to his strategy and his chances of success; but he showed no consciousness of the existence of Lenin or Stalin or Mussolini or Ataturk or Hitler; and though every reader of the *Seven Pillars* knows that he suffered torments from what Ibsen called a sickly conscience, he was always a law to himself and never connected his scruples with any form of belief.

He was keen on all sorts of technical subjects and on art and literature and music, as many soldiers are when they are not hopelessly stupid; but he had no use at all for politicians and propagandists and diplomatists as distinguished from strategists. He had an immense store of knowledge up his sleeve — sometimes on the most unexpected subjects; and he was both handy and inventive as a mechanic; but he will be remembered as a guerrilla general and as one of the greatest descriptive writers in English literature.

You must keep in mind that he was not like Haig or Allenby or Foch or Ludendorff, giving orders and seeing little or nothing of their sanguinary effect. He had to do the most diabolical things with his own hands, and see their atrocious results close up. He had to lay the mine, watch the approaching train, press the contact, and see truckfuls of Turks blown to screaming bloody fragments about his own ears. He had to take his pistol and personally execute capital sentences in cold blood because no Arab could do it without starting a blood feud.

A highly sensitive and imaginative man cannot do such things as if he were doing no more than putting on his boots. I once asked him whether he felt badly about such horrible exploits. He said, of course he did, very badly indeed. His steadfast refusal to make money out of his experiences even when he was in actual want shews how he felt about them. He chose to enlist in the ranks to earn sixpence an hour rather than write best-sellers in Arabian and Turkish blood. For a time after the War I believe it cost him a struggle to preserve his sanity; but that was before I knew him.

He had a perfectly ridiculous adoration of literature and authors; and my efforts to break him of this by pointing out that such a feat as the creation of the *Seven Pillars* took him for ever out of the ranks of the amateurs and the dilettanti only frightened him off the subject. Though he has been described as a shy man I never saw any sign of it. He went wherever he wanted to, whether into a workman's house to ask whether he might share the family dinner instead of going to a restaurant, or into a king's palace to give the monarch a piece of his mind. He was a very strange fellow, a born actor and up to all sorts of tricks: you never knew where to have him.

The very curious arrest of his physical development was puzzling: at forty he still had the grinning laugh and artless speech of a schoolboy; and powerful and capable as his mind was, I am not sure that it ever reached full maturity.

SIR HERBERT BAKER, K.C.I.E., R.A., F.R.I.B.A., architect.
1862-1946. Designed Cecil Rhodes's house; Government
Houses for S. Africa and Kenya; S. Africa Capitol; Secretariat
and Legislative Buildings, Delhi; India House and S. Africa
House, and Bank of England extension, London. Author of
Cecil Rhodes, Architecture and Personalities.

frail Form

A phantom among men . . .
A pardlike Spirit beautiful and swift —
A Love in desolation masked; — a Power
Girt round with weakness; . . .
It is a dying lamp, a falling shower,
A breaking billow; — even whilst we speak
Is it not broken?

SHELLEY — *Adonais*

Have you ever been a leaf and fallen from your tree in
autumn?

T.E.S. to KENNINGTON

I FIRST met Lawrence shortly after the War at Oxford, in a
New College Common Room. I was at once fascinated by
his laughing, roving, blue eyes and his high domed forehead,
which gave the distinction of intellect and an assurance of high
character with the power of both thought and action. Two
sculptors, who modelled his head, record an unusual projecting
ring round the centre of the forehead. I saw afterwards how
those eyes could change to a piercing look of command.

To me it was love at first sight; he radiated some magnetic
influence, such as long ago I experienced in the presence of
Cecil Rhodes. I felt I would have followed him, had I been
younger, in any adventurous quest; just as we all felt a compelling force to do the tasks Rhodes set us to do. In this first
talk he warded off my questionings about his experiences in the
War with counter-questions on art. We talked of Syrian
archaeology; how discoveries had pre-dated civilization by
thousands of years. We made friends then and there.

When he was being mercilessly hunted by the hounds of

Press and Film he found a haven of peace in the attic of my office in quiet secluded Barton Street, Westminster. It was 'the best-and-freest-place I ever lived in', he wrote when he ceased to live permanently there; and 'nobody has found me, ... despité efforts by callers and telephones'. He refused all service and comfort, food, fire or hot water; he ate and bathed when he happened to go out; he kept chocolate — it required no cleaning up, he said — for an emergency when through absorption or forgetfulness he failed to do so. He worked time-less and sometimes round the sun; and once, he said, for two days without food or sleep, writing at his best, until he became delirious. He wrote most of the *Seven Pillars of Wisdom* there; he usually slept by day and worked by night; in airman's clothes in winter cold. We who worked in the rooms below never heard a sound; I would look up from my drawing-board in the evening sometimes to see him watching, gnomelike, with a smile; his smile that hid a tragedy. On sum-mer evenings we would tramp the traffic-free London streets, talking of our likes or dislikes of buildings old and new; returning to a late supper; or alone through the streets he would wander in the shadow of the night. In his criticism of archi-tecture he would search for the naked truth regardless of tradition or fame. He saw the faults of St. Paul's — not indeed its faultless dome — as Wren no doubt himself knew them, being bound, as he confesses, by the rigid Palladian standards of his day. He was equally critical of the nihilistic tendencies of the 'Modernist' who, in revolt against the atrophies and pedantries of traditional styles, ignored the eternal verities of his art.

He never showed signs of illness and seemed salted against colds; when paying a visit to friends in the rain he would put on a greatcoat reluctantly, saying 'They don't like me wet'. He had steeled himself to a rigid asceticism and kept his mind in complete control of his body. He denied himself all the lusts of the flesh and seemed as free from any thought, as he was from talk, of vice. He never smoked, and said of water that it seemed a priceless drink after the brackish and putrid thirst-slaking in the desert; that he could enjoy the delicate and varied flavours of water as an epicure could the tastes of various wines.

He could not be induced to tell of his adventures in the War, except in his kindness to my young son; or as a bait to draw out the adventures of others. Thus I heard for the first time stories of warfare in Arabia in countertalk with an Indian frontiersman of experiences in Tibet and of adventures and escapes from the Bolsheviks in Turkestan. But in such talk on Lawrence's side there was always the search for knowledge of the country and its people. He learnt, as a small instance, that the yak thrived better on the moss licked from the barren rocks, as the Arabian camels on the desert scrub, than on the best commissariat fodder. So also when meeting Conrad he probed him on the methods of his craft; Conrad admitting but little conscious design. Lawrence would say that he himself had over-studied his own craftsmanship. He loved the company of creative people, those who did something; but he successfully avoided society, 'that unrest which men miscall delight'.

He had a profound knowledge of medieval architecture. He could describe in vivid and full detail the military science and the town-planning of the fortified towns of the Crusading Kings. When I took him to see the brasses of Cobham Church, with which I was familiar, I found that he knew, for instance, all about the number, place and condition of the rare early type with the beautiful inlaid Lombardic lettering.

He had, it seemed to me, a wide insight into the arts. In literature and music he soon led me far out of my depth. I could not agree with all his views on art. Standards, tastes and emotions changed so much since the War with the younger generation. His state of mind in relation to much post-war art can best be explained, perhaps, by his own comments on some of the illustrations in the *Seven Pillars of Wisdom*. As we turned over its pages he would explain their meanings; but of some of the stranger woodcuts at the ends of the chapters he would say, 'I don't know what they mean; they're mad; the war was mad'. Were they meant to relieve the tension of the drama, as the Fool's grim and gay humour in Shakespeare's tragedies?

Or to express his own sublime smile at the actors in the war-drama, whom he calls 'sentient puppets on God's stage'?

His more extreme war-bred views on art as on other things, impish and often paradoxical as they seemed on the surface, and modernist, as far as so penetrating a mind could bend to any passing fashion, softened and, it seemed to me, became more rational with the passing years and renewed vigour. I came to marvel at his insight into, to use his own words, 'things' essential radiance'.

He confesses in his book that he 'had a craving all his life for the power of self-expression in some imaginative form', but had been 'too diffuse ever to acquire a technique'. Others will weigh his mastery of military science and the practice of war: of air-craftsmanship: of the art and mechanics of speed-boat-building and testing their efficiency in sea-worthiness and as targets in air-bombing: of archaeology: of scholarships: of writing and making books — the beauty and artistry of the *Seven Pillars*. The artist in him is shown in that book in the composition of the photographic views of the street-scenes in Jidda, exposed at the same hour for several days; and in that Tintorettoesque masterpiece, 'Entering Damascus'. But he had the divine discontent of the artist, being never satisfied with his work; even the *Seven Pillars* he would say was a 'poor book'. The drama, he thought, was overwhelmed by the artistry; though by that it may live! His talks to me on all subjects to do with my work were often of value and an encouragement. As I was leaving for East Africa, he gave me unasked a note on the principles that should order the laying-out of towns in the tropics, which differing radically from those of professional town-planners, proved of some value.

Before the air drew him as a magnet to its service, he intended to work at the science and art — the two were to him insepar-able — of writing, printing and binding books in a house-workshop he planned in his Chingford hill-top, on the fringe of Epping Forest. On entering the Air Force he sold the land — at the price he gave for it, not at its increased market value. This was, I believe, his only remaining capital.

The mysterious personality of Lawrence, the power girt round with weakness, will be best understood from his own books and his many letters to his friends. He was fond of self-analysis, but too fond of paradox; the light of his swift mind varied like the prismatic colours of an opal. While often a severe and indeed impish critic of the proud or pretentious, he had a catholic tolerance and sympathy with all workers and doers; and I believe a wide compassion, though it was deeply and deftly hidden.

My interpretation based on my personal knowledge may add but little, I know, to the testimony of those who may have had more intense experience of him. Segregation from his fellows in his school days and at the University, acting on his sensitive and high spirit, tended through his life to a boyishness and independence — as before to Shelley and others — the shades of the social prison-house never closed on the heavenly visions of youth. These deepened and matured in the solitude of the Arabian desert, ever the breeding place of saint and prophet. When to the Crusader the call for action ended and the wave of his energy broke, the instinct for abandonment and sacrifice took the place of ambition, and there came the temptation of abnegation and of bearing, in his own words, 'a cross from which to contemplate the world'.

War-shock; wounds in battle and air-crashes; disease, privation, sun-blasting, scourging, stoning; reaction of nerves long self-steeled against physical pain; living-surrender to the lives of alien people — which he said came 'near madness' — ; disillusionment and the vanishing of his long-cherished romance in the hour of triumph — 'honour lost', he calls it, through breach of faith — not due to him — ; the sum-effect of these, acting on his body — weakened and steeled by will alone — and his awake and super-sensitive soul, lessened for the time the vital forces of his mind and body. But was it only for a time? Would he recover these vital forces when the opportunity and the incentive came?

When book-making in a cottage seemed to him insufficient he enlisted in the Air Force, which was, he said, the nearest thing in the modern world to a life in a medieval monastery. He would find there a physical rest-cure in a passive regimen and a mind free of any reproach of arrogance or self-seeking in the blood-guilt of the War and in writing of himself and of fellow actors in it. He had, he wrote in 1927, 'taken pleasure in divesting myself of everything anyone could be found to accept, before I shut myself up. So accusations of selfishness will fall harmlessly off triple armour of assurance.' We should not perhaps take him too seriously when he talked of 'a penance for too rich and full a life'.

I have always felt that in the complexities of his philosophy there was the ulterior object of learning the ways of living and thinking of the men in the Air Force. Human sympathy and understanding from his personality would, he knew, help and exalt the Service and by his example the youth of the nation. It was thus by a living-surrender to the lives of the Arabs he was able to influence them to his will, and so lead them to victory. The Air Service he thought was the determining force in the future strategy of war; and the conquest of the air, 'the biggest thing to do in the world to-day'. 'You may think it a useless life,' he wrote to me, 'that's a grave judgment, for there are 25,000 of us leading it. You may think me better than the 24,999: I do not agree, if so. They seem to me very much my sort of fellows; perhaps they could do better: perhaps I could. But if ever there is a man squeezed right out and dry by over-experience, then it's me. I refuse always to say 'ever' or 'never' of myself, or of anything alive: but I don't think that I'll ever be fit for anything again.'

It was no hasty decision. He wrote to me from India in 1928 when he was about to sign on for another seven years: 'Do not think me perverse — or at least give me the credit of being consistently perverse. My ambition to serve in the ranks dates — concretely — from 1919: and nebulously from early 1917, before there was an Air Force.'

His weakened nerve-batteries, as with so many but less sensitive war-shocked men, required recharging with the alcohol of speed. Hence the need of the latest speed-bike from which at last he was thrown to his death — the instant made eternity, as he would have wished. Speed stimulated his creative thought. He wrote, he said, the chapter of his book that pleased him best by its rhythmical prose, in an aeroplane flight to Egypt.

Was the life he chose due wholly to this urge to a form of monastic life and interest in the Air Force? Was it not also the realist in him that led to the revolutionary conversion of the creative artist to the mechanical age? In a medieval monastery he would have been a master-mason. Another artistic spirit at Oxford, Ruskin, of imagination all compact, revolted from art to social ethics: from healthy plants alone could art flower. The creative artist in Lawrence was given power of expression in the making of speed-boats. He knew that his work was good when he told us that his boats by their speed had saved from wreckage sea-planes and their crews.

There is no doubt that when finally he left the Air Force his health in mind and body had immensely improved. He seemed to have gained a stronger and healthier intellectual and spiritual outlook. He hardly showed his years and seemed happier too, though one never knew the steeling-force of his mind's control. This renewal I think was due, apart from the rest and the healing years, to his sea-faring life, the experience, in which he revelled, of testing the sea-worthiness of his boats in all weathers. He then gave his friends hopes that he would rise superior to the forebodings which so often filled his letters and conversation. About a month before the end he enjoyed two consecutive meals and our surprise at a second helping, unknown before, evoked a cry 'Now you will do something great yet!' And in after-talk on national defence-strategy he expressed with an unwonted enthusiasm a desire to serve in the guiding of it; 'Hankey has too much to do'.

He came up a few days later, full of sound and fury, such as I had never heard from him before, against the agents of Publicity, who disturbed the peace of his country cottage. I am sorry that he was angry, as it was the last time I saw him.

Could these hopes have been fulfilled if the opportunity

and the stimulus of an ideal came to him? Or must we believe the mass of contrary evidence? In the words of his Epilogue to his book, were 'the springs of action exhausted' still? Had his soul 'grown old before his body', as he said of the souls of others and 'most of ours'? In his letters to me from India in answer to my offers of introductions, knowing that he must hunger for intellectual companionship, and assuming that he was brooding over some literary or other work for the future, he wrote: 'I am an extinct volcano, a closed oyster, and I must discourage treasure-seekers from the use of tin-openers. If there aren't any pearls the poor mollusc will have died in vain': that he had 'no seeds germinating . . . it will be miraculous if any activity ever revives in me': he was 'as high and dry . . . as the ship Argo . . . drawn up by Jason after the Fleece quest, and excused further voyaging'. And he ends pathetically 'I am so tired'. Again he wrote: 'My rackety life makes me expect an old age full of aches and ailments . . . always there's a feeling that perhaps I'll miss old age by some happy accident.' And prophetically he wrote to me in November 1928, 'I'm forty now, and six years may be enough to see me out'.

These extracts from his Indian letters to me may be of interest. He had dreaded the voyage out. He said there was room for few books in a Tommy's kit; he had acquired a habit of long hours of thought all alone. He found Karachi camp, a mile around, beyond which he never went, more dreary 'than any deserts of Arabia'. When on the frontier at Drigh Road and at Miranshah he never went beyond the barbed-wire fence — he wrote, in answer to my inquiry, 'So do not ask me about Waziristan, or Wazirs' — at a time when rumour whispered that he was stirring revolt across the border! He saw nothing in India but what was sordid and mean and regretted he could not go to Delhi. He 'mooned about within the wire fence, thinking of Hogarth and Hardy, who have died'. The modern fort at Miranshah with all its 'medieval apparatus' of fortifications interested the student of the Crusades.

Were his mind's self-sufficiency and his books alone enough to satisfy his spirit in the primitive life he contemplated in the two-roomed servantless cottage at Clouds Hill? Would he ever recover again the inner springs of action, some vision splendid such as inspired his youth; 'a hidden urge refluent as air' which 'present every hour of the day' strengthened him through the evils and miseries of the War? The chance had come to him to realize the ambition of a youthful dream as it had come to Cecil Rhodes — veld-bred as he was desert-bred — miraculously as it must have seemed to both: to him the Arabian war, to Rhodes the power which great wealth gave. Rhodes ever held tenaciously to the far-off object of his vision, saying when misfortune befell, 'My life-work is only just beginning'. Lawrence made no such disastrous mistake as Rhodes. He calls his Crusade 'a triumph'. Like Perseus and St. George, mythical hero and medieval Christian saint, whose shrines were in Syria and Palestine, he freed the country from the Dragon of misrule. Yet he humbled and defaced himself as though his life-work had failed and ended. Would a call to action have come to him again? Or would he no longer 'do things creative — partaking of the spirit'? 'Mankind is no gainer by its drudges,' he said: did he fear to become a drudge, or was he but waiting for the opportunity? If faith or love for a far-off vision or ideal, some going out of his nature and identifying himself with some forward movement for the betterment of the world, such as inspired his Arabian campaign, had again inspired and controlled his all-powerful reason, what yet might not his genius have achieved!

Whom the Gods love die young before their work is done, it may seem to us who remain. But it may be best for us too. His legendary fame may be a light to future generations, not so much for the greatness of his talents and achievements, but for his victory over the Body of the Spirit of Man. In the bright company of the sublimely mild Sidney and meek crusader Gordon his

> 'soul, like a star,
> Beacons from the abode where the Eternal are.'

LIONEL CURTIS, c.h. Fellow of All Souls College, Oxford. Born 1872. Called to Bar; served in South African War; Town Clerk of Johannesburg; Transvaal Legislative Council; Lecturer in Colonial History, Oxford; Secretary to the Irish (Peace) Conference, 1921; Adviser on Irish Affairs, Colonial Office, 1921-24; Institute of International Affairs. Author of *The Problem of the Commonwealth*; *The Commonwealth of Nations*; *Dyarchy*; *The Prevention of War*; *The Capital Question of China*; *Civitas Dei*.

I was first introduced to Lawrence at the Carlton Hotel soon after the Armistice by Lord Winterton who had served under him. He was dressed in khaki with an Arab head-dress and took me to see Feisal who was staying in the hotel. In 1919 I saw more of him at the Hôtel Majestic in Paris. It was there one night that a full-blown British general started an argument with him on questions of strategy. 'Now let us suppose,' said the general, 'that you, Colonel Lawrence, were commanding one force, and I were commanding another against you...' 'In that case,' Lawrence intervened, 'you would be my prisoner within three days.' The story explains why the young archaeologist was not always loved by professional soldiers. Allenby was a conspicuous exception.

It was in this year, I think, that he came to stay with me at the cottage where I was living near Ledbury. There were two or three other ex-officers as well. After supper a fruit grower, Bickham by name, happened to drop in, but did not catch Lawrence's name when I introduced him. Bickham remained, listening to the talk for about two hours, and when he had to go made a sign that he wished to speak to me alone. When we got outside he exclaimed, 'Who on earth is that amazing human being?' Then I told him who Lawrence was and what he had done.

A similar thing happened to me in 1929. I was asked to lunch by two Chinese friends in Shanghai, and was introduced to a third man at the party whose name I did not catch. When the unknown man left to keep an appointment I asked my hosts who their astonishing friend was and found I had been talking to Hu Shih. I mention this because I have just been told that Lawrence was talking to Archibald Rose one night in his room in London when Hu Shih happened to come in. After introducing them Rose discreetly withdrew and returned after many hours, about three o'clock in the morning, to find the pair still deeply absorbed in conversation. To have missed the chance of hearing what these two particular men from opposite sides of the globe had to say to each other was an act of self-denial to which I personally would not have been equal.

Some years ago my wife and I were going to see Lawrence at Clouds Hill. On the way there I said with some bitterness that he might be Prime Minister if he would. There was nothing he could not do better than anyone else, except, I added as an afterthought, doing what he is going to do this afternoon, giving a tea-party to a lady.

On the way home I took back the exception. The party, confined to ourselves and two privates from the Tanks, was a work of art, so quietly conceived for our pleasure that we had not noticed the skill behind it till we came to look back on it. Whether it was archaeology, raising a rebellion, leading an army, writing a book, organizing an air-race, or designing a speed boat, he did it all with supreme excellence.

He once told me that as a child he conceived the dream of freeing the Arab people from the Turkish yoke. This was why he learned Arabic. He could learn a language in a fraction of the time that an ordinary mortal would take. Dr. Hogarth told me that he discovered Lawrence by looking over his shoulder in the Bodleian and finding him reading an Arab text. [*Editor's note:* They had met before, I think; see p. 29.] Lawrence himself also told me that he spent some of his vacations tramping Syria and thinking out the campaigns of Saladin. When the War broke out his strategic thinking was already done.

His success in the War, like his other achievements, was, I think, due to two faculties which appeared in everything else that he touched. He could grasp the matter in hand, whatever it was, so clearly that he made everyone to whom he explained it feel that they understood it as well as himself. I remember feeling this when during the Conference of Paris he described a fortification built by Richard Cœur de Lion in France. I have never seen this fortification, but I have in my mind to this day a clear picture of the fort and why it was planned as it was. I had much the same feeling when I afterwards showed him a prehistoric camp buried in woods on the top of a hill. He saw in an instant what I, who had known it for years, had never been able to see; things which were obvious the moment he pointed them out — where the main entrance to the camp had been, and why it was rightly placed and designed.

He understood the situations he handled, and then brought to their management some idea so fresh and original that no one else could foresee it. When Feisal was called to appear before the 'Big Five' in Paris to state his case he asked Lawrence to act as interpreter. 'I,' said Feisal, 'will recite a chapter of the Koran verse by verse while you will make the necessary speech.' I guessed when Lawrence told me the story that he himself had put this idea into Feisal's mind.

Another thing that struck me about him was his intuitive judgment of values in letters, architecture, art, machinery or men. For politics in the narrower sense of the word he never displayed the slightest interest.

His respect for men like Hogarth and Allenby who had known how to use him was immeasurable. I once asked him what sort of a mind Allenby's was. 'It is like the prow of the *Mauretania*,' he replied. 'There is so much weight behind the prow that it does not need to be sharp like a razor.'

But all this does not help to explain the faculty of leadership which Lawrence exercised during the War, but never chose to exercise again. No one could meet him without seeing that it was there. Shortly after the War he agreed to tell a group of undergraduates about the Arab revolt. The largest private room in Christ Church was packed to its utmost capacity. Punctually at the appointed hour Lawrence crept in like a mouse, shyly sat down on a sofa and without a note told the whole story in exactly an hour, never moving a muscle as he told it.

Every sentence was simple, clear and perfectly phrased. Had anyone taken his talk down in shorthand, the uncorrected transcript would have been a literary and historical masterpiece. Most or all of his hearers had served in the War and hated the thought of it; but if, at the end of the evening, he had asked them to follow him on some wild adventure into the heart of Asia or Africa, one saw that all of them would have done so unquestioningly.

His ascetic vein, no doubt developed by early contact with the East, was another side to his character. His one over-mastering purpose, in which I think he wholly succeeded, was to keep his superlative mind in absolute control of his body. It is not perhaps correct to call this asceticism. I have never met anyone more entirely devoid of vice. The power of physical self-control he attained may perhaps be illustrated by an incident. A stranger whose car had come to a standstill in the road asked him to crank it. Just as Lawrence was pulling the lever, the driver advanced the spark. The engine backfired and broke Lawrence's wrist, but somehow the engine started. The driver thanked him and drove on, and Lawrence never allowed him to know that his carelessness had broken his wrist. The accident cost him months of pain, borne with a never-changing smile.

After the War, any career that he chose was open to Lawrence. Why did he turn his back on the great opportunities he had made for himself? An experienced medical adviser would be able to answer. The nervous strain he had undergone can be judged by anyone who reads the *Seven Pillars*. Of even greater significance is the fact that after the War he wrote that book, and wrote it twice over. He put the first manuscript on a seat in Reading Station, and it vanished. At first he declared that he would never re-write it, but at length we persuaded him. Night after night he sat in his flying suit in an attic above Herbert Baker's office in Barton Street, writing the book. On one occasion he wrote for forty-eight hours at a stretch.

A Harley Street specialist once told me that it is easier to bring on a nervous breakdown in writing a book than in any other way. One symptom is the loss of all sense of enjoyment in anything. Life becomes so unbearable that the sufferer is tempted to end it and too often does so. Lawrence was conscious of this temptation and sought the severest discipline he could find as an aid to resisting it. Colonel Stirling who served as Chief of Staff in Arabia has said that 'Lawrence was a man guided solely by his conscience'. Had he been a Catholic I have no doubt that he would have joined one of the strictest monastic orders. He told me that he would have got into prison if he could have done so without committing a crime. As these severer forms of discipline were closed to him, he sensibly chose the life of an aircraftman in the Air Force. And the treatment he prescribed for his own case was effective. In one of his letters he wrote, 'At Farnborough I grew suddenly on fire with the glory that the air should be, and set to work full steam to make the others vibrate to it like myself'. Those words are evidence that his exhausted nervous system had begun to recover its tone.

Lawrence was always giving, himself, his friendship, his time, his brains, his possessions, and especially money when he had it, but unwilling to accept service or gift from others, a princely giver but a chary receiver.

Hogarth once said of him, 'People call Lawrence an Arab. Lawrence is a street-Arab.' One side of him lived and died the incorrigible undergraduate. Yet he could read Spinoza faster than I could read a detective novel, mastering the meaning, and also retaining it.

One cannot reduce to a single coherent picture the various sides of his mind and character, utterly diverse as they were. I have never met anyone like him, and can think of no one in all history with whom to compare him. If Prospero, ere he broke his staff and buried his book, had spirited his daughter Miranda from the *Tempest* into *Midsummer Night's Dream* and then married her to our English Puck in a temple of Athens, his grandson might perhaps have been comparable to Lawrence.

ERIC H. KENNINGTON, a.r.a. Born 1888. Official War
Artist, 1916-19 and 1940-43; Art Editor, *Seven Pillars of Wisdom*, subscribers' edition, 1926, and to Jonathan Cape's edition,
1935; Sculptor of the bust of T. E. L. in St. Paul's Cathedral,
London, and of recumbent effigy of T. E. L. in St. Martin's,
Wareham. Author of *Drawing the R.A.F.*, etc.

THIS writing tells much about E.H.K. and all too little of
T.E.L., but he would have wished it so, for he veiled himself, and revealed those with whom he worked. Sometimes losing his self-assurance, he liked certainty and positive
life in others. What they could see in him was often only a
reflection of themselves, as they might be. So they could grow,
and might not know him, as plants grow in the sun's rays, but
cannot say what the sun is.

I first saw him in Lowell Thomas's film at the Albert Hall:
glorious photography, glamour and oratory. I came out drunk.
But nobody seemed to know anything about Lawrence of
Arabia, and I began to forget, till a picture dealer said 'There
was a Colonel Lawrence in here this morning. He has bought
two of your soldiers and left his address'. There it was. 'All
Souls, Oxford.' (This was in 1920.) I wrote immediately and
followed the letter.

He was on the platform, and had to introduce himself, for
I could not connect him with Lowell Thomas's screen-seraph.
I met a small grinning, hatless kid, bothered by a lot of untidy
hair falling over his eyes. He seemed apologetic, and made me
a superior and most distinguished person. He let me plaster
him with the Lowell Thomas romance, gently protesting that
it was far from the truth. In his rooms he explained that he
had done very little, had been extremely lucky in having good
men to work with, and that he preferred buying pictures to
fighting. That any creative artist was a much finer creature
than any soldier, and managed to suggest that I was really the
uncrowned king.

He giggled often. 'I've written a book . . . a poor thing
without illustrations to help it through. Do you know any

artist who could make portraits from photographs?' I said they would be no good. The artist must see the person. 'What a pity. For my sitters are in various parts of Arabia.' I asked, Did he wish me to go out and draw them. He giggled: 'You cannot have any conception of the difficulties. I should have to be your guide, and it would be expensive. I have no money.' How much? I asked; I could make some. 'Well, six hundred pounds would make life easy for us for ... would six months be sufficient?'

So the plan was made in fifteen minutes, and during the next month I earned exactly £600, for there was, most conveniently waiting, a large official portrait. During that month, working in London, I lived in a fantastic Eastern romance: a jumble of Feisal's tents, desert prophets, camel charges, muezzins. Lowell Thomas had done his work on me well and quickly.

I presented myself (and £600) to a slightly different person. Very quiet, giggling less, with serious eyes, and I knew I was being commanded. 'I must forgive him — but how was he to know that a respectable artist could make £600 ... Surely there was no precedent ... He was exceedingly sorry if he had given me grounds for hope ...' All my respect disappeared in rage, and I caught his coat to shake him, but was pulled up by his remoteness. He was not there to be shaken ... Next, he was planning the details of our trip.

What was happening? I asked myself in the train. This wasn't the Circassian dancing girl (see Lowell Thomas) nor the spotless white-robed descendant of the Prophet (see ditto). A person was coming through. There was something in the bright definite eyes as they glanced past, a dignity of form, an easy authority ... I bought the tickets (which, by his orders, were not via France) and handed him one. He was gracious, but could not go with me. He must go in a battleship to a conference in Cairo. I could sell the tickets ... perhaps next year — or in 1923 ... But my mind was too fixed, and finding there was a possibility of catching him at the conference if I started a cross-Europe journey at once, I told him I was going alone. He then gave me all help possible in one hour's talk about Arabia and the Arabs. He was most eloquent and I think he used mesmeric power (later, he strongly denied doing so). He led me, stumbling after his mind, through Nejd, Yemen, Jerusalem, Damascus, Sunni, Shia, Ashkenazim, Saphardim.

I goggled, and I am sure he enjoyed painting his great mind pictures, to replace the wooded panels of the University room. But it was not the story telling that left the clearest impression, but the teller, with his male dignity, beauty, and power. He moved little, using bodily presence just sufficiently to make brain contact. I had never seen so little employment or wastage of physical energy. The wide mouth smiled often, with humour and pleasure, sometimes extending to an unusual upward curve at the corners, a curious menacing curve, warning of danger. The face was almost lineless, and removed from me as a picture or sculpture. However gracious its attitude, it remained distant. ('He's like a fine Buddhistic painting,' I thought. 'The lines have just the same harmony.') The eyes roamed round, above, and might rest on mine or rather travel through mine, but never shared my thoughts, though noting them all. He stayed higher on another plane of life. It was easy to become his slave. These crystal eyes were almost animal, yet with a complete human understanding. And at moments of thought, when he would ignore the presence of others, retiring into himself, they would diverge slightly. Then, he was alone, and as inscrutable as a lion or a snake. He would return, and graciously attend to one with limitless patience, dealing with our slower brains and limited understanding, our hesitations and fears, apparently never exasperated by our inefficiency.

It was at this meeting I realized both his bodily strength and his sensitiveness. Though not broad, he was weighty from shoulders to neck, which jutted, giving a forward placing to the head, and a thrust to the heavy chin. Graves has called his eyes maternal, and I think rightly so, but a near contrast was the power of the frontal bones, and their aggressiveness. It was in their form, for I never saw him frown. Carlow says, 'He always seemed to be looking out from under a tent'. The fearless eyes were protected by a fighter's bones above and below. It was the face of a heavy-weight boxer, and in all circumstances, dynamic. Above and round and behind this fighting machine was a full development of brain, deep from back to front, and more high than broad. I was puzzled how the head could be at once so strong, and so sensitive (not knowing that the strength I was admiring was the shadow of a burly youth 5ft. 6 in. and over 11 stone. He must have once been as strong as a gorilla). He stood up, and I thought — 'Boxer's face, and tightrope athlete's body. He stands as if he were floating — like a fish.' My mental portrait drawing was sharply cut short, and conversation was made light and extremely humorous.

Cairo: The hotel, and signs of conference: crowds, but how to find Lawrence? There he was coming down some stairs, very small, the centre of a group. A new sight of him and his public mannerism — slight nods of the head, slight turn of the body, almost no movement of the hands but the blue crystal eyes moving always, seeing everyone and everything, halting a second, passing on, quickly penetrating — never tiring, never idling. I thought he had not seen me, and began to fear for myself and my plan; fool that I was. He appeared ghostlike, next day, in my room. Work would keep him, he said, some weeks in Cairo. It would profit me to tour Arabia, Palestine, and Syria by car. There were two Americans in my hotel planning a trip. Sea to Beirut, car to Damascus via Baalbek, and return south along the coast to Jerusalem where he could meet me and do something to make my portrait-painting raid inland a success. Meanwhile would I draw Allenby, and perhaps Churchill? And Ironside? 'Ironside is great. Six feet four, and sixteen stone. Brains too.' Why such a point of his having brains? I asked. 'Have you ever met another big man with brains?' was his answer.

Perhaps, he added, I should like to see Cairo with him as guide. This meant three hours' intense interest and enjoyment. The Arab city, the excavated early cities, the great dumps.

He was impersonal, merely an illuminator. He would pick up a broken pot from the excavation rubbish, and give a wide description of life at the time of its making. — Another fragment, and another description . . . 1000 years earlier, from a patinated ring, another picture. To my ignorance, he seemed to have all past life in his mind. Not at the time, but afterwards, I noticed the range of his awareness. He fed me richly, but also, I think, attended acutely to the life around him, listening to all the conversation. Maybe I imagined this. (Lowell Thomas again — super spy.) I saw no one notice him specially — we were just two Westerners doing the round of the bazaars.

During this conference time, he sat to me for the drawing which he called The Cheshire Cat. Black-and-white chalk on dark paper. The Arabs disliked this; he afterwards told me why: they think the faces of the damned in hell are black. He would not use this for the *Seven Pillars* though he liked it best. Reason: it was too obviously the spider in the web of its own spinning.

Of course he was right. The good-hearted Americans added me to their ample luggage, and at Beirut, stuffed both me and it into a car and . . . There was Western Arabia. Camels, villages, baking desert, deep snow, rocky mountains, oleander, cactus, snakes, and *Bedawi*. A joyful trip and a fruitful one. At Damascus, I drew Nawaf Shaalan, possibly my best Arab portrait. From Damascus, we jogged down to Jerusalem, where I seemed in for a permanent halt. It produced a portrait of Storrs, however, and a friendship with him. But I wanted Feisal's men, not Jerusalem.

Then T.E. came, as usual, opening the door without noise, and everything was possible again, probable, certain, and delightful. A mass of Emirs, Sheikhs, and Bedawi were congregating at Amman. (Did he tell them to, specially for my benefit?) Why not hire a car, and have the fun of passing by Jordan, Jericho, Es Salt? Syrians were comparatively safe though spirited chauffeurs. He would get the British representative to put up a tent for me, and give me a list of the men he wished drawn. Many of them would be there. Perhaps he would visit Amman . . . How simple; T.E. had explained how to do it, and of course one did it. A look, a giggle from the man who had no self-seeking, and one could not fail to achieve the impossible.

So off we went, Arab driver, Ford car, self and drawing materials, and extraordinary months passed in extraordinary surroundings. He did come for one day. The weekly plane dropped in a long sunny spiral, bump, bump-bump. Stop. Again the loose-end multitude surrounded and swarmed on it, and their cries this time became a roar, AURENS — AURENS — AURENS — AURFNS! It seemed to me that each had need to touch him. It was half an hour before he was talking to less than a dozen at once. Recreating the picture, I see him as detached as ever, but with great charm and very gracious. I thought he got warmth and pleasure from their love, but now know his pain also, for they longed for him to lead them again into Damascus, this time to drive out the French. Easily self-controlled, he returned a percentage of the pats, touches and gripping of hands, giving nods, smiles, and sudden wit to chosen friends. He was apart, but they did not know it. They loved him, and gave him all their heart. By now, I did not question, Where do I come in? I knew he saw everything. After hours of deification, and (as I know now) difficult states-manship, he sat down in my tent, untouched and untired. Quite unmoved, he was the same as when in his Oxford rooms. He told me what chiefs were in the camp, and writing a list, gave it to young Kirkbride, asking him to bring them and me together (Kirkbride threw it away that night, deciding it was not important). Then it was time to return to Cairo. Without adding coat, gloves, or goggles, he climbed into the plane — seeming to walk into unapproachable solitude — and was gone.

Some months later, in Knightsbridge, I phoned him, early morning before he went to the Colonial Office. 'Awful failure,' I said, 'but they are here; can you come and see them?' He said, with a giggle, 'Wait till I put the receiver down', and was

round in an incredibly short time. He made a perfect entry
to a room, which I got to know as characteristic. No sudden-
ness. A silently opening door, a shape gliding in, and a
simultaneous closing of the door: eyes sweeping circular-wise,
like a searchlight, halting a moment on the most interesting
things. Then a direct look, straight at one, eyes passing
through, impersonal, but mouth in a social grin, slightly
humorous. He said nothing. There was no need: the floor
was wall-papered with Arabs. I was honestly ashamed; they
were too few, and not good enough. I said so. He began to
say illuminating things about some, and with some he com-
muned silently. There was no sign that the portraits affected
him (to which he has owned to several friends). 'Sikeini —
he has no self interest. Shakir — few men are loved as he is
and deserves to be.' At Abdulla, he giggled repeatedly but
said nothing. He spent most time on Ali ibn Hussein, and
seemed to me to be almost reverential. It was one of the
hundred surprises he gave me. To me they were drawings.
He exchanged with them as with living souls. 'Mahmas.
That means coffee spoon. Called so, probably, because the
parents happened to notice one during his birth . . . I'm glad
you got X. He is a homicidal maniac. He can't help it.
He killed three of my best camelmen, and finally I had to
disarm him myself.' 'Well, he nearly killed *me*,' I said, and
told him the story, while he gazed kindly, but distant as the
moon. Then he began to giggle and said, 'I am glad he did
not kill you, Kennington, because . . . if he had . . . I should
not have seen these drawings'. Then he giggled himself backwards, out of the room, and left me guessing.

Now, how was it that I was enabled to leave and return to
London with portraits of a score of the Arabians that he most
wished? (And I am not modest now about the quality of the
drawings.) He could not be personally present and surround
me with ease and leisured sitters, but he could be aware of
distant happenings and to some extent direct and shape them.
I believe that as he sat in the Colonial Office, he was consciously
influencing painter and sitters in Arabia, just as now he is a

living spiritual influence on some hundred or thousand souls in this world.

However, contact with T.E. meant shock on shock. His next visit — again the cat-like entry. Would I accept £720 for eighteen Arabs? How diffident he was at what *he* considered a *paltry* offer. I made attempts to refuse, trying as others did to give all to him, and take nothing. But he was exercising his will and I stopped any resistance.

The book I had not seen and began to get curious. The only things I had seen were one letter and the list of Arabs, given to Kirkbride, and I had no hint of his written-word mastery. He had gone out again to the East, and I wrote for a foreword to the Catalogue of Arabs soon to be exhibited at the Leicester Gallery. What came back from Aden was another shock. Such understanding, observation, and memory one seldom experiences. But such generosity leaves one numb . . . And the giggle is sent to the rescue . . . What a lot of work was done by that giggle! It was used to create an appearance of emptiness, silliness, triviality, when people brought reverence: to bridge the gap of an awkward first meeting; mostly to remove tension, sometimes naughtily, a flourish following a knock-out blow: or a bodkin to explode false dignity, or fraud, or, nervously, to prevent thanks. Nearly always it was an instrument, and the best giggle was the spontaneous one — T.E. genuinely amused. Sometimes, alas, it was his own safety valve, when robbed of success by the failing of others, and at rare intervals painful, when it became hysterical, mastering him.

When he returned from this 1922 trip, I saw him often, and at each contact found richer qualities. No one could meet him, and straightway know him truly. Our focus had to be adjusted slowly. Common measures were too small. But he made the process of growing easy by constant joking, using our humour, just as he used our thoughts, and words. He also became our age, though certain that he was the world's grandfather.

Short remarks and conversations can be recalled:

'She is more of a person: when one does a big thing, one grows to the size of it.'

'It gives one great power to be always on the edge of something.'

Poking fun at me and my slow brain — 'I like to give Kennington an idea. He sets it up like a person and begins to draw its portrait.'

Looking at my war memorial of three soldiers — 'That front man is the physical. We've got one in our hut. Spits round his bed.'

He could condemn — 'Her fault. She should have known she had married genius.'

Looking at a pebble I had carved — 'Smooth, polished, civilized, night-clubby, horrible — what's the matter with you, Kennington?'

When he judged harshly — 'He's a bad hat. He's a four-letter man' — he had great dignity.

Old age to him was pathetic. He made a few exceptions. Doughty, Hogarth, G.B.S. and perhaps a few others. 'Who's that poor old chap?' I said my friend (aged 60) was in full mental and bodily vigour, and enjoyed life. T.E. hoped not to live to grow old. That meant anything over 45.

Once or twice, he showed sudden compassion. When he saw our two-year-old run barefoot across gravel, he felt the pain: 'He'll hurt his feet. He'll hurt his feet.' It was a really spontaneous cry. Very rarely did he allow his raw feeling freedom. He hooted gaily 'like a hen' when he saw me swing out 60 small geyser flares to light one cigarette. 'No, I don't smoke.' 'Well,' I said, 'may I? I know you have no vices.' He giggled. 'Oh yes I have — (giggle) — many vices.'

He showed me a blaze of feeling once. I was able to tell him that Ali ibn Hussein had been imprisoned for some months by old Hussein. He seemed to double his size. 'I'll have him out in a month.'

I never heard him raise his voice, and never saw him move suddenly or quickly yet he had all the signs of speed, and must have been like lightning, in a fight.

Often he would use his power and knowledge to help suffering and sometimes bodily suffering. He asked if he could have five minutes with my wife, critically ill and despondent. He talked with her for fifteen minutes and left, saying nothing. Upstairs I found a joyful person, who from that day had her face turned towards health. She had no setback. I afterwards said he could become a faith healer if he wished. Would he? I got no response. He could to some extent communicate his intelligence and sensitiveness. To listen to good music with him was to hear it afresh.

Up till now, I had made of him a happy king of men. Of course, disappointment followed, as he chose to show me his weaknesses and his suffering. 'No, I can't go there with you, Kennington, I should be spotted.' 'What matter?' I said. 'You don't understand. (Giggle.) You are a very robust person — I am nothing.'

I asked him if a certain Arab had killed four wives and two guests. He seemed to travel in his mind and answered: 'He has the reputation of killing wives, but there was not definite proof. He certainly killed two guests. He had them killed as they mounted their horses. To kill guests is a greater offence in Arabia, than to kill wives.' I told him an Englishman, an old teacher called Bowhay, who had hardly left his room for years, and had no contact with the East, knew the crimes from my pastel portrait of the Arab, by direct sight. T.E. retired into himself and said, 'It is possible to see the tendency, but not the act'. I thought, there is a greater man than you living. A year later he said, 'You are deeper, Kennington, wider. Is it your old teacher?' Two years later I said to T.E., 'Could we do our business in a taxi?' I was just off to an appointment with my old teacher. He read my motive and my hope to bring the two great people together and I was aware of a tautness, almost as if I were being paralysed. I nipped round and faced him. He had, by a psychic power, entered my mind and was in charge of it. Then he deliberately giggled. 'No, Kennington, no — I am not going to see your old teacher. He (a barrage of giggles here) might upset me.'

I had shown Bowhay one or two chapters of the *Seven Pillars* and he had said, 'Reading this book has made me suffer. The writer is infinitely the greatest man I have known, but he is terribly wrong. He is not himself. He has found an I, but it is not his true I, so I tremble to think of what may happen. He is never alive in what he does. There is no exchange. He is only a pipe through which life flows. He seems to have been a very good pipe, but to live truly, one must be more than that. He has told you his colour is black. It would be so, for all colours melt into black.' I was certain that the wise man could not err, and ejected his unwelcome verdict from my conscious mind for some years, but it took root subconsciously and asserted itself after T.E.'s death. Bowhay criticized in 1926, after reading one chapter of the book: possibly he would have modified or changed the criticism on contact with the power-boat expert and inventor of 1930-35. My own opinion of this: T.E. had, in youth, a spiritual harmony of such very great powers that he was selected, sometime about the taking of Akaba, to undergo the third temptation of the exceeding high mountain. Whether he yielded completely, partially, or not at all, he considered himself fallen from his sublime standard and made the rest of his life an intermittent struggle to reclaim or recreate his soul, by altruistic labour, self-denial and penance. By turns he gained and lost ground, his humble R.A.F. service granted him periods of purification and with them happiness, but never steady strength. The past kingship he had accepted and renounced remained an undefeated menace — an ever-present shame.

But I must go back. He did bring the book. Oxford version, first half, and as he put it on the table, more of Lawrence looked out of his eyes, and long serious face. We seized the book and he slipped away.

We implored him to produce the second volume. It was being bound. Days became weeks. Then he appeared, book under arm. For some minutes I was too greedy to notice him, then saw the change in him when he began to speak. He actually looked not well, and his still seriousness was frightening. 'It is an evil work . . . I could not refuse you after receiving the Arab portraits from you. It will not disturb you. Next morning you will start your day's work as usual, but you have an odd brain. It is in compartments. I have not let Robert Graves read it. It can never be published. I could not live if it was loosed abroad.' I began to fight. It had to be published. It was a grand, immense masterpiece. He looked more tired. 'How could I go on if it was made public? At Stamford Brook I did not know whether I was trying to throw myself under a train, or trying not to. I intended to throw these volumes off the centre of Hammersmith bridge. I have worked myself out and am finished. Every bone in my body has been broken. My lungs are pierced, my heart is weak . . .' I used any means to save my tottering plans, and said that every organ in his body was sound. I could see them all. I knew he had a droll belief in the artist's power of sight, and he paused. I went on, if only he would eat and sleep, he would be stronger than most men, and would be back at his real weight. At 18 he was over 11 stone. He sighed sadly, 'How do you know these things?' I said I could see. (It was a lie. His mother had told me so.) He began again, gently to prove to me how degraded the book was, and foreseeing defeat in a battle with that brain, I said the book had to be published. He said, more gently, 'Give me one good reason — *one only*'. It seemed the crisis, and I found one reason, and said it was a book on motive, and necessary at this moment of life; the world had lied till it was blind, and had to be re-educated to see its motives. It sounded futile, but he stopped quiet, and after a pause, said undramatically, 'Not bad' — (giggle) — 'Quite good' — (many giggles) — 'You win'. Then he laid the book on the table, giggled himself into normality, and backwards out of the room and house.

Food and a long sleep restored me; he had probably neither. Did he intend to destroy instead of publish the book? I do not know. Did he know? But if I had won a battle, it was at a price. He never spoke to me again of his suffering, save to jest.

From now, there was never a hint of turning back. He might sometimes change plans bewilderingly, but he carried out the work with even more thoroughness than I was aware of. He phoned, 'How did I like it?' I praised its humour. 'Ye giddy Gods. He thinks it's funny.' I said it was intended to be so in parts, and could prove my claim in a letter. Sent him the drawing of the Juheina crowding on top of a hill. He phoned again: 'Yes, it was a funny book, and all comic drawings in my letters, past and future, would be included.' He had several, and would send them back to me, to be zinc blocked. The gross baby (Temptation of necessary food) and the new-born (Us all) — portraits of my offspring, came back with his careful instructions. I was told to do a dozen. It was only this year, 1936, that I learnt exactly why he wanted them in his book. This part of a letter to Cockerell, October 15th, 1924, explains: 'Kennington was moved to incongruous mirth reading my book, and a dozen Bateman-quality drawings came of it. To my mind they are rare. Surprising and refreshing as plums in a cake (I've never had plums in a cake, but you know the sort of feeling it would be) and lighten up the whole. It's good that someone is decent enough to find laughter in a stodgy mass of mock-heroic egotism. My prose style is just a bad one, and Kennington's comment, unconscious comment, touches it to the mid-riff. (What is a mid-riff?) Of course they don't fit the page, or the style of print: why, they wouldn't be screamingly funny if they did. It's Kennington pricking the bladder of my conceit. Hip, Hip, Hip, you see, and then a long last fizz of escaping air before the poor frog burst.'

Till the incursion of these, the book was to have as illustrations, my Arabs and two or three Englishmen, John's Feisal, a pencil of T.E., and possibly some other portraits, but he got fun out of the new scheme, and began to juggle with artists and illustrations. Would I find a man to draw A and B? X and Y were drawing C and D. There must be masses of tailpieces. Roberts? Yes. Who else? All my artist neighbours. 'Yes, poor things, set 'em going.' More sitters were sent to me, Jaafar (who just fitted my arm chair, and unintentionally walked off with it), the fierce Boyle, who could still roar with laughter at the memory of his battleship a transport for camels, Wilson . . . in each of them, the fire of T.E.'s spirit. What initials should he have? Large, square, new. Wadsworth's satisfied him right away. X and Z were missing: we got Stanton to do them. There was no Arabian name beginning with X: T.E. invented one.

He made me hop — to-day, Chiswick; yesterday, Notting Hill (Pike's shop); to-morrow, Peckham (Whittingham and Griggs). A dozen corrections on one proof might not suffice. Whittingham and Griggs appealed to T.E. to stop my fault-finding. T.E. would giggle, and find yet more faults, and this he could do without having original handy to compare with print; I saw both together. He, in India, could correct a tone or colour, when he had not seen the painting for six months. Also he knew the processes and capabilities of the machines better than I, or Whittingham and Griggs. How much he taught Pike, is not for me to say. I concentrated on the illustration reproduction, and kept clear of the letterpress, and maps, and binding.

Several times he mentioned his intention of enlisting in the R.A.F., openly giving me his reasons, now well known; perhaps, because he knew he would get no advice for or against, and no pity, for my active service had been in the ranks. I said, 'You can lie about your age, but it will bother you on the square'. He did lie, successfully; his army age was given as something under 30, instead of 34. I asked if he felt older than his 20-year mates. He said, 'My age is more than the combined age of everyone serving in the R.A.F.' But it worked. He slowly regained his steady nerves and muscular poise. I was amused to see his hands grow from white to red and double their size. When I said so, he sighed in apparent despair: 'Yes, I earn my living by them.'

But how neat, fit, and trim he looked. Every line always perfect, from set of hat to spacing of the puttees, never a dull button, or speck on the boot, and how the well-cut uniform showed the strength of his neck and drive of his jaw. He brought well-being of mind, and body, and soul, to us each work-visit, and the anecdotes of his service life as a recruit were well chosen. Side-splitting humour, without hint of pain. Garnett knew the pain, and his words on it astounded me when I returned his copy of *The Mint*; we could not agree at all. I could never pity T.E. When Buxton so feelingly asked, 'Do you get him to eat?' I thought, 'But he mustn't eat when he comes to us. Every minute is given to work.'

He got me to arrange a meeting of Clutton-Brock and himself in my house. He chose Clutton-Brock to criticize, and possibly correct his metaphysics. No correction took place. They talked of other things for an hour, things beyond my understanding. I gaped, and afterwards questioned him. 'Who were the Gadarene Poets? What did you mean by . . . ?' 'Oh, that's intellectual acrobatics. Any 'varsity don can do it. It's our shove-halfpenny or dominoes. But (giggle) we can't paint pictures.'

His reverence for creative activity gave him unusual insight. He read the work (drawing, painting, poem, sculpture) and the maker of the work. He took infinite trouble over every illustration, and was never impatient with the fractiousness of the artists, attending to the opinion of each on rough proof and final printing; artists can be very insistent on the quality of reproduction. Also they are often hard up, and he was generous to appeals other than for work payment.

Being overfamiliar with art activity, I was puzzled by his reverence, and asked if he had ever done some creation with his hands, and how he knew he had no creative power. He said, 'I carved eight life-sized figures in soft stone in Syria, using knives, and forks, and a hatchet. My servant was my model. They had no merit. No . . . they are not there now. When we re-took the ground there was no trace of them, not even fragments. They are probably in the cellar of some German museum . . . labelled VERY RARE, SUPPOSED PRE-SUMERIAN'.

He called Michelangelo 'The last great child'. Repeatedly he voiced his disgust for children, but put high value on the child-quality in grown-ups. Indeed, sometimes, he seemed to enjoy arrested development in his adult friends.

I first went to Clouds Hill to introduce T.E. and Pike, his printer to be. The door was open, and Pike and I walked into a group of young men. T.E. had always seemed a separate thing, not speaking of other contacts, so it was a surprise. All in Tank Corps uniform, they were much at their ease, reading, talking, writing. A greater surprise was the condition of T.E. He was possessed of devils, visibly thinner, pale, scared and savage. He seemed to avoid looking at me, and when he did, his look was hostile, but he so soon gained his usual quiet, that this first impression went out of my mind for years. He got me a Tank man to draw, and dealt with Pike's hundred queries. While drawing, I noticed his speed without haste, and how he turned difficulty to ease, and puzzles to simplicity. Keenness and energy came to Pike's face, and a deep trust. The drawing absorbed me, and T.E. came, unnoticed, and giggled over my shoulder. 'Strange . . . odd . . . You've drawn a woman, Kennington.' I protested. He insisted: 'No, that's a woman's face.' The sitter was confused.

One thing, I am certain of. T.E.'s malaise — it was a daylight nightmare — so obvious to me, was not seen by any of the young men.

Though he had let me read his book, he had always hidden from me the nihilism, which was his recurrent curse. Maybe, he kept it from me because he knew that it would destroy a creative artist, maybe he knew that I should tire him by ridicule. I think from the former, the generous reason.

He joked about his Tank Town troubles, so that I did not guess at his protracted torture there, but it was during his tank service that he paid us the most strange visit, as usual without warning, and with a soldier on pillion. This time — for the first time — he dropped all defences. There was a wall of pain between him and us. We both felt helpless, for he looked his disappointment at us. He almost might have come specially to quarrel. It was as if T.E. was giving an impersonation for two or three hours. Everything was attacked. Life

itself. Marriage, parenthood, work, morality, and especially
Hope. Of course, we suffered and were unable to cope with
the situation. All we could do was to dodge and futilely make
light of it. The young tank-man was most positive. He
banged his fist on the tea table, and threatened. 'Now, none of
that. How often have I told you? Look me straight in the
face . . .' An animal tamer, and T.E. a wild beast that partially
obeyed him. I got some of our joint work going, and T.E.
attended to it normally. Aside, to my wife, the young man
revealed his grief at T.E.'s suffering. I don't know who that
was, but he had great courage and love for T.E. How did
T.E. recover from these crises? I don't believe that anyone
could give him help, yet he did seem to recover completely.

All its parts completed, the book was taken by T.E. to
the binders, and soon he came round with copy No. 1 under
his arm. He seemed to have rehearsed the presentation, so
non-committal, grave, quizzing, and humorous. He seemed
to say, 'A fine child . . . a trifle overweight, perhaps'. Three
more copies followed quickly, and these, four in all, were my
unexpected fee for art editorship. Choosing penury himself,
he wanted us all to be wealthy, and emphasized their money
value, giving the probable dates of their rise and fall. He was
right in date, but underestimated the price. I did not make
public my possession of four or try to sell, but received in one
day two telegrams offering £550 and £600 for two copies.

He was just now getting all his affairs in order, preparatory
to sailing for India, and I feared he might be too busy to grant
sittings — promised — for a bronze head. Of course he found
time, giving me at short notice about five half-hour sittings.
He looked much the same but was remote, and did not giggle
at all. Exceedingly still, he seemed to have done with every
barrier, and to sit naked. I had long wished to get a statement
from him, which would throw light on the spiritual difference
I knew there was between us. What was his God? He
answered without hesitation, and once more I missed his words,

so beautiful was his face. He had a glory, and a light shone in his eyes, but more of sunset, than sunrise or midday. What I think I heard in the flow of eloquence, was a record of process without aim or end, creation followed by dissolution, rebirth, and then decay, to wonder at and to love. But not a hint of a god, and certainly none of the Christian God.

A visitor (not a chance one) was Naomi Mitchison, for whose historical novels he had great respect. Without disturbing his sculptor, he told us both how the Greek temples were created, from the unquarried stone to the placing of the roof top. He only gave me a shell to work from, head up, silent, letting me use every minute.

The last sitting was his last day of freedom in England. From that night he was to be C.B. and perhaps to-morrow sailing. His eyes began to show turmoil. Their usual outward glide was repeatedly stopped and they would suddenly turn aside. I noticed a vibration of the head. Was he cold? I asked. I thought he shivered. 'No, it is not cold.' He shivered again, worse, head, hands on knees, trembling. Soon, he shook all over from head to foot. 'No, I'm not cold. I'm always like this before a crisis.' I concentrated, with an eye on the time. Then, from work to car, and I drove him, as fast as law permitted, to Uxbridge. He shook, off and on, all the way. I chaffed, Was he afraid of my driving? I had driven six years without a bump. He giggled (Thank God), 'I wish you'd had one yesterday'.

At the barracks, I was allowed to drive straight in. T.E.L. had left me before we parted. I stopped right against the double line of men standing easy. He joined the rear rank, almost last man; no good-bye; he did not see me or the car. For a few minutes I watched him shifting, chin thrust forward, turning blindly left and right.

On his return, he took refuge from the press, in our country cottage. To me he was just the same in appearance, and behaviour. He fed me with jokes and recounted, in great detail, the story of his visit to the House of Commons to beard the Socialists. It is well known, but I have only heard the finale, from his lips. 'Well, good night, gentlemen. I hope you all lose your seats at the next Election.' 'What should we do then?' said one simpleton. 'Join the R.A.F. — but no. They would not take you. There's not a fit man in the room.' (Giggle, giggle, giggle.) It was told to amuse me, and it did. But it bored him utterly.

We began to drift apart now the work-tie was broken. I saw him less, but what matter? More than others, he was always present. A week's absence, or six months were the same. Our contact now was *his* interest and help in *my* work. He did not want to say what he was doing, and I was quite ignorant of his myriad interests. When I pressed him, 'What did he do in India?' he replied, 'I made a translation of the *Odyssey*'. This seemed rather shocking to me, after the creation of the *Seven Pillars* and *The Mint*. How could he get interested in the *Odyssey*? I asked, 'Weren't all the characters bloody fools?' He looked past me, right through me, sighed, 'Yes, they were all bloody fools'.

His visits, joyful as ever to us, became less frequent, and all that I can recall of these, about 1929, is the grand picture of him, as he made each time the same departure. His confident ease, as he sat astride the monstrous bicycle. A few vigorous kicks on the pedal: the beginning of slow movement: a chuckle: a downward glance, and sensual grip of the rubber handles — like a cat taking its pleasure in claw-stretching: a conscious summoning of power, still latent in the horizontal machine, but active in the upright human body with its creased neck and jaw: a tortoise-like waddle, the head was raised, the eyes gazed at the horizon as if in ownership: the advance quickening snakelike, then the disappearance in a roar of dust. He was happy. He never looked back. Travelling twice as fast as his boats — nearly as fast as his brain.

But he could arrive less noticed, and often did. Nanny rushed out, and drove the soldier away from the baby he was teasing (the baby greatly approving of his disturber).

His happiness was not assured. He turned up again with fear in his eyes, and assaulted me right and left. I was much too weak to inquire into or consider his suffering and its causes, and flew to counter attack, and defence, picking, instinctively a rather deadly weapon, as I took down his new address. 'The other night, Lawrence, I gave a lecture on sculpture to hundreds of people.' He stopped and attended. 'How do you spell *Cattewater*? — Thanks — and there were two girls in the front row, who fell in love with me.' — He grew severe. 'Is Mount Batten one or two words? — Thanks — and after the lecture they came up and gaped adoringly at me.' (He was jumping with rage by now.) ' "Oh, Mr. Kennington", they said, "Please forgive us, do tell us, do you really *know* Colonel Lawrence?".' He hooted like a hen; 'So it still goes on', and left.

He never bore any grudge for cruel or malicious treatment, and so serene were his following visits, that one had to forget the pain. In the last year or two, I saw him rarely, he was continually present spiritually, with help, understanding, joy, and jokes. His physical presence, though it, like his letters, spelt happiness, seemed unnecessary. Certainly since that May morning, a number of us have for a period been stunned and shocked, but that does not matter. His great labours remain, transformed to spirit. He is marvellously alive. Often the prophet has been born in this world, has lived with us in the flesh, as one of us, and dying, has left us quickened by his spiritual message. How great, or wise, the message of T.E.L., each may decide for himself. But now, a prophet has left a record, so definite, that it cannot be falsified, of his almost every thought, feeling, word, and act, from first youth till death. Surely this is new, and happens for the first time.

E. M. FORSTER, c.h. Born 1879. Author of *A Room with a View, Howard's End, A Passage to India, Aspects of the Novel, Abinger Harvest*, etc.

T. E. liked to meet people upon a platform of his own designing. In my own case it was the platform of aesthetic creation, where I had to figure as a great artist and he was a bungling amateur. This did not suit me in the least, but protests were useless, and after all the important thing was to meet.

We met for the first time in 1921, but then the platform was political. I was having lunch at the Emir Feisal's in Berkeley Square — at him rather than with him, since my virtual host was an old Syrian friend who had gone on his staff. Feisal was absent through most of the meal, owing to business at the Colonial Office. He returned towards the end, and with him came a small fair-haired boy, who seems at this interval of time to have been holding a top-hat. This boy rapped out encouraging words about the Middle East: all would go well now that Winston Churchill was in power. Colonel Lawrence! I wrote a letter afterwards, and said how glad, how proud, I had been to meet him, and had no reply.

In 1924 he lent Siegfried Sassoon a copy of the double column edition of the *Seven Pillars*, and Sassoon asked his permission to send it on to me. He agreed, for he had read a Forster novel, *Howards End*, and it was the real thing, though was not the author long since dead? Better informed in all ways about himself, I was most careful not to praise the *Seven Pillars* when writing to him. I thought it a masterpiece, but to have said so would have been fatal. I restricted myself to detail, and analysed particular sentences and paragraphs, chiefly from the point of view of style. This was well taken, and a suitable platform for our intercourse was thus provided.

He was such an awful tease and so fond of pulling people's

legs that all this depreciation of his own work and deference about mine may have been a trap, in which, bland, I was to flounder. But I don't think it was. He was too serious over writing to set traps for writers: colonels were fairer game. He was most generous towards his contemporaries, helped them where he would never have helped himself, and maintained towards their work a very rare and noble attitude, which can best be described as a divine jealousy. Some authors do not mind being surpassed, others turn sulky; T.E. felt at the same time pain and joy, for his disgust at his own supposed inferiority was inseparable from his delight in the achievements of others. Praise from him was never mechanical; it gushed out of him with the violence which usually accompanies blame, and sometimes left the recipient gasping. He was not the benign pot-bellied critic who sees good everywhere; he praised to pacify an inward wound. He was like a god who envies mankind, and for that reason rains blessings upon us instead of shafts of disease, a god outshining any conception of Homer's.

As a result of my letter I went down into Dorsetshire and stayed at an inn, of course at his expense. By now he was a private in the Tank Corps. He turned up while I was having supper, rubicund, clumpier, and rather disconcerting. We must have shaken hands, but he had a bad handshake, and he did not like being touched (by me anyhow); in later years I realized this, and touched him as seldom as possible. Now he spoke: 'It is never very easy to make me eat' was almost his first remark. We were both of us shy. Presently he revealed the existence of Clouds Hill, and I called there the following day. From that moment things went pleasantly. I got on well with my fellow-guests, who were his fellow-soldiers, and felt very happy there. A good early-model gramophone, a night-jar on the roof, fires of rhody-wood, food out of tins eaten as we walked about the upper room, water or tea drunk out of black cups — those are some of my memories. I cannot arrange them, for I was at Clouds Hill several times, once without him. No alcohol, no low talk — and yet at moments T.E. could be bawdy, bringing it in so mischievously and quickly that one could hardly believe one's ears, and was left accusing one's own dirty mind.

After Clouds Hill, Plymouth leaves the chief impression. I sometimes stopped there with a great-aunt who had never heard of Shaw or Lawrence. 'Some celebrity, I suppose, dear. Ah!' she murmured, much to his gratification. He was with the R.A.F. over at Mount Batten. My visits to him were very pleasant, thanks to the kindness and hospitality shown by his officers, but he now seemed to belong more to them than to the men, his work was becoming highly specialized, and I did not feel so easy. I could appreciate him wanting to be under-dog as he had been in the Tanks; I could not understand him consenting to be bottom-monkey, and lending his ingenuity to the perfecting of war-gadgets. The popular explanation may be correct: namely that T.E. was intensely patriotic, lived for the Empire, and believed he could serve her best from beneath. But the deepest impulse I could ever see in him was not the Empire nor even England, only the desire to write well, so that all that boat-building activity of his later years presents itself to me as a side-line, which he pursued in order to distract himself. He hated Plymouth, except for the old houses round the Barbican. We went for several walks. One walk was round Mount Edgcumbe, to which he had private access. In the course of it I said that if there was another big European war, nothing would survive — no civilization, no poetry. T.E. did not mind about civilization but any menace to poetry scandalized him and he replied a little primly that poetry is indestructible. Another day we went for one glorious half hour in his speed-boat on the Sound. We were to have gone for a longer outing on the following day, but when I came down for it, full of beans, he told me that the boat had strained her back during the night. I wonder! This was not the only time I had to slink away from his explanations. Most certainly he did not always speak me the truth, though did it matter? one felt safe in his hands. I seldom asked questions because they involved him in answers, and though I was frank with him he was never equally frank in return, nor did I resent his refusal to be so. This explains, in part, why he was a great leader of men; he was able to reject intimacy without impairing affection. He had also extraordinary powers of encouragement: when we talked about the Arab revolt, he made me feel that I could almost have taken Damascus myself — almost, not quite: that was where he was so subtle. And when I was depressed over my own work, he would tell me that I had it in me to write just one good novel more — just one — which heartened me much more than any indiscriminate assurance.

Excluding Clouds Hill and Plymouth, we must have met about a dozen times. There was a week-end at Lincoln when he talked brilliantly about medieval sculpture in the lounge of the hotel, with the result that after he had left people said to me, 'That airman friend of yours must have been Colonel Lawrence, wasn't he?', and I had to tell a lie. There was a day when he called at my rooms in London, and stood patiently outside them for hours until I returned. There were several walks about London at night, avoiding the cenotaph, because he was in uniform and would have been obliged to salute it. There was a chance encounter in Queen's Hall, where he was with some men whose faces I instinctively distrusted. (All his friends will agree that he had some queer friends.) There was a walk on the downs in Surrey, where he blew the gaff on the Secret Service, gave me the names, addresses and telephone numbers of two personages who thought their own incognito vital to the national safety, and suggested I should ring them up any time.

The last meeting of all was by the turnstiles of the National Gallery. He was in civvies — a stocky quizzical figure, turning his head slightly until I recognized him. He was out of the service at last and had been hurting his hand against a reporter's face at Clouds Hill. He invited me to stay there again — we hadn't met for a couple of years. We went on to see Epstein's 'Christ' which he remarked would be publicly convenient for birds and then we ate an omelette at a French restaurant in Wardour Street. Our talk was of the impending prosecution of James Hanley's novel, *Boy*. I think that he allowed me to pay for the omelette and that we parted for ever outside another picture gallery, but our last moment together held no more significance than the first moment at Berkeley Square. What was vivid to me was that I liked him as well as ever and should stay with him soon. The date of my visit was fixed but by the time it arrived his life had ended; I have been once to Clouds Hill since then, and was glad to see the improvements he had made — the leather-covered divan, the turfing, the carved doors to the reservoir — but that is the end.

I do not want to sum T.E. up. These are only a few notes, to be added to the common stock. I will finish them by recording that he was pleased by what I wrote to him about the *Mint*, and that he was also pleased when I helped to sell the proofs of the *Seven Pillars* for the benefit of another friend of his, to whom he had given them.

All these are scraps. The real framework, the place which his spirit will never cease to haunt, is Clouds Hill, and the gay motto over its doorway is the one beneath which I see him at rest.

[*Editor's Note:* T.E.L. carved ου φροντις on the lintel at Clouds Hill. The Greek is not readily translated; 'no matter for thought', 'no care' are approximate equivalents. The quotation is from a story told by Herodotus, of a young Athenian aristocrat, Hippocleides, who was chosen among many suitors to marry a king's daughter. The king announced the decision at a banquet, but revoked it when Hippocleides danced and stood on his head on the table; told 'You have danced away your bride', he replied, 'No care to Hippocleides', and went on kicking his denuded legs in the air.]

SIR WILLIAM ROTHENSTEIN, painter. 1872-1945.
Official war artist; Professor of Civic Art, Sheffield, 1917-26;
Principal, Royal College of Art, 1920-35; Member of Royal
Fine Art Commission. Drew portrait for *Seven 'Pillars of
Wisdom*. Author of volumes of Portraits; *Paul Verlaine*; *A Life
of Goya*; *Drawings by Hokusai*; *Ancient India*; *Men and Memories*,
etc.

MY wife, returning from a party in the autumn of 1920,
spoke of having met Lawrence. A day or two later he
came to the house, a small shy youth, fair and blue-
eyed — I was surprised, as were most people at his unheroic
appearance. He returned from time to time, sat to me for a
drawing, and I began a painting of him in his Arab dress.
W. H. Hudson, coming into the studio one day when Lawrence was sitting, was at once taken with him; and Lawrence,
when Hudson came to be drawn, asked if he might sit and
listen while Hudson talked. And one evening, coming to meet
Hudson at dinner, he brought with him a copy of *The Purple
Land*, in which he asked Hudson to write his name. For he
regarded this as one of the great books of our time.

Then there was Frederic Manning. Lawrence, who
seemed to have read everything, knew Manning's *Scenes and
Portraits* almost by heart. Like Max Beerbohm, he thought
this book contained the strongest and subtlest prose of recent
times. I have already described elsewhere how the two met
(*Men and Memories*, Vol. II); how Lawrence, eager to interest
Manning, started to talk again and again of his Arabian days,
and was interrupted each time by Manning, equally anxious to
talk of himself. This was the only occasion on which I knew
Lawrence ready to spread his peacock tail; but he was not
given the chance. Hudson had tried in vain to get Lawrence
to talk of his exploits. Lawrence, deeply respectful, was
determined to listen only.

I always felt there was something tragic in Lawrence's youth.
Most remarkable men have a period before them during which

236

their characters can form slowly themselves. It was not so with Lawrence. To acquire a legendary reputation when scarcely out of the twenties, to be pitchforked into fame so suddenly, that the ordinary courses of life are choked, as it were, with doubts and hesitations, is handicap enough for the strongest character. There was no doubt of the strength of Lawrence's. But to act when there is a call for action is one thing; to act when there is none is a more difficult matter.

Now Lawrence was only in part man of action; he was also scholar, thinker, artist, and critic. Moreover, he felt drawn to the more adventurous spirits in art and literature; and such are apt to be revolutionary, contemptuous of authority, of acclaimed reputations, in their attitude to society. When Winston Churchill pressed for Lawrence's co-operation for his Middle East Department, he jibbed against bureaucratic harness. Though Eddie Marsh coaxed and persuaded, what would Wyndham Lewis or other of his artist friends say! When he was finally persuaded and had an office in Whitehall he was a little self-anxious and uncomfortable. 'Who would have believed,' he said to me, 'a year ago, that you and I would be officials!'

If he was shy of becoming an official, he was pleased to be elected a Fellow of All Souls. I stayed with him there for a week-end, and he clearly found his austere rooms to his taste. He had his few fine books carefully arranged; he cared much for good printing and spoke of trying his hand at a press, of becoming a printer, in fact. The other Fellows appreciated his company. Lord Haldane and Sir William Robertson came to stay while I was there, and I noticed more men sat round to listen to Lawrence than gathered about the statesman and the soldier.

About this time he was getting together his illustrations for his *Seven Pillars*. He was still sitting to me in his Arab dress. Generous with his time, he never seemed to object to standing for hours together — once, when I was painting the folds of his outer garment, he remained standing for two hours without a rest!

He talked much while he was standing. But how little of a man's talk, even of the most famous wits and talkers, remains! — a few sayings, repeated again and again in the biographies. He had not yet overcome his bitterness about the promises that he made, if not on the initiative of the British Government, at least with its sanction, to Feisal — promises invalidated by the secret Picot agreement. His disillusionment had much to do with his shrinking from the many things life had to offer in which most men find satisfaction. He was critical, too, of the conduct of the War, alike by statesmen and generals; above all, he deplored what he held to be the needless sacrifice of the lives of splendid men. Allenby alone, in his opinion, lost no lives needlessly during his campaign, and for Allenby's character, and for his strategy, he expressed a warm admiration.

When my painting was done he brought his mother, and his youngest brother, to the studio. He told me afterwards that his mother preferred this to his other portraits. But I knew better. John's pencil drawings came near to perfection as records of his appearance and character. He used to consult me (and others too, of course) about the artists he had in mind to undertake the portraits and other illustrations for the *Seven Pillars*.

When the book appeared, I was critical about its form, and some of the reproductions. 'For the brutality of the plates I must plead guilty,' he answered. 'The politeness of margin makes me very angry. Kennington's page pastels could be ruled down, so, into normal pictures; but by running them to the edge they jumped out of the book, and so became monstrous, and their originals. John and the rest (including you) had to follow suit, in self-defence. It was my deliberate intention to make the pictures appendices, not illustrations, and to rouse with them just the feelings you expressed. Regard my *Seven Pillars* as a protest against the illustrated book, and you'll feel what I was driving at.'

But I have never been reconciled to the reproductions, without margins, out of tune with the printed page. No matter. To me the *Seven Pillars* was and remains one of the great

238

books of our time. But once it was done Lawrence turned to other matters.

Perfect self-knowledge he had not — hence his uncertainty; he was neither giving himself to action, nor to thought. There was a division which irked his spirit. At times indeed, his spirit seemed broken. He could not walk with the crowd, yet the excitement of adventure was no longer within him. He was disillusioned, a little worn with his fame; and small wonder he was undecided about his future work. If he wanted his mind freed from the immediate problems that beset him, and chose for a while to be relieved of responsibility by serving as a private, carrying out whatever task was set him, who had the right to assail him? Returning tired and disillusioned after a long period of unnatural strain, no wonder he was unable to find himself at home in a distracted world. It is usual to hear him criticized for the choice he made, always in the same terms, for one meets with no originality in unimaginative clubmen's comments. A consistency of attitude, to fit comfortably into the easy ways and thoughts of men dulled to the finer gallantries and indignations of a sensitive spirit, torn and sore, shrinking from mental contacts as the sore body shrinks from rough touch, is scarcely to be expected. What call was there for the rare powers which, in a manner, stifled Lawrence's will as denial of exercise poisons a man of unusual physical energy? While writing the *Seven Pillars* his powers were fully employed. David Hogarth and I, too, pressed him again and again to go on with his writing. While Lawrence felt that, through the written word or the painted image, man has ever put his deepest intuition into concrete form, yet he was drawn to live with the average man, troubled by something of the same sense that lay at the back of Conrad's mind, deeming the exercise of the finely tempered will, in the face of the blind forces of nature and the vulgarities and stupidities of mankind, as perhaps as decent a way to follow as any that life offers. He was at heart an aristocrat, who disdained the privileges generally offered, rather than claimed. Hence in part, I think, his self-abnegation, his decision to share the lives of rough and humble

men. 'No one will offer me a job poor enough for my acceptance,' he wrote. 'It has cost me great pains to get admitted to
low life again and my wish is to progress downward, rather
than up the ladder once more.'

So it was with his writing. No one more than he respected
high achievement in art and letters, and had an alerter
understanding of excellence. Yet here again, having once
essayed his powers in the *Seven Pillars of Wisdom*, he
was contemptuous of work which his critical sense told him
was imperfect. 'About my writing,' he wrote, 'you are over
kind. I don't think much of it. My style is a made-up thing,
very thickly encrusted with what seemed to me the tit-bits and
wheezes of established authors. So, for book-learned people,
the reading it constantly, but not too sharply, tickles their
literary memory, by half reminding them of half-forgotten
pleasures. There isn't any good, a permanence, in such a
derivative effort.' He must do the best, or nothing. When he
was often perplexed and uncertain, I would tell him he was by
nature an artist, that he was denying an inner need by refrain-
ing from creative work, an opinion which Hogarth supported.
Hogarth was distressed at Lawrence's retirement from the field
of letters, and vexed at his going out as a private to India.

Most men of talent have to wait many years before they win
general acceptance; but here was a mere youth whose name
was famous, whose personality roused the interest of young
and old alike. It is the unsuccessful who incline towards
assertiveness and arrogance; modesty comes easily to those
whose fame is secure. So Lawrence could afford to think
lightly of his success. I call to mind with what amusement
he told me he had been sending articles to the newspapers,
anonymously, for which he asked two guineas, and which were
regularly returned to him, while he was being offered fabulous
sums to write under his own name. I thought it rather a waste,
seeing what he had himself to say, to be translating the *Odyssey*,
the more so since, unlike Macaulay, who preferred the *Odyssey*
to the *Iliad*, he thought little of the original. 'Homer? a pot
boiler,' he wrote, 'Long ago done with ... The Greek isn't

very good, I fancy; and my version is frankly poor. Thin, arty, self-conscious stuff, the *Odyssey*. I believe the *Iliad* to be a great poem — and to have fragments of a great poem embedded in it, rather. But the *Odyssey* is pastiche and face powder.'

And again: 'About the *Odyssey*. I fully agree with you. My version is fustian. But so is Homer, I think. The more I dwelt on the Greek and struggled with it and its story the more possessed I became with a view that here was something too artful for decency. It tries by surpassing pains and skill to simulate the rule-leaping flood of authentic greatness. All the talent in the world never approaches genius; the two things are incompatible . . . I am a translator definitely, in my version; and you can see through it, I hope, easily; as a mawkish fraud.' But what a waste of his own genius, if he felt so!

He was really happier doing hard physical work. 'I've been in Hythe now for nearly a year, testing motor boats, and watching over their being built. A difficult, occupying job; that I am glad to do, for it needed doing and no one else in the R.A.F. had any experience to do it.'

I was amused, since he had chidden me over a book of memories, that 'I needed more venom in my ink', to find, in reading through his letters, how much they contained of praise of his contemporaries. But so anxious was Lawrence not to get entangled in social relationships, to keep his spirit hard and apart, that he was careful to avoid anything like sentiment. Yet there was a layer of solid affection for his friends in the strata of his nature.

'Wasn't it delightful to find Manning coming out so suddenly as a real flesh and blood figure. Beautiful as are *Scenes and Epicures*' — he means *Scenes and Portraits* — 'ever so much more worth while is *Her Privates We*.' It was over Manning's death I last heard from Lawrence. When Manning died early in 1935, there was no obituary notice in *The Times*. I drew the Editor's attention to this neglect and telephoned a short notice to the office, at the same time telegraphing to Lawrence, urging him to follow up the lines which were printed. Not only did I receive no answer, but Lady Manning complained of Lawrence's silence. I again wrote, addressing my letter to Mrs. Hardy's care, and this time heard from Lawrence in terms which were strangely foreboding.

'Dear W.R.,' he wrote from Clouds Hill. 'Manning died as I was on my way to Bourne, to visit him. I turned off and rode down here. Your two letters came. Between them I had to go to London and I called at Airlie Gardens: vainly, as usual. I suppose you are still chained to your College. Now Mrs. Hardy has sent me your last note. I am sorry to appear so remiss; but my discharge from the R.A.F. (which had to come) has rather done me in, so that I no longer have the mind or wish to do anything at all. I just sit here in this cottage and wonder about nothing in general. Comfort is a very poor state after busyness.

'As for Manning, I cannot say how sad the news made me. He was a lovely person, and it is hateful to see him go out, unfinished. But gone he very definitely is. It makes one feel as though nothing can matter very much.

'If I come to London again soon I shall ring your bell once more. Patience will tell, in the end. Only I do not expect to come up yet awhile.'

He had written previously in a similar spirit. 'It is a sorrowful thing when a Hogarth, Hardy, or G.B.S. dies; but it satisfies another facet of my mind. It's all over and they are out of it without failure; we are safe with them. Men run about always on the edge of the precipice and when they are safely dead we breathe again; if we have cared for them.'

A fortnight after getting the letter about Manning, Lawrence himself lay dead at a military hospital in Dorset.

LIEUTENANT-COLONEL RALPH H. ISHAM,
C.B.E., F.R.G.S. Born, New York City, 1890. Secured James
Boswell's private papers and MSS. from Lord Talbot de Mala-
hide in 1927. Publications: *Private Papers of James Boswell*,
etc.

BEFORE lunch one day in the summer of 1919, Sir Ronald
Storrs dropped in to see me at my flat at 1 St. James's
Place. He had with him a very small, shy, ruddy-com-
plexioned young man, in a very new uniform, which bore no
ribbons; presumably he had missed active service. We all
drank sherry and he seemed perfectly at ease in the light conversation, listening rather than talking, for Storrs and I were
voluble. I had had an immediate feeling of liking for this
young man, which grew during the conversation, as I perceived his keen intelligence and saw how quickly the expression
of his eyes, large, clear and blue, reflected the passing thought.
When he noticed my case of old books and went to examine
them with obvious pleasure, I liked him more. We were on
common ground; his neat and sensitive appraisals delighted
me.

About this time I caught sight of the insignia of Lieutenant-
Colonel on his uniform. This was a shock; if Storrs had
introduced him as Colonel, I had not heard.

We arranged to dine together and during the course of the
evening the usual questions of service arose. When he said he
had served in the East, I asked him if he knew his namesake
of Arabia. He grinned hugely and said, 'I'm afraid I know
him much too well'. He enjoyed my discomfiture. I said,
'Well, anyway, you don't look like him.' He replied, 'I know
I don't, and I don't feel like him'. And we both laughed.
It would, I think, never have occurred to anyone that this
sensitive, retiring and inexperienced-looking youth might be
Lawrence of Arabia, of whose power and achievements one
had heard so much. Here I might mention that Mr. C. E.
Harmsworth recently told me that when Lawrence visited
him in the Foreign Office to urge the Arab Cause, they

were amazed to discover that such an apparent freshman could be *the* Lawrence and could have the grasp and determination of a Leader of the Opposition.

During the next six months we spent many evenings together. We always met at my flat in London; sometimes we dined at places like Claridge's, sometimes we went to little Soho restaurants. Invariably we returned to my flat and talked the night out. We both liked poetry; we both liked tall stories; we both believed anything could happen, and we both had a feeling of having lost roots by serving another country. (Regarding poets, he once remarked that most of the moderns did not let themselves go, for fear of giving themselves away; that for fear of being laughed at, they tried to laugh at themselves first.)

He had a sense of proportion and a sense of humour about everything except the insignificance of his body and his own attitude regarding it. He felt he had got fitted into an absurdly small case; a strange neurosis prevented him from enjoying the comedy of his own smallness. Thus the battle of spirit and body started early in him and rendered him inevitably knotted, constrained, self-conscious and eccentric. When his body claimed attention and refreshment, it pleased spirit to ignore it. When ambition and genius, knowledge and will power, led to great achievements that excited attention, he fled in absurd fear lest praise be turned to laughter at sight of him.

At times nerves and self-consciousness led him to act in a manner that gave an unfavourable impression, and people who expected to see a flaming personality found what seemed to be a second-rate person. He could switch off the great current of force that was in him, and then his face took on the set, self-obliterated look of soldiers on review.

Some of the apparently foolish things he did are attributable to his lack of self-confidence and his fear of letting people down. I think the fear he had of a woman's love came mainly from his sense of unworthiness. It was this same lack of confidence that made him decline jobs that were offered him and seemed, to others, suitable. Thus to me, in two letters of 1927:

'Do realize that I have no confidence in myself', and 'I cannot accept your offer of a job. It would not do to work for any friendly person'. I think it can be said that no one could have been so bad a judge of Lawrence as he was of himself.

Relief from self came gloriously from music, from reading, from beauties of colour or countryside, from single companionship, from submergence in a strange crowd. He loved speeding through the air or plunging deep in water because, he said, it gave him the illusion of becoming actually part of those elements. The Air Force gave him the perfect sense of submergence and participation; his years in it, alone but never lonely, he held to have been the best of his life, bar some black days in Uxbridge and India.

The war years had cheated him of his young time; they took him 'to the top of the tree without the fun of swarming about the middle branches'.

He resented his body's permanent immaturity. He did not, I think, realize that his personality also would not quite grow up. His hatred for his body was a boy's hatred; his fear of women was a boy's fear; his terror of being noticed was a boy's terror. He liked pranks and stories as a boy does.

His perceptions and reactions were those of a boy. His powers of intuition had, I suppose, been exercised and increased by much listening to conversation in languages he understood only imperfectly. His awareness amounted at times to clairvoyance.

Man's instinctive reactions have so degenerated, as now to be vastly inferior to those of the other animals. He no longer senses danger in the dark. The course of intellectuality and of scientific thinking has led to the disuse and weakening of the intuitive powers or even to disbelief in their existence. Here I believe that Lawrence had the advantage of being thousands of years behind us, but feeling powers within him which were uncommon and suspect, he feared their insistence. As they were too strong for suppression, the taught habits of logical thought made him at times doubt his sanity.

This was part of the fermentation of contradictory elements

that boiled within him, permitting no ease, only the hope that none would notice. To take another instance, people inspired in him a deep desire for fame, but they saw in him a shrinking, amounting at times to horror, from any recognition of that which he had accomplished. Some rationalists imputed to him a desire to draw attention to himself by appearing to avoid it. They had no conception of the emotional tension within him, or how interwoven were pain and shame with memories otherwise intensely gratifying.

If he had not been inhibited, if he had been able to talk about his emotions and conflicts, I believe he would never have written the *Seven Pillars of Wisdom*. In that book he found the relief of the confessional. Then he could overcome his reserve and let others read it.

So great was his knowledge, so clear his perceptions, and so forceful his conceptions, that it was difficult to know where one ended and another began.

I asked how he happened to do what he did in Arabia. He said, 'I meant to do it from the beginning'. 'How could you? You were neither soldier nor man of action.' He said, 'True. But I felt it as something already *done* and therefore unavoidable. I felt on sure ground'.

Once he listened with great interest while I told him about my acquisition of James Boswell's papers and my work on them, and how they made me feel that I knew Boswell better than any man alive or dead. I added extravagantly, 'In fact, I think I should not be surprised if Boswell appeared in my room one day'. Lawrence's expression, which had been one of amusement, became serious. He said, 'Oh, but I feel certain he will'.

His reactions were essentially those of a sensitive child immediate, intuitive, emotional; that is why he was comfortable only with people of simplicity, and that is why it was such a bitter shock to him to discover the world's wickedness and selfishness when the tides drew him forth.

One felt that he would be well with children. His brother tells me how, a day or two after discharge from the Air Force,

T.E. stopped to visit him in Cambridge and devoted a great deal of time to the play and interests of his daughter, aged eight.

It was obvious that the Desert would appeal to Lawrence and be a glad refuge. The infinity, the silence, and the physical cruelty of it sharpen man's sensitiveness to a point of spiritual predominance. Here nothing diverts human instinctiveness of God. Overwhelming bodily suffering is met by resignation and tranquillity; it is taken as God's will, and complaint would be blasphemous.

It was obvious, too, that desert people would be dear to Lawrence. In his description of the Arab character he describes his own, particularly where he says of them, 'Body and spirit were for ever and inevitably opposed'.

I know there were times when he longed to go back and lose himself in the Desert, but he told me that the Government would not let him, that they so restricted him that even when the Air Force recalled him from India, the boat was picketed against his leaving it for a moment at Port Said. He had been furious. He largely cursed the Press for this and similar troubles, such as his being refused a *visa* by several countries. He said that journalists were constantly yapping about him as a 'Man of Mystery' and attributing uprisings in whatever country to him, quite regardless of facts. That they would stop at nothing to gratify the morbid curiosity of the public, even though it meant the smashing of private lives.

Aside from the element of persecution, he got great fun out of the fantastic tales written about him. 'On the whole I prefer lies to truth, particularly where they concern me,' he wrote. 'I got discouraged trying to tell people the truth and finding they didn't believe it, so I told them lies.'

He did not lie in the strict sense, but he did indulge in fiction. And he was perfectly aware of it. His tales arrived full-blown, and appeased what he called his 'craving for self-expression in some imaginative form'. 'What does it matter? History is but a series of accepted lies.'

I did not agree that history is based on a foundation of lies.

They creep into history because people see things differently. For example, one biographer has made the definite statement that Lawrence never looked a man in the eye; now the thing I remember more than anything else about Lawrence is the directness of his gaze. Others have remarked that he never took alcohol, but when we dined together he drank wine of various sorts freely.

He was governed by principle, not by principles, and was too much of a realist to be patient with rules and conventions. He achieved fabulous things by indirection. At times he could believe in being ruthless. 'Ideas may ferment and poison men more than spirits. Then reason and good example are howled down and only the sword can preach.'

If he could discard the truth in favour of fiction, he could out-fiction fiction in performance. It gave him pleasure to ride his motor-bike through the tram tunnel under Kingsway or down the Duke of York's Steps. He suggested that the Prince of Wales might make more of a dash if he habitually drove his car up and down these steps.

Not only against convention did he rebel: he was doomed to battle, and made for battle. As his body was his spirit's bondage, it was to be fought. As the Turkish yoke was the Arab's bondage, it was to be fought. As the sordid martinet discipline of the Old Army was bondage of the air service it was to be fought.

He was completely unselfish. He needed money sufficient to secure his 'bread and margarine'. Beyond that he liked it only to spend lavishly and give away. Once, when we were talking of man's greed, he said, 'The fools don't realize that their possessions, in time, come to possess them'. But he wrote in 1927, 'Money is a jolly thing to give your children. Often I feel that that should be the first duty of fathers!'

In fact I think his unselfishness is too little recognized. To gain ends for others he would exhaust himself and be unscrupulous gladly, but where his own interests were concerned his sense of honour and fitness, and perhaps also of unimportance, led him to complete self-neglect. Even when he had arrived at the point of starvation he refused vast sums within his grasp. He wrote in a letter to me from Karachi in 1927: 'Did I tell you (I did not go about explaining myself) that I consider what I did in Arabia morally indefensible? So I refused pay and decorations while it lasted, and will not take any personal profit out of it: neither from a book about it; nor will I take any position which depends on my war-reputation.'

Sometime in 1919 a rumour ran about London that Lawrence had rejected a decoration that the King offered. [Compare the article by Winston Churchill.] Lawrence told me that the occasion had not been a public investiture but a private audience, that he had already declared his unwillingness to accept decorations, and that although he had been forced to decline some which the King offered him, he had given explanations with which the King seemed sympathetic.

In sharp contrast to this was the version of the episode which the then Prince of Wales (King Edward VIII) told me after dinner one night at Bayonne, in 1931. He said that Lawrence had definitely caused the King embarrassment by refusing the decoration at the moment of presentation, and that this lack of consideration — not for the decoration, but for the King's feelings — had made him, the Prince, refuse to meet Lawrence, although mutual friends had attempted to bring them together.

To King Edward's secretary, Sir Godfrey Thomas, I am much indebted for sending me the following: 'From what I have been told, you can be assured that the incident in question left no impression upon King George's mind of incivility on the part of Lawrence. His Majesty was naturally somewhat taken aback, and felt that the momentary embarrassment might have been obviated had Lawrence been able to intimate his reluctance at an earlier point.' [*Editor's Note:* He had however refused in the course of conversation, so the late Lord Stamfordham wrote on the evidence of notes made on the following day by Lord Wigram. The King's memory differed too in thinking that T.E. gave as one reason against accepting decorations that he might fight for the Arabs against the British. He had said, against the French. As a matter of fact, he returned the decorations sent him by other governments, with the exception of the *Croix de Guerre* of France, which he sent round the streets of Oxford on the neck of Hogarth's dog.]

His experiences with the French had angered him against them. He said they suffered from mental fermentation and had a genius for international dishonesty. They hated all people except the French, and, reciprocally, were loved by the French alone. They were always complaining and there was no appeasing them. The only way to deal with them was to say 'hoots' to them.

He told how once Mr. Balfour saw him in the street and said, 'The two great obstacles to the world's peace are the French Army and the American Senate'. T.E. said, 'May I quote that?' 'If you do, I shall deny it.'

I was in Brazil for most of 1920. Shortly after my return I had a meeting with Mr. Winston Churchill, then about to go to the Colonial Office, and was asked by him if I had seen Lawrence. I did not even know where he was. Mr. Churchill informed me that Lawrence had been made a Fellow of All Souls, Oxford, and was living there. He said that things were not going well in the Middle East and he believed that Lawrence was the one man who could put them straight; he had written to Lawrence and had asked him to come and see him. Lawrence's reply had been flippant.

Mr. Churchill asked me if I would try to prevail upon Lawrence. I said that of course I would, but that I thought it would help if I could indicate to Lawrence what the proposal might be. Mr. Churchill said that he meant to put the matter, in so far as he could, completely in Lawrence's hands; that he would make him Governor-General, and would back him to the utmost.

Accordingly I sent a telegram. Lawrence wired back that he would come and dine with me, which he did. I told him what Mr. Churchill had said. He smiled about the flippant letter. 'I like Winston. He writes well. But he's a politician. I'd rather be a chimney sweep than a politician. Their job makes them second-rate. Too much necessity for compromise. All ours that I know, are honest and devoted — but they have an eye on the weather and they reek of red herrings. I have finished with them. I don't want to go back to the East, I have bad memories of it. Also, I don't care to be Governor-General where I have once been Governor-General. The art of life is never to do a thing twice. Now I'm enabled to do nothing. I've always longed for that. I don't want to be caught up again.'

These objections seemed to me too personal and I argued that, if he left any stone unturned to improve the position of the Arabs, he could no longer justify his bitterness about the treatment of them. He grinned thoughtfully and said, in the peculiar slow manner of his when reflecting, 'Yes . . . yes . . . yes'.

After a bit, a stubborn resolve seemed to seize him. 'No — I won't do it. Big bugs are always getting themselves into jams and having to be helped out by the subordinates. I argued in Paris that we ought to back Mustapha Kemal and the Young Turk Movement. Had we done so, all would have been well, but it was like talking against the wind. Now I'm tired and I want to rest and forget.' However, when we parted he promised to reconsider. He wished to consult someone (Mr. Lloyd George, I think) before deciding. As is well known, he did go to Mr. Churchill and when he retired, he felt that, however tardily, Britain had satisfactorily fulfilled her moral obligations to the Arabs.

He was like Kipling in the intensity of his patriotism, but disliked the jingo tenor of Kipling's writings: Kipling, he said, had not portrayed the Victorian spirit but had created it. It had grown as he fed it. He said that Kipling had caught on early to the fact that it was good business. People liked to think 'This is us'. Lawrence had gone down to spend a day with Kipling and they had talked mainly of engines and argued as to the man who first invented the internal combustion machine. He was struck by Kipling's memory for dates and names. They had got on very well together.

·

My father's death in the spring of 1922 necessitated my spending most of my time in America for some years, and I fell out of touch with Lawrence until 1927, when, locating him in India, we had a correspondence which led to my asking him to translate the *Odyssey*. I did not see him again until April 1930. He had then the look of a man nervously exhausted and there was suffering in his eyes. He was, he said, too tired even to read anything but light casual things. He complained of what a long time it took to grow old. I was reminded of what he had written me from Miranshah in 1928, in answer to my offer to send him *The Boswell Papers*. 'I daren't own a set of them. I have no place to keep anything. The life in barracks is all a common life. Everything choice is ruined by rough handling. Also I am inevitably affected (I'd be a monster if not) by my six years' service: and I'm therefore like them. The very fine things are too fine for me, now.'

But youth seemed to be Lawrence's permanent possession. Whenever I saw him after a long interval I was impressed by this. We were together for the last time in March 1935. I remarked then with astonishment that he seemed not to have aged a bit since the day I first met him, sixteen years before. The bitter post-war disappointments, the poverty and hunger, the long years of service as a common soldier — all these things and more, seemed to have affected him not at all.

It had occurred to me that it would be an important contribution to literature if he could be persuaded to write a Life of Mohammed. I spoke to some publisher friends and they agreed and were willing to pay well for it. With this in view, I had timed a contemplated visit to England to coincide with his discharge from the Air Force, in March 1935. Upon arrival, I found that he had not returned to his cottage at Clouds Hill because the place was besieged by representatives of the Press. His whereabouts I could not learn, only that upon his discharge he had left Yorkshire on a push-bike, with a small bundle.

I sent my London address to await him at the cottage. On March 15th, I received a telegram from him saying that the

Press had cleared off and he had returned to Clouds Hill, where he would remain, and wondered if I could go down to see him there. On the 17th, I motored from London to Clouds Hill. As we neared the cottage I noticed a group of, perhaps, four men, talking earnestly together. They carried large cameras. They seemed very curious at my arrival. I knocked, then shouted for T.E., but there was no response. On the few feet of lawn that separated the cottage from the surrounding rhododendrons, I saw fragments of thick old tiles. One could see where they had been broken out of the roof. Then a local man came up and said, 'He's gone'. I asked what had happened. He said that a number of Press representatives had arrived, wanting to interview and photograph Lawrence; he had refused but they would not go away, and kept banging on his door and shouting at him, and at last he had given one man a terrific sock in the eye and driven them off. Lawrence had then taken his push-bike through a covered-over path in the rhododendrons and had ridden away on it, only shouting to the man, 'I'll be back when you see me'. The photographers, not having witnessed his departure, had placed some of their number in the bushes facing the door and others had gone to the brow of the steep hill rising immediately behind the cottage, and from there had hurled stones on to the roof, hoping to drive him out into the ambushed cameras of those below. [*Editor's Note:* A newspaper man told me two months later that no one had witnessed or knew the cause of the assault on his colleague, whom he afterwards saw stoning the roof.]

I left a letter for him, and drove back to London, sick at heart that the peace and enjoyment of his little home, to which he had so looked forward on his retirement, had been ruthlessly invaded.

Five days later Lawrence came to see me in London. As a rule I did not keep a diary, but occasionally after my meetings with him I made notes of his conversation. I have thought to quote here from my diary entry of this, my last, day with Lawrence. It will be obvious that some of the notes were made in moments of leisure, others jotted down hurriedly; they sit like marbles in a bag.

March 22nd, 1935. At 9.30 the valet woke me up with a note from Lawrence to say that he would call back at eleven. I was shaving, when he suddenly appeared in the door, wearing grey flannel trousers, brown tweed coat, no hat (as ever). Good and simple greeting. He stood at the bathroom door and we talked. He said he was sorry to have missed me at Clouds Hill, but the photographers had driven him out. I said I knew full well, as I had seen them and the damage they did to his roof. He said, 'Did one of them have a black eye?' grinning, 'I gave one of them a beauty, but it rather put my thumb out', and he rubbed the back of his hand reflectively. He was now going to see the heads of the three big newspapers with a view to persuading them to give orders that he should be let alone. We spoke of the cottage. He wished I had seen the interior, for it was there that his work was apparent. Big living room with his books ranged about. Bathroom with one of the gold medallions from the *Odyssey* set over the door under glass. The swimming tank across the road was more a reservoir against fire, which saved him insurance on his valuable books. He said the whole business had been made possible and paid for by the fee for translating the *Odyssey* and the one-third royalty from the American edition, on which he had received about £450. His income was now £2 per week. He had not served long enough to get a pension. He said he was now 46 and had probably 20 good years ahead of him, which he planned to spend reading and seeing England on a push-bike. 'England is the most beautiful spot on earth. You who dash through it in motor cars never get to see it properly.' I made the suggestion that he come to America first for a visit. He answered, 'Yes, I'd like to, but you see I have not got time. England is a much bigger place than you think'.

I told him that Simon & Schuster wanted him to do a life of Mohammed — as a modern biography. After considering a while, he said, 'No', because to do it would take his mind back to the East which he wished to forget. Besides, he couldn't bear the thought of work, was looking forward to complete idleness and didn't need the money.

He said the moving picture rights of *Revolt in the Desert* had been sold three times, but each time the business had petered out because he would not give his permission and threatened injunction against its production. They had last been sold to Korda who had been very decent. T.E. said he could prevent it anywhere and would, because the matter of all the biographies was mainly taken from the *Seven Pillars*, and he owned the copyright of that. Nor could they use any of his own words, nor put words in his mouth that he had not uttered. He said he would however co-operate with any film based on his Arabian career if it were done in the manner and spirit of Mickey Mouse. It would be perfect with that treatment. Example: a Turkish troop-train blown into the air in bits — re-forms in space — and perfectly united, lands gracefully and proceeds merrily on its way. Treated thus, his affairs would make a great picture. He said this without any irony or bitterness, but beaming and chuckling at the idea.

We spoke of the apparent threat of European War. The thing that worried him more was the possibility of war between Italy and Ethiopia. He seemed to think it very likely as Mussolini had to do something to turn people's minds from home realities. Having nourished their ego and their dramatic sense, he dared not stop. This war, if it came, would be the beginning of a conflict between dark and white races that would spread over the world. Every coloured race would be incensed at the arrogance of Italians (whites). In the end they would regard all whites as one.

We spoke of a mutual friend whose wife had let him down. He said, 'But women's emotions are too strong and various to permit them to hold to a course. Their dishonesty is not fundamental or conscious, as with men; it is the result of emotional sickness and there is no dealing with it'.

God is something one feels. Destroyed by intellectuality. He believed, but had no religion. Organized religions attempt to justify man's urge for God. It is silly and dangerous to try to justify natural feelings. Religions are mainly over-thought.

Leachman — brave as a lion — used to keep treacherous tribes in order by threatening and beating their chiefs. Got away with it by sheer courage and spirit. Lost his nerve six months before he was killed. So wrote to his family, but carried on. One day drove up to tent of disaffected chief. Cursed him, then seized him and spat in his face. Turned to leave. Chief shot him in the back before he got out of tent, which was violation of Arab hospitality.

—— (the author of a recent book on the East) had persecution complex. In Arabia they did all they could to help him but he complained bitterly.

Belloc's *The Jews* — 'good book, but I don't agree with him. I am very fond of the Jews. Belloc has real genius, but the necessity of keeping the pot boiling has strangled it.'

I spoke of the Tank Corps. '*Royal* Tank Corps,' he corrected. 'Don't you like the idea of royalty?' I asked. 'Yes, I think it is very valuable for Boys' Books.'

How the miracle of harmony was achieved in a man who was at once prophet, poet, jester, crusader, I am at a loss to understand. Yet I find it difficult to think of him as anything but a very simple, lovable and charming companion whose wit and comprehension made the hours with him delightful and memorable. Indeed, when he got going on some subject that particularly interested him (and there were many) he talked with such a rush of brilliance, and with such a force of comprehension of men and matters, that I, at times, experienced a sense of elation comparable to that which music can give.

PERSONAL CRISIS

CELANDINE KENNINGTON
FLORENCE DOUBLEDAY

CELANDINE KENNINGTON. Born 1886. Wife
of Eric H. Kennington.

THE first time I met T.E. I didn't know who he was, and
he made very little impression on me. He came to the
house as Eric's friend and I remember him sitting rather
apart from other people on a hard settee. He gave me a sense
of strangeness as he sat there, very beautiful, and very still,
like some lovely exotic bird or animal brought in unwillingly —
under perfect restraint, but longing to be gone. As we went
out, he took part gaily in a joke of dressing up cushions in a
coat and hat and leaving a dreadful dummy on the sofa to
puzzle someone who was coming later.

I had heard it said on all sides that he loathed women, and
that he had said 'Kennington's got married; we shan't hear
much more of him', and I was alarmed to hear that he was
coming to our house on Chiswick Mall. He had said jokingly
to Eric, 'I hope your wife does not collect negro sculpture'.
Eric made the most glorious mock African figure out of lumps
of plasticine and various household tools: we put it in a
prominent place in the dining-room, but T.E. did not bat an
eyelid.

I was shy sitting opposite T.E. and only remember the
extraordinary effect his scrutiny made on me. He might be gay
or remote, then there was a sudden blaze of blue from his eyes
and a most startling sensation of power, and one realized he
could know at will all there was to know about one; that he
could make one what he willed, if he willed. It was like mesmeric power not being used at the moment, latent and terrific.
This stopped my shyness because I saw it was no use, he knew
all about one and that was just that.

Not long after this I had a desperately bad miscarriage
and for days was terribly ill, and did not want to have to go on
living. Then T.E. came up to see me: he sat on a hard stool
leaning forward and gripping it with his hands; he fixed his

eyes on me and began, 'Of course you must be feeling very miserable, you feel you have failed in your job, and it's about the most important job in the world; . . . you must be feeling you are utterly no good and nothing can ever be worth while . . .' On and on he went, describing me to myself, clarifying all the nightmare fears by defining them, and doing it all from the woman's point of view, not the man's. He seemed to know everything that miscarriage could mean, even down to the shame of being laughed at for it, and as he talked warmth began to come into me, instead of flooding out of me for, besides putting things as they were, he brought a power to re-make them all afresh. My detestable nurse said, 'I can't allow visitors in here. She's too weak to speak . . . and look at the time that man stayed.' Then looking at me grudgingly, 'I must say you don't look tired . . . you look better'. It was a long job pulling round physically, but from that time I was well spiritually. Of course after this I simply loved T.E.

When we had visitors who might be tiresome, we secreted him in the woodshed on a chopping block, behind a screen of faggots. He turned up on his motor bicycle one summer evening at Holly Copse, and saw our supper set out in the garden; he smiled and said, 'I think I can bring my friend in here', and fetched the R.A.F. lad who was with him. We had a merry meal, T.E. knowing exactly how to give the conversation a turn in the boy's direction whenever he thought it desirable. After supper T.E. and Eric went off to talk business and it was easy to get the boy to talk. He seemed to regard T.E. as a great rarity, a very precious and rather incompetent one, who must be gently bullied for his soul's good and made to do some practical detail about their journey (I forget what: some overcoat or something) against his will.

Was he a woman hater? It is so often asked. I don't think he was at all: but he had not the usual interest in them from the sexual point of view, and he deeply disapproved of what many women do, that is they hamper a man in fulfilling his destiny: they tend to make him non-adventurous; they hold him back to attend to their comfort. This he fought steadily and relentlessly. After some people have heard Eric talk about him, they often say to me rather pointedly, 'And what do *you* think about Lawrence?' This question always brings the same rush of inescapable feeling and I find myself beginning to answer by blurting out, 'Well, you see . . . he saved my life'.

FLORENCE DOUBLEDAY. Of New York. Widow of Frank N. Doubleday, founder of the American publishing house of Doubleday, Page & Co. (now Doubleday, Doran & Co.), the other original partner being Walter H. Page, later Ambassador to Great Britain.

WHEN we came to London in December 1918, Sir Evelyn Wrench invited my husband, F. N. Doubleday, (known to his friends as 'Effendi') to a dinner, at which he was placed by the side of a young small, blond gentleman in khaki; on his place card was 'Colonel Lawrence'. My husband had a delightful time at dinner and, when it was over, he said: 'I am so sorry that we shall not see you again.' Lawrence replied, 'Why not?' My husband said, 'Because I am just passing through London'. Lawrence said, 'Aren't you staying at an hotel?' And the answer was: 'Yes, at Brown's. Will you come and dine with us if Mrs. Doubleday writes and invites you?' 'With pleasure,' replied Lawrence.

As my husband was going out of the room, he stopped and said to Sir Evelyn: 'Who is that delightful man that sat next to me at dinner?' Sir Evelyn replied, 'Why, Effendi, don't you Americans know about Colonel Lawrence of Arabia, who is one of the most sought after men in London and whom Lowell Thomas is exploiting in every way which may assist Lawrence in his cause for Arabia?'

Next morning Effendi dashed upstairs to speak to Rudyard Kipling, his most intimate friend, who was staying at Brown's at the time. He asked Mr. Kipling if he and Mrs. Kipling would dine the following Friday. Kipling responded that he already had an engagement for that night, but, as he considered Lawrence the most romantic figure that had come out of the War, he would cancel his dinner and come to us.

Thursday night we had dined early and were going out of the dining-room at eight o'clock, when there stood Lawrence, who was introduced to me and said, 'But you asked me for dinner to-night'. We, of course, said 'Yes' with pleasure, and returned to the dining-room. When we had only been seated a short

time, he said, 'But you really *did* ask me to dinner to-night?'
And we said, 'Yes, of course, we are sure we did'.

After dinner we went up to our sitting-room and had an
enchanting evening. He was full of his Arabian campaign
at that time and had some hope that he was going to get
Damascus for the Arabs. One incident that he related impressed me very much; it was one of the many signs of his
kindness and consideration. He was speaking of blowing up
the Turkish-German trains in Arabia and how he could only
have sixty feet of wire to connect to the charge on the track;
he would sit there on his camel and wait to set the charge off.
When I asked him if it were not very dangerous, he said 'Yes'.
I said, 'Then why didn't you let one of your men do it?'; and he
responded, 'Why, he might have been hurt'.

After Christmas we went to Paris, where Lawrence met us.
One day Lawrence and Feisal came to tea and also Frank
Symonds, the well-known American correspondent for the
Tribune. Never have I seen two men so intent on trying to
persuade another to take up their cause in his paper —
unfortunately unsuccessfully.

In 1920 we were over here again. Lawrence at that time
was living at All Souls College in Oxford and invited us to
luncheon on a Sunday. We went up the night before and he
came to dinner. Then you felt his admiration for and devotion
to my husband, which grew with all the years that we knew him.

The next morning he came to take me through Oxford
and I was deeply interested to see how he never in any way
asserted himself; in most of the colleges he did not seem to
be known by the porter. This incognito lasted until we came
to one college where we were refused entrance into the Great
Hall. Then the Lawrence of Arabia came forward and we did
get into the Great Hall. Finally he took me to his chambers,
left me in charge of the manservant and went back to get my
husband and stepson and his wife. It was a delightful lunch
party and afterwards Lawrence pulled out his valuable books

and sat on the floor and showed them to us like a small boy. His simplicity was one of his greatest characteristics.

In 1921 we had a house in Green Street. One morning Lawrence turned up in time to go with my husband to the office, and then he returned to luncheon. My husband took me aside and said: 'What am I to do with him?' I said, 'Let him do as he wants,' and he went back and spent all the afternoon with my husband. It was almost as if he were trying to get help from him for what he wanted to do.

The next year he enlisted.

The first time we were in England after his return from India, he dropped in to see us and, when I suggested spending the night, he said, 'Yes, with pleasure'. Then we could arrange another time for him to come and go with us to Mr. Kipling's; we would lunch — picnic — on the way. On one of those picnics, it was suggested that what he was eating might give him indigestion; he answered, No, I think not, my stomach is my servant!'

One day, when we were motoring out, I said to him, 'T.E., why did you enter the Air Force as a private?'

His response was: 'In 1923 I was nervously, physically and financially broke.'

I exclaimed, 'Then you went in as a rest cure?' and with great alacrity he said, 'Yes, and don't you think it is doing it?'

He asked us to call him T.E., because he said that was the only part of his name which really belonged to him, and people who were fond of him should call him that.

When I asked why he had taken the name of 'Shaw', he said, with a smile, that he had chosen a name of four letters (unfortunately I have forgotten it) but found that the officer with whom he was to enlist had that name also. When Lawrence went up, the officer said laughingly, 'I'm not going to let you have my name,' and Lawrence replied, 'Then give me the telephone book and I will pick the first name of four letters that I see,' and the first was 'Shaw'. 'And,' he added,

'I have had to apologize to Bernard Shaw many times for having taken his name.'

As the years went on, my husband was not very well, and T.E.'s tenderness, kindness and attention to him were most beautiful. He had a way of sitting and looking at him that was most touching. It was rather like a small boy looking up at his father whom he dearly loved; and he was always full of consideration for everyone. He even let the trained attendant take a movie of him with my husband, because he thought it might amuse him.

In 1930 my husband had a very serious operation. I cabled to Lawrence and for the next six weeks he wrote Effendi the most enchanting letters. One was really a masterpiece, very much longer than any we had ever received before, and was written from a fisherman's hut up in Scotland. Some of the descriptions were perfectly beautiful, of 'the wind whistling down the stems of the dry heather' and of 'the disembodied voices of the gulls, the saddest sound in the world'. Then he described going to the Post Office or general shop and asking the woman for some books. Finally she offered him *The Boy's Book of Colonel Lawrence*. He told her that he knew him and that he was a wash-out, and the woman said he was very difficult to please.

In 1931 I suggested that we should go to Kipling's. I had been ill, and by the time we reached Sevenoaks, I was thoroughly all in. I said, 'I'm sorry but I cannot go any further', and though it must have been a disappointment to him because he liked Kipling so much, he asked with great enthusiasm, 'Will you let me telephone to say that we cannot come?' I have always felt rather unhappy that we let him pay for that telephone, for he had so little money.

He had a most unobtrusive, wonderful way of looking after you without appearing to do so and was such an enchanting guest because he talked on any subject, no matter whether it were politics or Air Force or social life of all degrees.

On one of our drives to Kipling, Effendi asked him why he had come back from India. He responded, because the Indians were accusing him of having instigated the revolutions in the neighbourhood and the Russians were likewise doing so. He said that he was stationed in an enclosure of barbed wire on a hill but that they sent a guard for him to bring him back to England. When he got on the steamer, he was told that, as there was no third-class accommodation they were giving him second class, but, being third class, he must speak to nobody, which amused him greatly. His guard was still with him, and when they reached Suez he was told that he must not get off at Aden; if he did he would be arrested, but he said he didn't want to. Finally, when they got to Plymouth, still with guard and attendant, he was taken to the R.A.F. quarters where the guard finally left him, and he was again a free man.

My husband said: 'T.E., when are they going to send you away again?' With a perfectly delightful chuckle he answered, 'I don't think they will send me away again because it cost the British Government £740 to get me back this time.'

He also told us about the wonderful boat he was inventing, which was to be bomb-proof, and he was so disappointed when the Air Force would not bomb it from the sky with him steering it, to see if it were going to be successful or not.

[*Editor's Note:* The bombing of manned armoured boats was regularly practised before he left the Service.]

The last trip that my husband made to this country three years ago, T.E. dropped in on him as usual and remained to dinner. My husband said, 'When do you think we had better go to Kipling's?' and I said, 'On Friday'. For once my husband did not connect the date. It was my birthday and I thought no lovelier thing could happen to me than to go with my husband and T.E. out to see Kipling.

When I came into the breakfast room that morning, I found my husband and his attendants had arranged a birthday breakfast. It was very amusing. T.E. came in in the middle of it, as he had arrived much earlier than the time set. When he found that it was my birthday, he exclaimed, 'I am so sorry

I did not know; I would have brought you a ninepenny present had I realized the occasion.' I said, 'Well, if you cannot do that, you can write in my *Odyssey*' and went off for my copy, which I had brought hoping to get an inscription in it. My initials are 'F.D.'; my husband's 'F.N.D.' T.E. could not quite stand not having him in it, so he put F, then a tiny little N in parenthesis, then D. It was such a nice touch of thoughtfulness that Effendi had to be there too. The inscription was long and amusing.

We started out and Frere Reeves and his wife joined us. They had a small car. We drove out quite a long distance and then I thought it would be nice for Mrs. Frere Reeves to be able to talk to Effendi and T.E., so we changed cars. Shortly afterwards it rained — and it poured. Mrs. Frere Reeves said that Lawrence was in a perfect state of mind for fear that I was getting wet and wanted to stop and get out and give me his place in my husband's car.

We hunted for a long time for a place to picnic and finally found one on the left-hand side of the road where we turned in, left the cars, opened the gate and spread out our picnic. Effendi did not walk very well at that time. We had him comfortably fixed, the seat taken out of the car and everything made right for him, when two men appeared from the woods near by, one evidently an ex-soldier as he had only an iron hook for his right hand. They came up to us and said: 'You will have to get out of here because a bull and twelve cows are coming here in ten minutes.' 'But,' I exclaimed, 'we have just started our picnic.'

'We can't help that; we can't keep the cows and the bull out on the road.'

'Very well,' I said, 'we will have to hurry,' and I looked up and found Lawrence had gone.

In a few minutes he returned and in a most casual way said:

'You can stay here as long as you like. I have been to speak to the head herdsman who is employed by a friend of mine. He will keep the bull and the cows on the road until you are ready to leave.'

It was so characteristic, the quiet way he did it; and, when we drove away, there were the twelve cows and the bull by the side of the road.

T.E. came down to see us off at Southampton. He remained with us for a long time that evening, talking to Effendi and I asked him while he was there, 'Won't you take me out on your motor cycle?' He did not look awfully happy and my husband said, 'No, something might happen to you', so I did not get on it, much to my disappointment.

I went up to the gangway with him — it was the only time that I ever did, and, as he shook hands with me, I felt he had something to say. I think he realized what I was fighting against, that my husband's condition was very serious.

He wrote Effendi a beautiful Christmas letter and in it gave a full description of his house and wound up with that he 'hoped we were coming back to England in the spring, which was pure selfishness on his part because he wanted to see us'.

After my husband left us, he wrote me what is surely the most beautiful letter that could be received about anyone. Then he wrote me again on his own birthday, just a year and a month after my birthday in London. One of the things he said was: 'Do not be pulled down by people lesser than your past tradition.'

That seemed to be the keynote of his character. For years he lived in a hut with eighteen other men, slept on what is the regulation bed — a sheet of iron with a little pad about an inch thick on it; even the holiday he went on, when he wrote the wonderful letter I have mentioned, was spent with two of his Air Force companions, yet he never lost himself in any way. His breeding, his intellectual attainments, the kind of work he was doing, all lifted him up above where he was and yet he was most loved by all. So what he wrote to me was what he practised himself. And in that birthday letter he put a little postscript in which he said that Clouds Hill would be his address, where he had a tiny cottage in which he hoped to live and be happy. What really describes him completely is what he said of my husband in the letter after Effendi left us: 'Only a very strong man could have meant so much to his diverse friends.'

OXFORD AND LONDON

ROBERT GRAVES
SYDNEY COCKERELL

ROBERT GRAVES. Born 1895. Author of *Goodbye to All That, I Claudius, Claudius the God, Count Belisarius, The Long Week End, The Common Asphodel,* etc., besides the authorized biography, *Lawrence and the Arabs* (1927) and *T. E. Lawrence to his Biographer* (1938).

THE first time I met him he was in full evening dress. This was in February or March 1920. It was a guest-night at All Souls, where he had been awarded a seven-years' Fellowship. The formality of evening dress, when everyone is wearing it, concentrates attention on eyes, and Lawrence's eyes immediately interested me. They were startlingly blue, even by artificial light, and glittered; also, they never met the eyes of the person he was addressing but flickered up and down as if making an inventory of clothes and limbs. I was only an accidental guest and knew nobody there. Lawrence was talking to the Regius Professor of Divinity about the influence of the Syrian Greek philosophers on early Christianity, and especially of the importance of the University of Gadara close to the Lake of Galilee. He mentioned that St. James had quoted one of the Gadarene philosophers (I think Mnasalcus) in his Epistle. He went on to speak of Meleager and the other Syrian-Greek contributors to the Greek Anthology, and of their poems in Syrian of which he intended to publish an English translation and which were as good as (or better than) their poems in Greek. This interested me, and I said something about a morning-star image which Meleager had used in rather an un-Greek way. Lawrence then said: 'You must be Graves the poet? I read a book of yours in Egypt in 1917 and thought it pretty good.' This was embarrassing, but kind. He began asking me what the younger poets were doing now: he was out of touch. I told him what I knew.

I was then an undergraduate at St. John's, but the War had interrupted my education, and I was already twenty-four years old, married, with two children, and not living an ordinary

272

University life. My chief interest then (as now) was poetry and this was the common ground on which Lawrence and I met. He had not long finished with the Peace Conference, where he had been acting as adviser to Emir Feisal, and was now tinkering at the second draft of the *Seven Pillars of Wisdom*, the first draft having been stolen from him a few months before. The Fellowship had been granted him on the understanding that he would devote himself to writing the book as a formal history of the Arab Revolt. As a matter of fact he found it difficult to work at Oxford and it was only when he had resigned his Fellowship and moved to London that he got going again.

I used to visit his rooms in the mornings, but not before eleven o'clock or half-past, because he worked only at night, not going to bed until dawn. I knew nothing definite about his war-time activities, though my brother Philip Graves had been with him in the Intelligence Department at Cairo in 1915, making out the Turkish Order of Battle. I did not ask him to tell me about the Revolt, partly because he seemed to be sensitive on the subject — Lowell Thomas was going about lecturing on *Lawrence of Arabia* — and partly because there was a convention between him and me that the War should not be mentioned. It was too recent and we were both suffering from the effects of it, and enjoying Oxford as a too-good-to-be-true relaxation. So though the long closely written foolscap sheets of the *Seven Pillars* were always stacked on a neat pile on his living-room table, I restrained my curiosity about them. He occasionally spoke about his archaeological work in Mesopotamia before the War, and one day gave me a full account of his famous interview with King George; but poetry, especially modern poetry, was what we talked about chiefly.

He was anxious to meet what poets there were, personally. I didn't think that there were many about, but through me he came to know, among others, Siegfried Sassoon, Edmund Blunden, the present Poet Laureate and, later, Thomas Hardy. He was not a poet himself and frankly envied poets. He felt that they had some sort of secret which he might be able to learn for his own profit. Charles Doughty was his chief hero and he came to know him through Hogarth, Curator of the Ashmolean Museum, with whom he had worked in Syria and whom he regarded as his second father. (Doughty's *Arabia Deserta* had been twenty years out of print and Lawrence had asked for a new edition to be published: he was now writing the introduction to it.) The poet's secret Lawrence envisaged as a technical mastery of words rather than as a particular mode of living and thinking. I had not yet learned enough about poetry to be able to dispute this. And when I did begin to learn some years later, I found him difficult to convince. To him painting, sculpture, music and poetry were parallel activities, differing only in the medium used. He had asked Doughty his reasons for the Arabian journey, and Doughty had replied that he had gone there 'To redeem the English language from the slough into which it had fallen since the time of Spenser'. I think that these words of Doughty's made a great impression on Lawrence and largely account for his furious keying-up of style in the *Seven Pillars*. *Arabia Deserta*, by the way, was used as a geographical text-book by the Arab Bureau at Cairo and many of the official reports made by Lawrence and his companions show clear traces of Doughty's style.

Vachel Lindsay, the American poet, an extremely simple man, and one of the best bad poets of the day — Middle-Western clay with a golden streak — came to Oxford, and I persuaded the Professor of English Literature to give him a room to recite his poems in. Everyone enjoyed the performance. Afterwards Lawrence invited Lindsay and his old mother and myself to lunch in his rooms. Mrs. Lindsay had been warned by friends to comment on nothing unusual that she met at Oxford. Lawrence had brought out the college gold service in her honour and this she took to be the ordinary thing at a university luncheon-party. Lawrence apologized for it as of no great antiquity: but the College had been patriotic during the Civil War and melted down all its plate to help pay the King's campaign expenses.

Lindsay, who was ambitious in an old-fashioned way (and eventually committed suicide when he seemed to be losing favour with his public), regarded his Oxford visit as the peak of his poetic career. He had enjoyed great fame in America recently and his successes at Oxford seemed to crown it. He said that Oxford was the cultural centre of England and England of the world. Lawrence said, 'I believe that, geographically, Daventry is the central point, but in the *Mabinogion* it is Oxford. Do you know the *Mabinogion*? There is a yarn there about two fighting dragons that were captured in the reign of King Lud. They made such an outcry with their fighting that Lud made them drunk with a cauldron of the best mead, into which they toppled; and then wrapped cauldron, dragons and all in a great piece of satin and buried them in the strongest kist-vaen in his dominions, which happened to be on Snowdon (near my birthplace). But he set the trap at Carfax, at the top of this street, because having measured his dominions by length and breadth he found that it was the exact centre of England. And so it still seems to us at Oxford.' Vachel Lindsay started rhetorically about Arab architecture. Lawrence corrected him on a technicality. Vachel Lindsay switched to safer ground — Mayan civilization in Yucatan. Lawrence again corrected him on a technicality. So Lindsay talked about Middle Western politics, and prohibition, and Lawrence listened with interest. He said later: 'I like a man to stick to his own subject. Lindsay's best poem is the one about the 1896 election — "Bryan, Bryan, Bryan".'

His rooms were dark and oak-panelled. A large table and a desk were the principal furniture. There were also two heavy leather chairs, simply acquired. An American oil-financier had come in suddenly one day when I was there and said: 'I am here from the States, Colonel Lawrence, to ask you a single question. You are the only man who will answer it honestly. Do Middle-Eastern conditions justify my putting any money in South Arabian oil?' Lawrence, without rising, simply answered: 'No.' 'That's all I wanted to know; it was worth coming for that. Thank you, and good day!' In his brief glance about the room he had found something missing; on his way home through London he chose the chairs and had them sent to Lawrence with his card. Other things in the room were pictures, including Augustus John's portrait of Feisal, which Lawrence, I believe, bought from John with the diamond which he had worn as a mark of honour in his Arab head-dress; his books, including a Kelmscott *Chaucer*; three prayer-rugs, the gift of Arab leaders who had fought with him, one of them with the sheen on the nap made with crushed lapis-lazuli; the Tell Shahm station bell from the Hejaz railway; and on the mantelpiece a four-thousand-year-old toy, a clay soldier on horseback from a child's grave at Carchemish, where Lawrence had been digging before the War.

He behaved very much like an undergraduate at times. One day I happened to go up to the top of the Radcliffe Camera and look down on the roofs of the neighbouring colleges. From a pinnacle of All Souls a small crimson Hejaz flag was fluttering: Lawrence had been a famous roof-climber when he was up at Jesus College before the War. He told me two or three of his schemes for brightening All Souls and Oxford generally. One was for improving the turf in the quadrangle, which he said was in a disgraceful condition, nearly rotting away; he had suggested at a college meeting that it should be manured or treated in some way or other, but no action had been taken. He now said that he was going to plant mushrooms on it, so that they would have to re-turf it altogether. He consulted a mushroom expert in town, but found that it was difficult to make spawn grow. He would have persisted if he had not been called away about this time to help Winston Churchill with the Middle-Eastern settlement. Another scheme, in which I was to have helped, was to steal the Magdalen College deer. He was going to drive them into the small inner quadrangle of All Souls, having persuaded the college to reply, when Magdalen protested and asked for its deer back, that it was the All Souls herd and had been pastured there from time immemorial. Great things were expected of this raid. It fell through for the same reason as the other. But a successful strike of college-servants for better pay and hours was engineered by Lawrence. Lawrence also proposed to present the College with a peacock which, once accepted, would be found to bear the name Nathaniel — after Lord Curzon, with whom Lawrence had had a row and who was Chancellor of the University.

One morning I went to Lawrence's rooms and he introduced me to a visitor there: 'You will dislike each other,' he said grinning. It was Ezra Pound.

'They tell me that he's Longfellow's grand-nephew, and when a man's a modernist that takes some living down.'

At the same time Lawrence was getting to know the painters and sculptors. They had a secret for him too. He used to offer himself as a model to see what they made of him. He knew a good deal about himself and wanted to know more. The various portrait treatments they made of him he found informative both about himself and about artists. Nobody painted the same man. One day in 1921 I was at Paddington Station with him waiting for the Oxford train. We met (Sir) William Rothenstein: he had tea with us in a refreshment room. Rothenstein said that he had just been doing a portrait of Lawrence. 'Oh,' I said, 'which Lawrence?' Lawrence kicked me under the table. It is only recently that I have seen Sir William Orpen's version, or rather a photograph of it. It is a curious, almost libellous magnification of a seldom-seen element in Lawrence's character — a sort of street-urchin furtiveness. A counter-balance to John's too sentimentally heroic portrait.

Professor Edgeworth, of All Souls, avoided conversational English, confidently using words and phrases that one only expects to meet in books. One day Lawrence returned from a visit to London, and Edgeworth met him at the gate. 'Was it very caliginous in the Metropolis?' 'Somewhat caliginous, but not altogether inspissated,' Lawrence replied gravely.

I remember having tea at Fuller's once with him, and the scandal he caused by clapping his hands for the waitress in the Oriental fashion. And one afternoon he rang the station-bell out of his window into the quadrangle. I said, 'Good God, you'll wake the whole College up'. 'It needs waking up.'

We planned to collaborate in a burlesque on contemporary writers, in the style of a Government Blue-book. I said: 'First we must get a Blue-book and study it.' He said, all right, he would buy one next time he went to London. He did. He asked at the Stationery Office for a Blue-book. The clerk said: 'Which Blue-book? We have hundreds here.' 'Which ever you like.' Mistaking his indifference for guilty embarrassment they handed him the report of a Royal Commission on Venereal Disease.

I teased him once for standing on the fender over the fire: I said that he did it to make himself look taller. He denied this hotly and said that the onus of proving oneself of any use in this world lay with tall people like me. This encouraged me to a ragging pretence of physical violence; but I immediately stopped when I saw the look in his face. I had surprised his morbid horror of being touched.

SIR SYDNEY COCKERELL. Born 1867. Fellow of Jesus College, Cambridge, 1910-16, and of Downing College, 1932-37; Secretary to William Morris and the Kelmscott Press, 1892-98; literary executor of William Morris, Wilfred Scawen Blunt, and Thomas Hardy. Director of the Fitzwilliam Museum, Cambridge, 1908-37.

HOW SHAW MET SHAW

THE first of my many meetings with T. E. Shaw took place on March 25th, 1922. It had come to the ears of certain friends of Charles Doughty, to whom and to whose *Arabia Deserta* Lawrence and I were both devoted, that the failure of his investments had involved him in a financial crisis. Lawrence, then a well-paid official of the Colonial Office, was determined to find a remedy. In order to discuss the possibilities; he invited me by telegram to lunch with him in the grill-room of the Carlton Hotel. We met at 1, and soon hit on a plan for giving Doughty temporary assistance in such a way as not to injure his pride. Lawrence was to raise £400 to buy the manuscript of *The Dawn in Britain* for the British Museum. As soon as this transaction was complete, I was to write and reproach Doughty for not having first thought of his old University, and was to pledge myself to obtain at least as great an amount for the purchase for Cambridge of the Note Books from which *Arabia Deserta* was compiled, the manuscript of that work itself no longer being in existence. This joint project was brought to a successful issue within a few weeks.

As soon as it had been decided upon, Lawrence and I turned to other topics, literary, artistic, political and typographical. When at 2.40 I rose to leave I mentioned that I was going on to Bernard Shaw's flat to bring away one of his three portraits by Augustus John which, after many friendly appeals, he had at last consented to give to the Fitzwilliam Museum. Lawrence immediately expressed the utmost admiration for Shaw, but on my proposing that he should accompany me to Adelphi Terrace as furniture remover, he resolutely declined.

He said that he made a point of avoiding his heroes and that nothing would induce him to meet Shaw for fear of disappointment. However, it was a Saturday afternoon and I was able to assure him in good faith that the Shaws would have gone to their house in the country, and that we should have the flat all to ourselves for our predatory visit. His objections then vanished and we walked together through Trafalgar Square to our destination. But, as good luck would have it, the Shaws had been detained later than usual and we entered just as they were preparing to leave. I introduced my companion. Great warmth was shown on both sides and a friendship was there and then started that was fraught with happy consequences for all three of them. After half an hour the owners of the flat departed and we were left to our job.

We unhooked the picture and I observed a white patch in the background. Moreover, it was unsigned. As Lawrence and I carried it between us to a taxi I proposed a visit to John's studio in Chelsea that these omissions might be repaired. He had been twice painted by John and this time he agreed with alacrity. We were again fortunate. The artist had not gone week-ending. He was busy putting finishing touches to his portrait of Suggia and he showed us this, as well as other works in progress.

But a painter's time is precious towards the end of March and we forbore to occupy too much of it. We left the picture with him.

We were both in high spirits and, as we descended the outside steps of 28 Mallord Street, I said, 'What next?' Lawrence replied, 'We have seen the biggest English dramatist and the biggest English painter of our day. Let us finish up with the biggest English printer!' He had a passion for fine books and I did not need to be told that he alluded to his friend and mine, C. H. St. John Hornby, whose famous Ashendene Press was attached to his house on Chelsea Embankment. It was within an easy walk. He too was at home for us for tea and dinner and this memorable day ended with a feast of medieval manuscripts and of printed books, both ancient and modern, in his splendid library.

ROYAL TANK CORPS

ALEC DIXON

ALEC DIXON. Born 1900. Bank Clerk; Private, Royal Tank Corps, 1919; Corporal, 1923, when he met T. E. L. (then Private Shaw, R.T.C.); Sergeant; Detective Inspector, Straits Settlement Police, 1926-31. Author of *Tinned Soldier*, *Singapore Patrol*, *Extreme Occasion*, etc.

T. E. LAWRENCE went to the Royal Tank Corps Depot at Bovington Camp, Dorset, in the spring of 1923, a month or two after the conclusion of his first spell of service with the Royal Air Force. With the permission of the War Office he joined the Corps as a recruit, giving his name as 'T. E. Shaw'.

No doubt the senior officers of the Depot knew who he was, but some months elapsed before any of the rank and file discovered his identity. Few of the non-commissioned officers and men then serving at Bovington knew very much about the Arab campaign, and what little they may have known they had gleaned from press reports of T.E.'s enlistment in the R.A.F.

Nevertheless, T.E.'s prowess as a motor cyclist soon aroused the interest and curiosity of the camp. His Brough motor cycle was the only machine of its kind in the district, and it was a luxury which represented about two years' pay to his fellow recruits. T.E. was a skilful and fearless rider, and as such he could not hope to escape notoriety among the men of a mechanical corps. (Even when his identity became generally known at Bovington the troops were not unduly impressed by 'the Lawrence legend'; it was 'Broughie' Shaw who claimed their admiration and respect.) At that time he had a side-car attached to the Brough, and he seldom went out for a ride without taking one of the recruits as a passenger. He appeared to derive as much pleasure as his passengers from these jaunts, but I do not think that he took men out in the side-car, as some have suggested, merely to watch their reactions at high speed. T.E. frequently worked and schemed for others' pleasure; seldom, if ever, for his own.

A few days after his arrival at the camp one of the corporals told me that he had been talking to 'that man Shaw' who, in his opinion, was 'just another of those bloody ex-officers chucking his weight about'. This was the common attitude of regular N.C.O.s towards ex-officers who enlisted in the ranks. There were several ex-officers among the recruits, and most of them made themselves extremely unpopular by talking largely of their past military glory. Thus it was that Shaw, whose manner and accent suggested an ex-officer, was at first regarded with suspicion by the N.C.O.s.

However, it soon became apparent that Private Shaw, whatever his past history, had no wish to discuss it. Neither did he attempt in any way to impress N.C.O.s with his scholarship or to exercise any influence over his comrades. He offered no explanation of his presence in the ranks — indeed, why should he? — and devoted himself wholeheartedly (it seemed) to the job of learning to be a soldier. Despite this self-effacement his personality asserted itself: his fellow recruits treated him with respect, even with deference. It was clear to me that T.E. had far more influence over the men of his squad than had the sergeant who commanded them.

Soon after his first appearance on the parade-ground I heard a story that Shaw had served during the War years as a Major on the Intelligence Staff. This turned out to be so near the truth that I imagine — although I never thought to ask him about it — that it must have originated from some hint T.E. had dropped to satisfy local curiosity.

I first met him about three weeks after his arrival at Boving-ton. One day I was standing outside the camp garage when Shaw stopped to buy petrol. He was wearing a black flying-suit and close-fitting helmet, a disguise as effective as the ill-fitting khaki of the recruit. For want of something better to say I suggested that his 'Brough' must be a difficult machine in slow traffic. He grinned. 'Yes,' he said, 'a wild beast! But it gives me an opportunity to see Dorset in my spare time.' As he spoke I was struck by the quality of his voice, and the quiet precision of his speech. There was nothing casual or super-cilious about him. When he grinned, his grim, strained appearance (characteristic of him at that time) gave place to one of boyish eagerness.

This opening led to a long conversation about the surrounding country, and he said that, in his opinion, Dorset was the most delightful of English counties. 'There are moors, downland, sea; and one is within easy reach of an excellent cathedral,' he explained. Then, as an afterthought, he said judicially: 'Of course, it's an oil painter's country.' This talk was scarcely what I had expected from a recruit, even from one who was reputed to have been a major in the Intelligence Service. I was puzzled; and to hold him in conversation I asked why he thought Dorset an oil painter's country. He answered slowly, in short sentences, choosing his words carefully and giving his reasons as one who is not idly interested in the subject, but has thought it over at some length.

We went on to talk of art generally and I was astounded at his wide knowledge of contemporary painting and sculpture. He was, I remember, most enthusiastic about the work of Augustus John, Henry Tuke and John Nash, but doubted whether painters like Orpen, Sargent and Lavery were more than able craftsmen. He admired Epstein's sculpture and said that his head of Joseph Conrad was a delightful character-study. Suddenly, in the midst of some talk about modern etchers, he asked if I were the corporal who went in for sketching. When I told him that I had done a few sketches of the surrounding moorland he asked if he might come to my hut and look them over; of course, I agreed.

As we stood there talking I had a feeling that I had seen Shaw on a previous occasion, in very different surroundings; but, try as I would, I could remember neither the time nor the place. His face seemed familiar, for I had seen several good photographs of Lawrence — yet my memory of those pictures did not help me to identify him.

That evening he came over to look at the sketches, and studied them closely for some time before venturing an opinion. He was inclined to be rather encouraging and said that, for a 'prentice hand, they were very fair work. When he had seen them all he smiled and said decisively: 'Yes; you think in line, and that may not be a good thing . . . always.' Then he caught sight of a pile of manuscript on the table and said quickly: 'Ah! So you write, too?' I was rather more self-conscious about those early literary efforts than I had been about the sketches, but T.E. was not to be put off. He asked if he might read through the MS. in his hut and explained that he was particularly interested because he too was 'learning to write'. (When this conversation took place the 'Oxford' version of *Seven Pillars* was already in print.)

So began a long conversation about books and their writers and I soon discovered his admiration for such men as William Morris, Swift ('hard and brilliant: he wears well!'), E. M. Forster, Thomas Hardy, Norman Douglas, Pater and Cunninghame Graham. I had a small collection of books in my room and, realizing that such a man must find barrack life very dull without books, offered to lend him whatever took his fancy. He grinned and thanked me, remarking that, surely, it was immoral to indulge in 'adventures of the spirit' when one was learning to be a soldier. However, he ran his eye over the books and presently picked out Conrad's *Mirror of the Sea*. He had read it once or twice before, he said, but thought that it might be a safe antidote for too much 'spit and polish'.

I had read everything that Conrad had written and we discussed his work for some time. T.E. called his writing 'slow music' and very dangerous stuff for a young writer to have about him. (T.E. frequently spoke of literature in terms of music and once told me that every novelist should study the movements of a Beethoven sonata before spreading his theme on paper. I believe a similar suggestion is made in one of G. B. Shaw's prefaces, and T.E. may have quoted it unconsciously.) He thought *The Mirror of the Sea* Conrad's best work, fine enough to stand with Melville's *Moby Dick* as the greatest sea book of our time. On another occasion when we were discussing the question of personal honour which Conrad elaborates in *Lord Jim*, T.E. said in a decisive voice: 'Of course Conrad wasn't a gentleman!' I was puzzled by the remark, for it was made without any attempt at irony; and to this day I am not sure about his meaning.

Next day he came to my room with the MS. and, without preliminaries, said that he thought my writing better than my drawing. Then he advised me to break away from the essay form and to try something in the creative line. 'You write too easily,' he said; 'and, as in your drawing, you sometimes think in line. Read plenty of Swift, and some Shakespeare every day — he's sheer music, you know! But you must practise writing, too. Write as if you were using the last drop of ink and the last sheet of paper in the world.' T.E.'s standard was very high, and he applied it in his criticism of everything I wrote. Even when he was working hard on the revision of *Seven Pillars* he was never too busy to read and criticize anything I had written and frequently asked if I had anything more for him to read. His criticisms, if devastating, were always helpful and were often of greater length than the MS. itself. On one occasion, when I had used an adjective of which he disapproved, he wrote in the margin, 'Golly! This is rich — you've out-sheikhed *The Sheikh*'.

That summer we had several outings together on the Brough, two favourite runs being to Salisbury and the Portland Bill. Another favourite spot of his was Corfe Castle, and he usually went there for Sunday morning breakfast if he happened to be free of church parade. Salisbury never failed to delight T.E. and he loved to wander round the Close pointing out the various periods represented in the architecture of its houses. T.E.'s conversation at such times was anything but dull, for he illuminated those architectural talks with amusing, and often ribald, asides on the habits of medieval priests and nobles. Our visits to Salisbury invariably concluded with a run out to Stonehenge, particularly if there had been rain in the late afternoon. He liked to see the place just before sunset when the wet stones took on a purple tinge against the dull sky.

During one of these visits a fleet of charabancs drove into the city and set down a crowd of boisterous sightseers. We had some difficulty in getting to the Close that afternoon and I

remarked, casually, that charabanc trippers were a nuisance.
T.E. took me up at once on this point, saying that the charabanc was a heaven-sent gift to the poorer folk of England since
it gave them an opportunity to see something of their country.
He seldom discussed social problems, and when he did it was
with detachment, for he seemed to be strongly opposed to any
kind of organized social reform. But for the under-dog, as an
individual, he had the keenest sympathy, which he frequently
displayed in queer, angry little comments as we passed through
a village or the dismal slums of some coast town.

It was not until our first visit to Salisbury that I discovered
his identity. We had been discussing life in the R.A.F. and comparing it favourably with our parade-ground antics at Bovington. I went on to say something about 'that fellow Lawrence'
who had enlisted in the ranks of the R.A.F. and speculated as
to his reasons for 'de-moting' himself. I asked T.E. whether
he thought it had been some kind of 'stunt' on the part of the
Air Ministry to stimulate recruiting. This idea struck him as
being amusing: he smiled thoughtfully and said that he didn't
think it could have been that kind of 'stunt'. After a brief
pause he looked me in the eye and said: 'That was a difficult
question. You see . . . I *am* Lawrence.'

After that confession, conversation fell rather flat for a few
minutes. At last he said that, although he knew that the truth
must come out sooner or later, he hoped he would be allowed
to remain T. E. Shaw. And there, for the time being, the
matter ended. I never mentioned Arabia to him until some
weeks later, when he introduced the subject himself and talked
quite freely of his work as archaeologist and soldier. By that
time I had become so friendly with 'Private Shaw' that the
'Lawrence legend' could do little, if anything, to distort my
view of the man himself.

It was obvious to me that legends would follow T.E.
wherever he went, whether he turned brigand or evangelist.
His whole life was a legend; and one had but to watch him
scrubbing a barrack-room table to realize that no army table
had been scrubbed in just that way before: he was the most

conscientious man I have ever known. Neither could he escape becoming a schoolboy's hero, for he never grew old; and he might well have stepped from the pages of Malory. As a soldier in the ranks he was, possibly, unique: he neither drank, smoked, gambled, nor took any interest in women; he played no games, backed no horses, and filled in no football coupons. Yet no one could accuse him of priggishness. T.E.'s unworld-liness gave him a tremendous influence over his comrades; they had no time for 'good' men and knew nothing of saints, but they knew a man when they saw one, and Shaw was their ideal of a man. It is no exaggeration to say that, in his day, Shaw was the most popular man in the camp. Certainly those who professed to dislike him were regarded with suspicion by their comrades.

After telling me of his enlistment in the R.A.F. Shaw went on to say how much he had enjoyed his life with the airmen. He had a great affection for the R.A.F. and hoped that if the War Office was satisfied with his conduct in the Tank Corps he would be permitted to re-enlist at Uxbridge. He had enlisted, he said, because he felt that the barrack-room was very much like a medieval monastery. And, as he explained with a grin, the medieval monastery provided a convenient refuge for disillusioned warriors.

Some time after this conversation I suggested that he would be wise to take advantage of whatever offers of promotion were made to him and pointed out that as an N.C.O. he would not only have a small room to himself but would be free from the more annoying restrictions. He waved the suggestion aside. He was afraid that, in those surroundings, too much freedom would not be good for his peace of mind — 'I am trying to get the taste of Arabia out of my mouth'. He liked the rough-and-tumble of barrack-room life and appreciated the Elizabethan honesty of its talk. Once, when I said that he might find that 'honesty' rather overwhelming at times he pointed out that it was helping to restore his sanity. While I was on leave at Christmas (1924) he wrote to me describing the orgies which had taken place in his barrack-room during the holidays. On

Christmas night all the men of the hut had been 'fighting' drunk, and he admitted that their 'animal spirits' had been too much for him. 'On the following morning,' he wrote, 'they wished for death, and I heartily wished they could have had it.'

From time to time T.E. talked to me of Arabia and particularly of its effect on him. Frequently he impressed on me the folly of prostituting oneself to an alien cause. (His conversations on this theme followed very closely along the lines of his preface to Doughty's *Arabia Deserta*.) He had, he said, learned so well to play the Arab that he found it extremely difficult, if not painful, to return to an outlook or frame of mind that was unaffectedly Anglo-Saxon. I doubt whether his service in the Tank Corps helped very much towards restoring his peace of mind. During those two years at Bovington he seemed strained and, in some moods, ten or fifteen years older than he really was: Arabia seemed to cling to him like Sinbad's old man of the sea. I sometimes felt that his Beduin taste showed itself in his love for the barren, wind-swept moorland of Dorset. He had a particular affection for Egdon Heath and talked delightedly of its 'clean emptiness'. He was not, I think, a man of gardens, although he would ride miles to see rhododendron in flower or to admire a stretch of heather blooming on the fringe of the moorland against a dark wall of pines.

During the first two or three months of his service with the Tank Corps T.E. was not a happy man. He disliked the routine of the depot, with its endless procession of drills and guard duties which were like those of an infantry regiment, and which he had not expected to find in a mechanical corps. Nevertheless, he was a good soldier, although sorely tried at times by those whose delight it was to make life miserable for any recruit who showed more than animal intelligence.

On one occasion I went to his hut after the last parade of the day and found him in bed. He looked haggard and seemed very depressed. When I sat down he apologized for his state and said that he had a touch of fever. He explained, apropos of nothing, that his visit to the Hejaz in 1921 had been almost too much for him and that the mental strain to which he was subjected during the negotiations had been worse than anything he had known during the campaign. He went on to discuss politicians, the War Office and, finally, the Army. He spoke bitterly of 'the stiff professional officers who expect their men to be accomplished housemaids'. Then he became critical of the Tank Corps, saying that it was run by a gang of superannuated infantrymen which overruled those who were trying to build up an efficient service. Tanks, as weapons of war, amused him; he thought them 'museum pieces' and a burden on the taxpayer. He had a weakness for armoured cars, and thought well of the Rolls-Royce model then in general use.

After finishing his recruit training T.E. was sent to the quartermaster's stores as clerk and storeman, and there he found life more to his taste. Conscientious as ever, he applied himself to the new job as wholeheartedly as he had once devoted himself to the cause of Arab freedom. There were no half-measures about 'Storeman' Shaw. Without exaggeration it might be said that he was one of the most efficient storemen the Army has ever seen. The Lieutenant-and-Quartermaster was an old soldier who had risen from the ranks, and he was not slow to realize that T.E. was the type of man who works well without supervision. The atmosphere of the stores suited T.E. and he soon made a friend of the lieutenant. Not only did he make the old man smile at his witticisms — a feat hitherto regarded as impossible by everyone in the depot — but even went so far as to persuade him to listen to a Beethoven sonata played on T.E.'s gramophone in the store.

Soon after this transfer to the stores T.E. settled down to work on the *Seven Pillars,* the revision of which was to occupy most of his spare time for the next two and a half years. This work, and the large amount of correspondence relating to it, prompted him to look for rooms outside the camp area where he might keep his books and to which he might retire in his spare time. Eventually he found a ruined cottage (Clouds Hill) on the southern edge of Egdon, hidden away among the trees and rhododendron bushes. With the help of the Depot Pioneer-Sergeant Knowles, this ramshackle dwelling was converted into añ excellent refuge, the expense of its renovation being met largely by the sale of T.E.'s massive gold dagger. When all was ready T.E. moved in with his books, a few pictures, his new 'Columbia' gramophone and a large quantity of records.

I spent nearly every week-end and two or three evenings a week at Clouds Hill in T.E.'s company. For me this was a very happy time, and it lasted until T.E. left us to rejoin the R.A.F. in August 1925. Two or three other men — sometimes more — of widely differing types were among the regular visitors to Clouds Hill in those days. T.E. was an expert at 'mixed grills' where men were concerned. He presided over the company, settling arguments, patiently answering all manner of questions, feeding the gramophone, making tea, stoking the fire and, by some magic of his own, managing without effort to keep everyone in good humour. There were many picnic meals (stuffed olives, salted almonds and Heinz baked beans were regular features) washed down with T.E.'s own blend of China tea. Some of us used chairs, others the floor, while T.E. always ate standing by the end of the wide oak mantelshelf which had been fitted at a height convenient for him.

Our discussions were many and various and T.E. invariably had the last decisive word. One day, when we were talking of Communism, T.E. shocked the troops by remarking, casually: 'When history comes to be written, Lenin will probably take his place as the greatest man of our time.' To a cavalryman who was bemoaning the passing of horses from the Army, T.E. pointed out that such animals were out of date — 'their acceleration is bad,' he explained solemnly. Once the talk came round to women and someone sought T.E.'s opinion. 'Ah!' he said with a grin, 'women are like horses: they need a large field'.

Sometimes we talked of foreign affairs and of home politics. T.E. thought party politics rather like a circus and he rarely discussed them seriously, although he was keenly interested in individual members of the government. He doubted whether the soldier's vote was anything but a joke, pointing out that the troops were talking football on the night when the post-war Lloyd George government fell. It so happened that T.E. was in London when the new Conservative cabinet was formed and he was one of the first to hear of Winston Churchill's appointment. On his return to camp T.E. came to my hut to tell me all about it. He was in high spirits and more impish than usual. 'Winston's got the Exchequer,' he said as soon as he entered the room. 'There'll be fireworks soon, you'll see. He's very excited about it. When I saw him he was strutting about with a large cigar in his mouth saying 'I'll make the blighters save! I'll make 'em save!'

Once or twice during his service at Bovington T.E. was offered official posts in the Near East and elsewhere, all of which he refused flatly. Only once did he show any interest in these offers. One day at Clouds Hill he said to me: 'They've offered me Egypt.' I suggested that he was just the man for that job. 'No,' he said decisively; 'Egypt would make me vicious. I believe they're talking of Ronaldshay as an alternative. If so they're barking up the wrong tree. George Lloyd's the man for Egypt, and I'm going to tell them so.' This, I believe, he did.

Most of our talks together were of literature, art or music. One day when we were discussing humour in literature T.E. rather surprised me by declaring that the only books which could make him laugh after he returned from the Hejaz were the 'Berry' stories of Dornford Yates. He was fond, too, of W. W. Jacobs and George Birmingham, but his prime favourite was, I think, Richard Garnett's *Twilight of the Gods*. During his stay at Bovington he was very friendly with Mr. and Mrs. Thomas Hardy and visited them frequently. I well remember his delight when G. B. Shaw first came on a visit to Clouds Hill. I was on leave just before this visit and T.E. commissioned me to scour Sussex for eight Jacobean candle-sticks to light the cottage. I managed to get hold of some passable reproductions for the occasion. On returning to camp I heard from T.E. that 'the Great Spadebeard' had warmly approved the housefitting. 'He came in,' said T.E., 'sniffing the air and taking stock of everything like a sergeant-major. I really think he liked it, you know.' He went on to relate how, with some misgiving, he had introduced the Shaws to the Hardys. But the meeting was a success or, as T.E. put it, 'a gorgeous mixture!'

Later, when Mr. E. M. Forster came down for a week-end, we were all impressed to spring-clean the cottage and chop firewood. In the midst of our bustle T.E. sat at a table in the upstairs room fiddling with a wireless set. I said nothing at the time, although I knew that T.E. professed to be contemptuous of wireless sets. But when he put up an aerial and installed the set on a corner table my curiosity was too much for me. 'What's the idea of the wireless, T.E.?' I asked. He looked round with a grin and said: 'It's for Forster ... it occurred to me that he might like to hear Big Ben strike while he is shut out of the world down here.'

T.E. was a very busy man during his last few months at Bovington for he was beginning to print the final (private) version of *Seven Pillars*. He had piles of. correspondence by every post, and all kinds of unlikely people were offering to subscribe to the limited edition. Among these was a major-general at the Staff College who asked if T.E. would pay him a visit some Saturday afternoon. T.E. went to Camberley and arrived at the house just as the general himself was stepping out of his car. T.E. marched up to him, saluted smartly, and said: 'Excuse me, sir — are you General So-and-So?' The general looked T.E. up and down and then snapped: 'Who are you — damn you?' T.E. looked him in the eye and said 'I'm T. E. Lawrence, and damn *you*!' Then he saluted smartly and rode off. Needless to say, the General's name was not on the subscription list.

T.E. collected a large library of gramophone records at Clouds Hill and there was always music there when he was 'at home'. Beethoven, Mozart and Bach were the composers to whom he most frequently turned. Mozart, as he would say, was for his delight, and Beethoven for 'excursions of the spirit'. More often than not he would come into the cottage and put on a record peculiarly suited to his mood of the moment. I knew, for example, when he was feeling particularly disgusted with the animal side of camp life — then it would be either the Bach Concerto in D minor or, if he felt particularly rebellious, a Boccherini minuet which he called 'music on tiptoe'. In the evenings we had a good deal of Beethoven, his favourites at that time being the 5th ('the immortal Fifth'), the 7th, and the Emperor Concerto. Another piece which delighted him was Josef Hofmann's piano solo from 'The Ruins of Athens'. I do not remember that he played a great deal of Bach in those days, although he was fond of slipping concertos and quartets by Haydn in between the longer Beethoven pieces. I don't think T.E. cared very much for Wagner's work, although he liked the 'Meistersinger' and 'Götterdämmerung'. He had a great affection for Delius and was very fond of the 'Hassan' music. It seemed to me, at that time, that T.E. was exploring the world of music, for he was reluctant to name his likes and dislikes among the minor composers. He would, for example, play a Stravinsky piece over and over again and say, finally: 'I don't know that I'm quite sure about Stravinsky.' His attitude to Gustav Holst was similar, although he never seemed to tire of 'The Planets'. Haydn he thought 'restful', but he was not very enthusiastic about Grieg. Although T.E.'s taste in music was excellent, it was unpredictable. One thing, at least, is significant — I never heard him mention Chopin, and as far as I remember there were no Chopin records in his library.

Among the singers he found his greatest pleasure in records of Clara Butt ('that woman's an organ'), Elena Gerhardt and Frieda Hempel. Galli Curci he could not abide. Among the men he liked Caruso, Chaliapine, Hackett and Gervase Elwes — the two favourites being Caruso and Elwes. He loved the older English songs, two of his favourites being 'Cherry Ripe' and 'The Lass of Richmond Hill'. Kreisler, he said, stood head and shoulders above all his contemporaries as a violinist, but he thought that such a magnificent player should play with the background of a full orchestra. T.E. thought that Josef Hofmann was 'the Kreisler of the piano'. He chose his records with great care and almost the only ones that he bought out of hand were recordings of the Lener Quartet.

T.E. seldom talked much of the theatre, although he was enthusiastic about the plays of G. B. Shaw. He would have liked Hardy's *Dynasts* as a film, he said, if it could be produced on similar lines to the Walt Disney cartoons. He suggested that it could be done — at enormous expense, of course — by leading artists: it would encourage British art and would be the first really good film ever made. I think he was quite serious about this because he had, on a previous occasion, pointed out that the Disney method of film-making was the only one possible if the cinema was to be taken seriously.

Just before I left England for the East (1926) I saw T.E. for the last time. We met in the Mall and he was in R.A.F. uniform. He came towards me swinging his swagger cane and looking more cheerful than I had ever seen him. He told me that *Revolt in the Desert* would soon be coming out as a public and abridged version of *Seven Pillars*. When it came out he hoped to be away on the North-West Frontier of India. 'What will you do with yourself there?' I asked. 'I think', he said, 'that if I go to India the safest thing to do is not to see India!' We talked of this and that for a few moments and then apropos of nothing, he said: 'Journalism — I could do it rather well, I fancy, but that is because I have no hope of ever writing anything that matters.' When he discovered that I was still writing a little he advised me not to 'overestimate the importance of doing something — there is no virtue in a long bookshelf.' Before we parted I asked him how he felt about life in the R.A.F. Did he still like it? Was he recovering his 'sanity'? He looked up and grinned. 'I grow older ungracefully,' he said, 'but that is too gradual for me to note, except that my hair is getting frosty, and often I feel tired.'

From a sketch (in oils) of T. E. Lawrence
by Augustus John, 1929

LATER FRIENDSHIPS

MILLICENT CANDY
LORNA NORRINGTON
JAMES HANLEY
H. H. BANBURY
H. E. E. WEBLIN
R. G. SIMS

MILLICENT CANDY. Born 1862. Writes of her late cousin, Miss L. M. P. Black (born 1850, died 1936), who lived in Italy in the wars of Garibaldi and was therefore especially interested in the Arab Revolt; she wrote to T.E.L. after reading the *Seven Pillars of Wisdom*.

IT has so often been said that T. E. Lawrence shrank from making friends, especially with women, that perhaps it may show a different side of that complex but sincere nature if the friendship with an old lady of eighty is revealed.

In 1928 she ventured to write to him sending good wishes for his birthday. He was then in a little fort with twenty or thirty airmen keeping watch on the North-West frontier of India.

In the letter the writer expressed the hope that when he returned to England she might one day see him at her home in Devonshire. He wrote in reply. This was in August, and the press informed us a month or two later that he had been brought back to England.

On November 24th, 1929, a very stormy, wet Sunday, about 4.30 p.m. 'Mr. Shaw' was announced. He came in quite naturally, and did not seem perturbed at finding three old ladies instead of one, was introduced to each and to the dog, who promptly accepted him and licked his hand.

He said he should have come sooner, but the authorities put him on business with the Schneider Cup race and for six months he had been busy about the flying-boats and got so sick of it all that when the race took place he sat in a boat and read a book and did not look at it.

After tea he began to talk about the *Seven Pillars of Wisdom* and said he would much like to see my cousin's copy, as he had none himself, and had not seen the book bound; he left England before it was ready. [*Editor's Note:* Some copies were bound before he left. His own were stored for him.]

We brought it out and had a most interesting talk about it.

He said he had intended to put maps at the beginning, but Kennington said, 'I will do you something better than that,' and produced 'The Eternal Itch', which represents the seven follies of man, and the World, the Flesh and the Devil. The Devil is represented by great swords, against which a little figure with a sword in each hand is battling through to a great light. And when my cousin said to him, 'That is you battling through to the light', he murmured, 'If we don't get burnt up first'.

We talked of many things and subjects and found many mutual tastes, but when I asked him what writer of fiction he placed first he said E. Morgan Forster, and I was obliged to confess I had not read him. 'What should I read?' '*A Passage to India*.' It was a great pleasure to hear him talk. His language was so good and his voice so pleasant, and one realized how far apart the mentality of the half-civilized Arab must have been from his, yet he could enter so wonderfully into their minds.

But he did not want to talk of the East; 'I have done with all that.' He stayed for an hour and a half, then had to leave and rode to Plymouth on the famous motor cycle against a strong head wind with heavy showers, but wrote afterwards saying he had enjoyed it, 'so all the memories of the visit were pleasant'.

He told us if we cared to see the seaplane station at Mount Batten, we were to say we were friends of his and they would find him, or if he was away the Adjutant would show us over.

It was a year before we saw him again, but my cousin and he exchanged letters, for busy as he was he managed to write to her several times in the year.

T. E. Lawrence's next visit was on November 30th, 1930. He had ridden from his cottage in Dorset and looked in at tea time for an hour and a half on the way to Plymouth. He was in good spirits and full of interest in the cottage; the planning of this little home seemed to be giving him real pleasure. He told us he had not been out of camp for three months.

We did not see him again until August 17th, 1931, when he came at his usual hour, and this time it was daylight and he could see the garden and admire the view, which he did.

On this visit my cousin ventured to ask his acceptance of a copy of a book she had written several years before and he took it very graciously and said, 'I shall tell you what I think of it quite sincerely'. I said, 'That is what she would wish'. And he wrote quite a long letter afterwards saying it was a pity she had not written a second book, 'Every first book is over careful of its manners and freedom comes only after it has been bought. Your second book would have been your test. It is everybody's. However, there it is. I cannot preach, having myself ceased after the drudgery of learning to handle words was surmounted'.

When we knew how very busy he was and what a lot of writing and detail his work involved, we were more and more impressed by his kindness in writing the letters which were such a wonderful pleasure to his old friend. I told him once something of that which his kindness and friendship had meant to her and he said, 'Funny, isn't it? But *very nice*'.

The fourth, and alas! as it proved, the last visit he was able to pay us was on Sunday, November 20th, 1932, when he was once more in transit from Dorset to Plymouth.

He had been working very hard but we were all struck by his good spirits and I hoped he was getting over the strain of the War years which had been only too apparent when we first met. He seemed in the prime of life and though he was beginning to talk of 'when he left the Air Force' one felt there must be some future task before him. He could not settle down permanently to the life of a recluse in a two-roomed cottage though for a time the pleasure of making it as perfect as could be would afford the necessary occupation of the leisure to which he looked forward with mixed feelings. We heard of the black cups that were to be made at the Poole pottery to his design and how the furniture was to be built in but no comfortable chair was admissible such as my cousin wished to send him. However, he was to have four cups as sometimes visitors would want tea, so spoons might be the friendship's offering! They were duly dispatched and gave pleasure.

Letters came telling of his work and the constant moving, and as the time drew near the end of his service in the R.A.F. he wrote (January 18th, 1935): 'This going out makes me sad, for I shall miss the work and the companionship . . . After I am free, I shall make Torquay a very early port of call.'

LORNA NORRINGTON, school-girl. Born 1920.
Daughter of Flight-Lieutenant Norrington, Marine Craft,
Air Ministry.

IT was four years ago, when I was eleven years old, that I
had the honour of meeting T. E. Shaw, known of course,
throughout the world as 'Lawrence of Arabia'. He was
serving in the Royal Air Force as an aircraftman, assisting in
the construction of fast motor boats, and was working at Hythe
near Southampton. As I had a half-term holiday from school,
my parents and I visited Southampton. My father promised
me that if the weather was fine I should be able to go out in
one of the boats.

Directly I met Mr. Shaw he fascinated me by his quiet,
determined manner and pleasant demeanour. When my father
asked him if there was a boat available for testing as he wished
to give me a run, Mr. Shaw volunteered to take me out himself
in what is called a dinghy. On this occasion we were out for
about an hour. When we got out of the boat-yard and in
Southampton Water he asked me if I would like to take the
wheel. Naturally I was delighted and before we returned he
had taught me to drive a motor-dinghy. After two or three of
these trips he allowed me to take a boat out on my own while
he followed in another boat to see that I came to no harm.

This half-term holiday at Southampton was followed by
many more. Every time Mr. Shaw took me out in one of the
boats, although his cottage often called him during the week-
ends, he would stay late to give me a run.

The whole time we were out he talked about the surroundings and the boats, but not once about himself or his past.
He told me all about the liners we passed, the year they were
built and anything interesting about them.

On the fifth of November another friend purchased some
fireworks which he took great delight in assisting to explode.
He could talk to me in child's language and always interest me.

JAMES HANLEY, novelist since 1930. Born 1901. Seaman, 1914-24; railwayman and journalist, 1924-30. Author of *Drift* (1930); *Boy*; *Ebb and Flood*; *Aria and Finale*; *Captain Bottell*; *The Furys*; *Men in Darkness*, etc. First met T.E.L. 1930.

THIS is not a criticism, but a reminiscence of Dix's Field, 1931. From my various associations with T.E. I have taken one particular afternoon which we spent together in Devon, and I remember this best because I felt that for once Lawrence was unarmed, that is to say it was the one occasion when I felt he laid himself open, and I rather put this down to the sheer ordinariness of the afternoon. I imagined and I felt too that he had left the various other Lawrences behind him. This seemed excellent to me. For one thing it allowed of quite ordinary conversation and at the same time it gave me a clue to his character. I would even say that I believe that T.E. on that summer afternoon really felt happy, and I may add that he later admitted it. I had heard so much about the man, from so many different sources, that I was completely at a loss to know which of the Lawrences had arrived until some few minutes after we began tea. Well he had left Arabia far behind, his scholarship and his literature. All to the good, there was no thought of 'getting at Lawrence', he hadn't hidden himself anywhere. Our conversation began with ships. This seemed a good omen indeed. He liked ships, little ships, dirty tramps. Getting seawards, so to speak, I had thought of asking him a rather pointed question which had just come into my mind. What were his opinions about the tremendous wave of humanitarianism that was sweeping the modern world? Life was a desperate affair anyhow, but did this humanitarianism blur the real outlines, and so on? But I did not ask him. When I looked across at him the question quite left my mind. He was simple, charming, unaffected, quite ordinary-looking with a cap on, quite the reverse un-hatted. He looked well, and I asked him how he liked being at the aerodrome Was he happy with just ordinary people? 'Quite,' he said, 'I am content, Hanley, I like living with these men.' The essence of a human was still there. 'They may be quite ready to like you, but do you feel one with them? That's the essential thing?' He was. That sounded genuine. Not that my sheer *naïveté* bowed in blind obeisance to his complexity of character; he did seem to me in that hour a happy man. Yes, he liked the Service, he enjoyed every minute of his work. He asked me if I enjoyed writing, and when I said 'Yes', he smiled and shook his head. 'Only people who are worried about something write,' he said. He said this with such sincerity, such genuine conviction, that for a moment I was tempted to believe him, and then it seemed rather silly and we changed the subject. We had a common interest in Hugo Wolf and talked of him for some time. Talking of Gerhardt's singing of his songs he remarked, 'She's good, but she lacks devil'.

He sat in an arm-chair drinking a cup of tea and eating a slice of bread and butter. A small terrier belonging to the house sat on his knee, but he would not have it removed, and it seemed to prefer his knee to anybody else's. During the course of conversation he said he felt best when he was moving about amongst crowds, thinking of nothing in particular, excepting patterns, shapes and colours. This merging of a single identity in the mass seemed to me a clue as to what he was after. He does not want to advance, I thought, but is slowly retreating, as though he were moving quietly back now over old ground hitherto traversed too quickly. He had about eighteen more months of Service life still to go — eighteen months of a rhythmical, austere and ordered state of being that he hated to give up. He said he should go to his cottage in Dorset and clean it up a bit, but beyond that he did not seem to wish to speak. Neither did we talk about the past, except that he mentioned the Arabian campaign as something he would like to forget. Books of course we talked about, it is impossible to keep them out of conversation nowadays, but mostly we talked of things, ships, countries, motor boats, aeroplanes, waves, forgotten roadways and canals. I enjoyed that meeting. It had a kind of effortless simplicity, neither of us was ready for the other, so to speak, neither was armed with poise. He said he would come and stay with us in Wales, but he never came, and I never worried him to come. So my last vision of Lawrence was roaring away on his motor bike, under the chestnut trees of a little square in Exeter.

REGIMENTAL SERGEANT-MAJOR H. H. BANBURY, Royal Tank Corps; Military School, 1900; enlisted 1905 (Dorset Regiment); Tank Corps, 1917-35. Meritorious Service Medal, Long Service Medal. First met T.E.L. 1924, in Dorset; also with him at Miranshah and Razmat.

I WAS one of the half-dozen who came under T.E.'s influence soon after he joined the Royal Tank Corps. A chance appointment with E. M. Forster gave me the introduction to T.E., and no second invitation was required when he asked me to come again, for he exercised a hypnotic effect on me. The impression persisted in every meeting, and having then been among soldiers for twenty years, it was not a feeling to be imagined. There was no propulsion in this feeling, but rather the sensation that he was deliberately playing down to me to lead me: yet in doing so he slowed my brain and tied my tongue: always there was an intense self-consciousness, a littleness of mind in the presence of a great brain force. I felt a mental pigmy in his company, even to our last meeting shortly before his end. Others of the circle have told me that they felt the same, and my wife, after her only meeting with him, spoke of the magnetic attraction of his eyes.

T.E. gave me great kindness, and I found, and saw, that his pleasure was to please others. From him was received the greatest of all gifts, the opening of the book of learning, leading me to the things that had been beyond my reach. Knowledge of him can be summed up in his intense concentrated energy; his generosity; his love of the beautiful, and his simplicity.

With him, time never lagged, he was always busy with books, music, talk or writing. He never fussed, and as time passed, so an understanding came of how he was able to carry out his many activities. When writing he tolerated no interference; 'I am busy' killed any further question, though once at Miranshah he left even his writing when he found that my

307

visit was for only half an hour. His intensity was far more evident when he was checking the proofs of the *Seven Pillars*, for he would sit with bowed head and clasped hands searching for the exact word or phrase that he sought till the sweat stood out on his forehead and neck. There was physical and mental agony in those hours of silence. He questioned me once to check the date of the eclipse when he was dealing with the attack on Akaba: 'Some people will be severe on that!' he said, and seemed relieved when I referred him to *The Times* or the nautical calendar for the year. A magnificent gesture of ignorance, giving the simpleton power to shine.

Even his jollying in our company was a trial of strength, for every energy went into these wrestles, and his spare frame took all our efforts to subdue; and competition with a pistol was severe, for he concentrated to overcome my highest standard: and succeeded everywhere.

The greatest pleasure was to get him to turn to books, for there he gave me freely of his time and learning. His criticism was always comparative; it was not sufficient for him to laud a book for itself, but where it stood in comparison with others, so that he was for ever leading me into wider fields. And books were not for adoration, but for enjoyment, for the giving of pleasure over the widest area. He lent freely — 'many fall by the wayside: I hope into better hands than mine' — and gave as freely. Knowing that my collection of Montague was incomplete he offered me his copy of *Dramatic Values* to complete it; my pleasure to refuse. He felt for the heart of beauty in books, and added to it as he read aloud some particular passage that appealed. As he first read Binyon's *The Sirens* he fairly purred over the second chapter of the first part. 'How Thomas Hardy would enjoy that; may I take it to him.' He would send me a parcel of books when in India with an admonition to 'bestow the load on whomsoever you please'.

In all our conversations he gave the impression of being self-less; his thoughts were constantly devoted to others. Only once did I know him to deviate, and that when discussing marriage. 'I suppose I should become bored with her in six

months, as with all things. And then where would *she* be?'
By the ending he regained his standard.

His hours at Miranshah were as busy as those at Clouds
Hill, for he was the clerk of the small detachment, besides
being the ration clerk. He was happy there, for he was
immune from visitors. The discomforts of the barren place
were overcome by the translation of the *Odyssey*. The limit of
his travel was to the post office situated in the barracks of the
Tochi Scouts, his private walk being over the dividing wall,
across the roof of the servants' quarters, and so to the post
office — about two hundred yards. He kept fit by walking in
the compound, generally spending two hours a day bareheaded
in the sun. This he practised in case of emergency — 'active
service in Mesopotamia or elsewhere, where I could not wear
a sun helmet. Our heads are harder than the natives; certainly
more useful!' His opinion of Indians was not high, while he
refused to use the common Urdu — 'a filthy language' he
termed it.

The insufferable heat of the room or office in the fort never
disturbed him; he spent the hours at work while most of his
comrades slept during the day. My visits to him were joyous
for both. Greatly he laughed at my criticism of *Imaginary
Conversations*; and he finished his talk with a description of
Landor as 'a grumpy old caviller; a man who argued with
everyone and then had his last fling with a gorgeous poem',
referring, of course, to 'I Strove with None'.

T.E. was a perpetual mask, hidden behind the actual
present. There was no past, no remembrance of things which
did not concern what was being done or discussed while we
were together, and no amount of leading would ever get him to
talk of things done. Only the present and the future mattered
to him, and the realization of this saved him from many painful
questionings. To me, it seemed that there was intense agony
of mind in discussion of the past, and as the history of the Arab
campaign was opened to me early in our acquaintance, I knew
the physical and mental anguish endured, and so refrained
from asking for information. There was no pose in this. Soon

after our meeting, we discussed Lucas's 'L'Envoi', and he read it over to me. The last line, 'Only our pain is never masquerade', was spoken with such force and intensity as to make me realize that there was an expression written by another which he felt fitted with his own feeling, and in uttering it he expressed his own self. Strangely enough they were the last words I heard from him, for he looked them up to check a reference.

At that last meeting he was a changed man; he was showing signs of age, and expressed disappointment at leaving the R.A.F. 'I wish I could go on for another twelve years,' he said in a sad tone. He was restless and tired, and knew that he needed rest before recommencing writing. He busied himself with his hands, building over with brick and tile the wooden bungalow which so nearly opposed his own cottage, without plans, to make it different from any other house, jesting at the difference, and hoping to surprise the county surveyor when he came. In this he was as thorough as in all other things, for he had the mastery of stresses and angles that many a master builder would envy.

As he knew me, so he treated me. There was no affectation in his manner, for we were equals; he a studious airman, I a studious soldier. Rank counted nothing either way.

He summed us all up in one expression. 'There are the real and unreal,' he said; 'the real eat anything, while the unreal require chicken followed by a Napoleon brandy.' He bridged the classes: very successfully, knowing the strength and weakness of both.

His writings, and the knowledge of the man showed me how complete he was in all things that he attempted; while the friendship he gave me was so intense that it leaves a hole in my life never to be filled. To have known him is to be rich; to have served him my pleasure; and the memory of him has deepened my belief that 'God created man in his own image', for, except in his own unfruitful body he beautified life.

LIEUTENANT-COMMANDER H. E. E. WEBLIN,
R.N. (Retired), Air Ministry. Born 1897. Regular Officer,
Royal Navy, 1912-22 (submarine service after Gallipoli campaign); Royal Air Force, 1923-33 — served in 'Iraq and Egypt;
ground survey for Cairo-Cape Flight; in charge of Marine Craft
Detachment, Bridlington, when he first met T.E.L. and worked
with him daily there.

As an A.C.1 (first grade Aircraftman) on duty, T. E. Shaw was a model of correctness, always smartly dressed and punctilious over saluting, showing the utmost respect to officers and N.C.O.'s. In this he was serving intentionally the double purpose of setting an example to the airmen and disarming the criticism of those who disapproved of his position in the ranks. The day he joined the detachment he said: 'I feel it my duty to point out to you, sir, that I am only an aircraft hand and therefore not eligible to take any of your boats to sea, and I make a point of never doing so unless there is a qualified coxswain on board.'

By the example he set to the other airmen he definitely raised the standard of efficiency in the detachment and at the same time got on well with the men. After about two weeks at Bridlington, he said to me with a smile, 'I have only been here a few weeks but they are all doing exactly as I tell them already. I suppose one day some N.C.O. will tell me to mind my own business — but I doubt it!'

This influence was not confined to the airmen but to all who came in contact with him, whether civilians or serving officers. He was often present at conferences or discussions with officers of all ranks, during which he would listen quietly until everyone had said their say and then with a respectful 'If I might be allowed to suggest, sir . . .' he would present what was obviously the best solution of the problem under discussion. This suggestion was invariably adopted.

I saw many examples of the rapid conversion of officers of various ranks who were prejudiced against him due to his position in the Air Force. A certain officer was visiting the detachment and on being told that Shaw hoped to see him in order to put forward some suggestion, said curtly, 'When I want the advice of an A.C.1 I will ask for it', and added remarks about the whole position being ridiculous. The following morning having noticed the two together in the shed for about an hour, I asked Shaw if he had found the officer amenable. 'That is hardly the word for it,' he replied, 'he ate out of my hand, in fact, he is on the telephone to headquarters at the moment ordering everything we want.' I remarked, 'This is quick work, because only last night he said that when he wanted the advice of an A.C.1 he would ask for it'. At this Shaw smiled and said, 'He *has* asked for it, sir, and had it!' The following night they were dining together.

He was the greatest assistance in the detachment. His knowledge of every subject that cropped up, both technical and otherwise was astounding and could always be applied practically. This covered such diverse subjects as photography, wireless, handling of speed boats under all weather conditions and even such things as the most efficient colour for painting bombing targets. It was in each case backed by practical experience and I have yet to find an instance where it was not correct.

While at Bridlington he successfully avoided publicity and the manner in which he went about unrecognized was extraordinary considering the number of holiday-makers who were daily on the pier. The only occasion on which I remember his being recognized produced an example of his quick wit. He was in dirty overalls stripping an engine in the open hold of a vessel alongside the pier, when one of two sailors from H.M. ships visiting the port, remarked to the other 'You see that chap down there with fair hair? That's Lawrence of Arabia.' Shaw looked up with annoyance and instantly said, 'I thought you fellows belonged to the silent Navy!'

His visits to our house gave us great pleasure. He would come to tea often, and sometimes to an evening meal. Always in the same off-duty 'uniform' — a sport's coat, high-necked jersey and grey flannel trousers. He had one peculiarity which always amused us. If he were late for any reason, he never made excuses or apologies as would most people, and also when he decided he had had enough of us, without any preliminaries, he would get up and leave, sometimes finishing a sentence on his way out.

We found him easy to entertain, because he loved to talk, whether of art, books, music, politics — or himself. We had always understood that it was dangerous to mention the Revolt and so were careful to avoid the subject until we found that he was quite willing to discuss it. He told many an amusing and interesting story of his experience, and once remarked that his past was like a tin can tied to a dog's tail — whatever he did it rattled. Later I came across this same expression in a book by D. H. Lawrence, apropos of a character who was likened to T.E. I wondered if he had borrowed the phrase, or whether it was just a coincidence that he used it.

His opinions of public personages were freely expressed. He had no respect for 'big noises' as such, and told us many rather irreverent stories of some of them. He would repeat his stories if requested, with perfect good humour, always in the same detail and with the same sense of enjoyment.

His keen sense of humour is well known, and we saw many examples of it. I once had occasion to write and inform him that on running the trials of an engine, which he had fitted with another airman, a part was found to be missing and that the corporal in charge blamed him. This called forth the reply 'I am sorry about the manifold washer. Two great Oxford scholars, called Liddell and Scott, worked for twenty-five years and produced what is still the world's standard Greek dictionary, then Scott died. As time passed and the users of the book now and then drew the University's attention to a misprint or error in the book, Liddell used to sigh and shake his head, "Ah yes — poor Scott, still it may have been mine!" '

The things which particularly impressed me were his unfailing patience and good humour under all conditions; his readiness to give help or advice, and the fact that he never allowed his mental superiority and self-confidence to be obtrusive with people who were his inferiors in intellect and education.

We who met him during the last few years of his life, knew and loved him as a man called Shaw, and could never look upon him as 'Lawrence of Arabia' because in some inexplicable way he would not allow us to do so. I always felt that his greatness was entirely in himself and not in the spectacular achievements of his life.

FLIGHT-LIEUTENANT R. G. SIMS, Royal Air
Force (Retired). Born 1885. Bank clerk; secretary of engineering
company; Olympic Games gymnastic team, 1908; fitter, R.A.F.;
Engineer Officer, in France, 1918; Equipment Officer, Adjutant.

WHEN I was posted to Catfoss, the R.A.F. started armed
motor boat bombing, and to my great joy, I heard
that Aircraftman T. E. Shaw was coming to Bridlington to give any help he could in the running and policy of the
boats. One memorable day he came to Catfoss, and I saw and
heard him speak at a conference. He was a small, slight man,
singularly well developed, wearing no medal ribbons, but
otherwise in very smart airman's walking-out dress. He
spoke in a very low distinct voice — I have never heard him
speak otherwise — but there was no question that any officer
could speak to him, or get him to speak, except on the business
for which he had appeared.

Several times after this I spoke about Service matters to
him on the telephone, and I loved to hear that beautifully
quiet, distinct voice answering with 'Bridlington R.A.F.
detachment, A.C. Shaw speaking'. Then he would answer
very politely, giving the information required in the fullest
manner, and the fewest possible words, calling me 'sir' most
meticulously at every sentence. I never heard him address an
officer otherwise.

Whilst I was in 'Iraq I took a lot of insect photos with a
camera I had been at some pains to make, and later I wrote
a short description about each insect, and bound them in book
form. One of my friends told me that T.E. would like to have
my book. I packed it up and sent it on. I waited. Months
passed, I still waited. At last a registered parcel came.
Eagerly I unpacked it; with increasing dismay I looked
through page after page, thinking that there might be a short
note. There was nothing at all.

The next day I received a telephone message that Aircraftman Shaw was in Bridlington, and would come over and see the

Adjutant as soon as he could. I rang up Bridlington, and asked for A.C. Shaw. He was out on the boats, so I left a message saying that if he could not manage transport from there (I knew he could not) I would arrange it from here. (I had a baby Ford of my own.)

The next day I heard nothing, so I rode over and went to the large dark garage where the boats were out for overhaul under his charge as representing the Air Ministry. I saw two men standing in the lee of a boat, and went up, meaning to ask them where Shaw was. As I got near them I noticed a small man in a rough fisherman's jersey, reading a blue print nearby, and although I could not see his face, which he kept completely hidden with the print, I knew, without hesitation, who it was. I stood respectfully in front of the blue print. This was slowly lowered, and a pair of the bluest, most flashing eyes I had ever seen blazed forth, whilst a vast forehead, equal in size to the terrific chin beneath, simply radiated scorn and hate at me. Although this reception should have struck terror I afterwards realized that it did nothing of the sort. I was full of admiration and joy at the sheer beauty of his face. It was that of a very small boy, angelically fair, from whom another boy has just pinched an apple. I murmured that I was Flight-Lieutenant Sims of Catfoss. Instantly the glare disappeared, and a slight smile replaced it (incidentally, from looking like a very young boy, he assumed the appearance of a man of about thirty or so) and he said with an engaging air: 'Oh, I am so sorry, sir, but for a moment I took you for a reporter.' He then said how sorry he had been to have kept the book for so long, but that it was one that had to be taken in homœopathic doses, and that he did not want to return it until he had finished it. He went on to say that the cost of publication would be very high, although he would like to have it published.

After a few minutes I asked him if he would come back to Hornsea with me for lunch. He engagingly excused himself on the pleas that (i) he was not dressed for the part; (ii) he felt dirty and shopsoiled, having clambered over the boats for most of the morning; and (iii) he had to be back at Bridlington within two hours. I suggested use of our bath-room and indicated the baby Ford. He listened with gravity. 'Then all that remains is for me to say thank you,' he said.

I asked him if he would not drive, but he did not drive cars, he said. Fast motor cycles he liked, but a car was of too stable an equilibrium for him to enjoy driving. He gave me the impression that he was slightly nervous of cars, and I do not think I took my eye off the road then, or at any time afterwards when he was my passenger.

On arriving at Hornsea he looked at our cottage, and stood for a moment in a favourite position, holding his left fist tightly with his right, with the index finger of his right hand bent and pressed against his chin. He then said: 'Ah, yes. Cobble built, repaired with brick facings, about sixteenth or early seventeenth century. Nice cottage.' He had an attractive way of saying Yes, slightly biting the first part, and making the end a little bit sibilant. His voice and choice of words were both quite perfect.

He set my wife, child, and dog, all at ease immediately. After lunch we ensconced him in a large chair and listened open-eared to his tales of books, people, music, and R.A.F. experiences, and very much against the grain at 3.15 I reminded him of the time, whereon he pulled himself out of his chair in one movement like a steel spring unbending, and said everything had conspired to make him forget that there was such a thing as work. He shook hands very cordially, and thanked us.

I duly delivered him at his garage, and he again shook hands. On no other occasion did he — or of course, did we — offer our hands, and we got the impression that he did not like even to be brushed against or touched. We used to stand very clear from doorways when he passed through. We often speculated on the reason for his shaking hands on that first occasion: we could not imagine his performing the most insignificant action thoughtlessly or without a sufficient reason, and doubtless he had one in this case. Also I firmly believe that he meant to come to see us that day, exactly as it turned out, and he foresaw, possibly within certain definite limits, future events and occurrences in a manner that was perfectly normal to himself, but which in our ignorance we might term psychic.

Neither that night, nor any other night when he had seen us, did we get to sleep until the early hours of the following morning. Words cannot describe the terrific charm of T.E. He walked as on silent wheels, perfectly smoothly, without any perceptible jolt. In fact, he made no noise at all. I never heard him clear his throat, cough, sneeze, or even splash about in the bathroom. His voice was particularly quiet, but so clearly did he speak that one never lost a syllable. His face was roughened and red, or as he referred to it, sandblasted, but although we knew he was about forty-five or so, the vivid impression he gave us was of eternal youth, and very beautiful youth at that. He emanated a mental stimulus that affected everyone, especially if he spoke.

For three days I kept silent and then rang him up. He started at once to talk of the progress he was making on his boats, and we got caught up in a welter of detail as to stores and gear that he wanted. I suggested his coming over again, but he regretted that he could not see his way for a day or two, and then I mentioned that there was a Celebrity Concert, conducted by Sir Henry Wood, in Hull, on the following Thursday. He considered for a moment and seemed to think that was quite an important matter, but was uncertain how to get back to Bridlington. I made the obvious suggestion, or as an alternative, would he stay the night, and I would deliver him to the garage by nine o'clock the next morning? He then proceeded to do a little sum. 'This seems to be rather over-driving your car and kindness. It is thirty miles return to Bridlington, and doing it twice over makes that sixty miles, just to get me into Hull. Does not that seem a lot of miles to eat up?' Again I answered in the only obvious manner, and he agreed. He never again mentioned the sixty-mile journey his visiting us entailed on our car. I just called for him, and took him back to the hotel as a matter of course. He had a very subtle way of paying a compliment by *not* saying or doing. Also for the few little services it was our pleasure to render during that winter he gave no thanks: it was perhaps his unique manner of an admission of friendship.

The concert to which we took him was good. The Schubert, he considered, had 'just one piece of sugar too much'. We gathered he thought as little of singing as we did ourselves. One rather futuristic piece, that conveyed little to me beyond discordant notes, I said I was unable to appreciate, to which he replied that it was perfectly conventional music underneath. The overlay was modern style only, but it was quite good basically. He also said, looking straight at me, 'The tympanum's very good'. Now, I am not at all sure that I know what a tympanum is, although one guesses it is a drum of sorts, so I simply answered that I knew too little to judge either the piece itself, or the individual instruments. He continued to look at me for a second or so, and then looked away. I remember this very distinctly, and rather feel it was a test remark. Answering as I did only proved ignorance, with which he was never impatient, but to profess a knowledge which was absent, was one of the things he detested. Once or twice afterwards I think he made somewhat similar test queries or remarks. He loathed falsity and hypocrisy, but tolerated broadly all well-meant errors. The truth never shocked him, but the aping of truth seared.

After three or four visits, we noticed a certain relaxing of his manners and body. Before, he had talked almost incessantly except occasionally when one of us said anything; then he would turn to the speaker and gaze almost embarrassingly until one had finished.

He enjoyed quite large meals, did not seem to care what was given to him to eat, but always finished everything. We soon learned not to ask him if he would have so and so, but just helped him to what we thought he would like. Occasionally, when offered a choice, we could see it was an effort to decide and the later custom of giving him a good helping was obviously to his satisfaction. He drank nothing but water, tea, and coffee. Smoked only two cigarettes yearly — one on Christmas Day and one on Easter Day, not because he liked to smoke, but because whilst doing so, he could feel how lucky he was that it was not his habit as a general rule. He liked fruit, especially apples. These he would eat holding in his hands. After getting close to the core all round, he invariably ate that too, including the pips, but he once explained to us, he *never* ate the stalk.

Before he rose in the mornings, I took him up a cup of tea and some fruit. He selected one or the other — never both. It was a delight to knock at his door and hear that very low quiet voice say 'Come in' and see him, fully awake, not at all tousled, and smiling a greeting. My small son would seize the opportunity of rushing in; we would hear low voices, until we thought it only kind to call him away.

At tea, he would always take a very large slice of cake for my dog, giving it, if possible, without that polite animal thanking him. He was not an animal lover in the full sense. It may be that either naturally, or perhaps because he wished, he prevented people, animals, or things from becoming near enough to him to interfere with his perfect focus of them. It must be very difficult to be popular and to live one's own life.

The first week-end he came arrayed peerlessly in a French print shirt with starched collar to match. Then he was being very polite and formal. He never afterwards wore a collar. The fisherman's jersey was his standard attire. I mentioned that I would start wearing one of a gay colour myself, but he was comically impressive. 'No. You are in a very important position,' he said. 'It would never do.' This was accompanied by an engaging grin.

He complained that the neck of his jersey stretched and did not come back, so that a draughty gap was caused. He suggested that necks and wrists should be sprayed with cellulose or other elastic fluid, so that the yarn would always remain elastic. We suggested that there were jerseys obtainable

with an especial yarn woven into the neck which already had
that effect. On his next visit, we produced the actual article,
with which he was as pleased as a small boy, trying it on at
once and approving its quality.

He was worried as to what slippers or shoes he would wear
at Clouds Hill. If he wore socks, they would be more articles
to wash — he contemplated doing his own — and yet without
them, leather shoes were uncomfortable, but footgear would be
necessary, as he would have to go in and out of the cottage.
We said nothing, but remembered seeing advertisements of
high sheepskin slippers with zip fasteners and rubber soles.
We got a pair and he came downstairs the next morning without his socks, to 'show us how comfortable they were'.

We did not see him wearing a hat any time. He told us that
in India topees were quite unnecessary. A Warrant Officer
had rebuked him for not wearing his topee in Karachi, when
he admitted that he had only been in India for two days.
Afterwards this officer learned that T.E. had been in the East
for over twelve years, and felt that his leg had been cruelly
pulled, but discovered that T.E. was T.E., and dropped the
matter. Later, in Miranshah, T.E. taught all the airman to go
without topees, and he described how an officer, an old friend,
once visited the station, and on landing called T.E. up, and
said, 'Please, Shaw, may I wear my topee?'

We had solemn discussions as to his household arrangements in Clouds Hill. He would not have tea or coffee in the
cottage, except a certain brand of tea which he would obtain
from a friend. One pinch of it makes a pot of tea that fills the
house with its aroma. This tea he would screw up in small
doses, and put so many doses in a tin box, sealing the lid with
surgical plaster, so that he could keep it practically airtight,
and almost indefinitely. He was pleased when this idea had
been evolved, as otherwise he had thought of soldering a
large number of very small tins, which would have occupied
limited stowage space as well as being rather laborious.

He had two flea bags in the cottage. His own, with a needle
and red cotton, he had embroidered MEUM. For the guest who

blew in, he had prepared another, similarly embroidered TUUM. The bags were complete with all necessary sleeping clothes, and were zipped all round, so that to make your bed, you zipped, unzipping to have it all ready for use. The TUUM bag he would hand to his guest, to park anywhere inside or outside the cottage that seemed a suitable place in which to sleep away the night. T.E. himself would await his guest's selection and bed himself down in the next best place.

Eggs he would not include in his diet. Clouds Hill was remote, withdrawn, and utterly restful. Eggs meant chickens. Chickens meant noise. So eggs were ruled out. Milk he could obtain with ease. One meal daily he could foresee, obtained at the camp of the Tank Corps. For the rest he would eat bread, and water, from his own spring, would be his staple drink.

Washing up should present no difficulties whatever. All that is required is a gently sloping brick path. On this path you put the articles to be washed up. You then get a kettle of *boiling* water, and with a two-foot head, project a stream from it on to the articles, which are thereby not only washed, but dried. But the water must be boiling.

For amusement and recreation, he would have books. People sent him books for review, criticism, friendship, and the writing of forewords. Of all the books that had ever been written in the world, he had found that there were scarcely 1200 that merited re-reading. How to dispose of surplus books at Clouds Hill would be a problem. In town the method that he had evolved was to take a midnight stroll, and drop unwanted volumes in letter boxes. He marked out promising boxes of a large size on front doors during the day time, mentally measuring the slots suitable for the reception of books on his disposal list. He had one or two especially favourite letter boxes in town, that received his volumes with a very satisfying boom; these he frequently patronized.

We suggested that he would have to limit his correspondence, as a man with so small an income could not pay shillings daily on postage, quite apart from letter paper. Yes, that was certainly a matter that would become most important. A suggestion that he should not pre-stamp his letters, thus allowing the recipients the privilege of paying double postage on receipt, was dismissed after only a second's consideration. The suggestion that printed cards be obtained, telling all and sundry that he would pare his correspondence to the minimum in future was very favourably received.

One of our most prized possessions is a letter addressed to The Sims Family and Dog; it is written on a card, printed: — *To tell you that in future I shall write very few letters. T. E. S.* This printing he crossed out in China ink, whilst on the other side among other things, he says he has managed to live on 22*s.* weekly as far as Class 'C' stores are concerned. This is an historic Air Force joke. Class 'C' stores are within certain limits looked on as things that are completely expended in use, petrol, nails, oil, metal polish, etc. Hence Class 'C' stores are called consumable. It is a very good joke in the ranks to remark, in the hearing of the cook, that the meat cannot be a 'C' store because, as everyone knows, 'C' stores *are* consumable.

I think T.E. dragged in the old R.A.F. joke, for the sake of its association at a time when he was feeling rather at a loose end. He had just left the ranks. I think he had anticipated, when he joined as an airman, a twelve years' purgatory. To his surprise, after the first difficult year or two, he found that life was pleasant, ordered, free from worry, without responsibility, and that his brother airmen respected and admired him: they and most of the non-commissioned officers called him 'Mr. Shaw'. In addition, the beautiful fast motor boats, and the understanding officials at the Air Ministry, delighted his heart and enabled him to have a paradoxically important hand in developing that branch of the R.A.F. which still advances with little alteration along the broad path that he did so much to lay down.

On one occasion, an officer of very high rank came to inspect things. On that day, T.E. had arranged to let me call for him in the afternoon for the week-end. I arrived at the garage about three o'clock. It was dark, forbidding, and vast. At first it seemed nothing stirred or lived there, but when the eyes and ears lately confronted with sights and sounds of the busy world became more used to the gloomy silence, a faint light was visible at the far end, and a very low murmur became audible. On tip-toe I approached. Surely, one thought, the ceremony is taking place. A slight upright blue-clad figure stood high up in the bows of a boat, with one electric light turning his hair into gold. He was giving a masterly lecture on the major features of the boats. The officer was listening in rapt silence, supported by two other Air Ministry officers. Behind them stood the contractor and engineer, one or two workmen with bared heads stood hushed on each side, and a couple of odd airmen formed the rest of the congregation. With infinite solemnity the procession visited boat after boat. The Air Ministry officials and the contractor occasionally breathed a quick word to T.E., prompting him so that he should not omit to describe, to their delight, one or two little points, that they could never tire of hearing, and patently desiring him to show off their boats, of which they were proud, and also himself, whom they worshipped. It was a ceremony of pure delight. T.E., perfectly sure of himself, and of every detail in his boats, was the complete encyclopaedia, as well as the beautifully respectful airman.

He was very vague and undetermined as to his future, after R.A.F. days had terminated. He had heard of a possible job, as night watchman. Good pay, free lodgings and coals, hours such that he could always go to concerts in the day time, and see pictures in daylight. He would not accept any position as an Air Force officer. As such he could not put on overalls and work on engines, or handle tools. He loved tools. Once when examining mine, he approved a very nice stainless steel saw, and said, 'I have one in the cottage, only it is bigger than this'. My small son would exult similarly on possessing a pocket knife with one blade in it more than in that of another boy.

During the course of his service, he had acquired as perfect a fitter's tool kit, of his own, as could be possessed. As many as possible of his tools were made of stainless steel. It is curious how often he mentioned stainless steel, chromium plate, and zip fasteners. The cleanness of the two former, and the efficiency of the last, appealed to him. He said what beautiful things the world contained, in the way of materials. Steel. Unpainted woods. Bakelite. Coloured glass. How in a few years, people would insist on surrounding themselves with those things instead of the awful painted woodwork, coloured wallpaper, and common decorated monstrosities now so usual. People would insist on a large number of non-working hours. They would insist on Music and Art generally being available for them at very frequent intervals. He remained silent for a few moments, and then with a serious smile, and an impish twinkle in his eye, said: 'In a hundred years from now, no one would think of sitting in a squalid little room like this.' In our own drawing-room and before our very faces, if you please.

With children, his manner was perfect. I came into the room one day, and found T.E. and my small son discussing the comparative merits of certain persons included in a book entitled *Heroes of Modern Adventure*. He gave thumbnail sketches of each, as he came to them, and at last: 'Oh, John, what have we here?' he said. 'Not quite right. Bad shot. Very inaccurate.' He was reading 'Lawrence of Arabia'. 'Give me a pencil and let us make notes.' So John produced one of his very many pencils, and T.E. wrote in the margins.

It happened that a boy friend had lent us, that Christmas, three books of which one was identical with John's. To our horror, we found that T.E. had noted the loaned book. We dared not tell John, but the next time T.E. came, I explained, and would he mind? He instantly took a pencil and made notes in John's own book which are slightly different, and a little fuller than those he had previously inserted in the other book. Later, although we felt that he did not want to meet anyone at all, he agreed instantly that this boy should come and dine with us, to round off the affair, and that night, it seemed that there were three, very young and lovable little boys, who, as a treat, had been allowed to sit up to dinner with us.

As a rule, he seemed quite happy to sit still, talking or

remaining silent. Occasionally he would inquire about local places. As a result we took him to Beverley Cathedral of which he approved, especially of the pinched pillars. He had heard of The Land of Nod, and so we took him there. What would have been to us merely a squalid little farm in untidy surroundings leapt into life under his vivid description as one of the smaller Roman forts, complete with guard house, earthworks, ditches, and a very obvious straight Roman Road leading to it. York Minster he loved. 'Just fancy hearing Beethoven's symphonies in a building like this. It would again be crowded with people, instead of the handful that comes. These lovely old places should be used for music, and beautiful pictures.'

He said he would take a holiday in Iceland at some date. On our asking why, he gave a photographic description of the land that made it seem to be one of the most interesting to visit. In reply to our inquiry as to the language question, he mentioned casually, that as he liked the look of the words in some Icelandic sagas, he had taught himself Icelandic when he was twelve years old. The possibility of forgetting any little bit of anything he had once learned, appeared to strike him as an entirely novel idea.

Every time we saw him, he would give us fresh cause for admiration, respect, and love, and although sometimes he was obviously more troubled about some problem of his own than at others, he was invariably the courteous, wise, understanding, and utterly regal youth, in whose presence, the foolish became profound, the ugly, beautiful, and the unattractive, charming.

On Tuesday, 26th February, 1935, Shaw was 'struck off strength' of the Bridlington Marine Detachment. In the third week of February, T.E.'s gratuity due after completion of twelve years' service was credited to him. He asked about half a dozen brother airmen to indulge in a mild celebration, and chose a visit to a picture palace. T.E. was careful to see that his guests all had cigarettes, and he was not in the least different from usual. After the show, he said that he very seldom went to the pictures. The last film he saw was 'Cavalcade', in which the photography was excellent, but the acting did not equal it.

In the film shown, 'Cleopatra', he considered both photography and acting to be one hundred per cent.

He talked much to his airmen friends during that week of his cottage, describing his work in it, and discussing details for increasing his available power from the small spring which fed his bathing pool. He hoped by complete conservation of its energy to work a small dynamo for lighting, not only for convenience, but to decrease fire risk in his cottage.

The general impression was that he would be relieved and overjoyed to get to his cottage where he hoped to continue writing. He suggested once that he would write a biography of Casement, if he could tap the archives through the help of a friend. Also he would write a sequel to *The Mint*, dealing in particular with his life and experiences in the boat sections of the Royal Air Force.

On one of the last nights he was at Bridlington, a party of officers and all his brother airmen invited him as their guest to the local theatre where a play by Galsworthy was being acted. T.E. accepted very solemnly. In accordance with Air Force custom, a visit was paid to a nearby club for the purpose known as 'ginning-up'. T.E. never indulged in the process, but occasionally ate the red cherries on small sticks from his friends' glasses. One of the waitresses brought him an entire dish of these dainties, and he ate every one with the zest of a schoolboy raiding a tuck-shop.

During the play, he sat very quietly mostly with his head on his hand and gave a little giggle, sometimes when there was otherwise complete silence in the auditorium. He afterwards said that the play 'was good. Very good. It must have been, because I hardly understood what it was about.' When it was over, in the foyer, T.E. who had brushed his hair carefully for the party, and looked quite immaculate in his cheap ready-made coat, slacks, and blue fisherman's jersey, was crowned by a friend with a very large, hard, bowler hat. T.E. rose to the occasion nobly, and paraded round the foyer with lordly dignity and a gloriously fierce air which matched the bowler hat perfectly. It was fooling brought to a pitch of genius, and

T.E. showed that he felt happy in the love and admiration of every soul in the room.

One of the programme girls shyly asked him something in a low voice, whereat T.E. answered 'Certainly'. The girl produced a chocolate box and a pencil, for him to sign his name, and within a moment, two other girls appeared also with chocolate boxes and pencil, and again T.E. smilingly acquiesced.

He then very quietly faded away, and the party lacked further excuse for existence, and broke up.

On his departure, the officer in charge of the detachment looked up from his office desk, and saw a small, pale figure standing there, smiling nervously. 'I have come to say good-bye, sir,' he said. They then talked of boats and Clouds Hill. T.E. said how he would love to sign on for twenty-one years, but his age was against him. He could not do things, and live, at his present age, as he had when a youth and young man. The boats would go on and would continue to grow in size and numbers. . . .

The officer's attention was distracted for a moment, and T.E. with his push cycle was not there.

No one seems to have seen him actually leave.

LITERATURE

EDWARD GARNETT
DAVID GARNETT
JONATHAN CAPE

EDWARD GARNETT, writer and critic. Born 1868, died 1937. Author of *The Breaking Point*; *The Feud*; *Turgenev*; *Papa's War*; *Friday Nights*; *The Trial of Jeanne d'Arc*; editor, *Letters from Conrad*, 1895-1924, etc.

T.E. AS AUTHOR AND CRITIC

'MY critical power is stronger than my sense of creation. "A critic in action" — was it you who so described my *Seven Pillars?*' wrote T.E. to me in January 1924. I don't remember if it was I, but 'a critic in action' seems to me to define T.E.'s genius to a nicety. His extraordinary brain penetrated to the essentials of the subject before him, seizing the whole through the parts. By his close investigation of technique he became intimate with the nature of the problem. But I shall confine myself to T.E. as author and critic, as it was on that side of his interests we met and corresponded. He was always frank about his literary opinions, though not averse from pulling one's leg. I think that it was to irritate me that, at our first meeting, he animadverted on Turgenev, whose interest and absorption in the passion of love was indeed uncongenial to him. A little later, in August 1922, he sent me the proofs of the first (Oxford) version of the *Seven Pillars* and my praise at first upset him. Though a week or so later (7/9/1922) he wrote: 'More gratitude for your praise which came exactly at the right moment. I lap it up with both hands — the praise that is — the more greedily that it's the first judgment I have had.' I was at first struck by his suppression of his intimate feelings, in the book, and I had told him when we had met that the effect of the whole would have been much greater had he been franker. 'With whom are you comparing me?' he asked. 'With W. H. Hudson,' I answered; 'in his books Hudson does not hide his feelings.' T.E. surrendered at once: 'Yes! but Hudson is above us all,' he replied. And in his letter of 7/9/1922 he admits my charge: 'The personal revelations should be the key of the thing: and the personal chapter actually is the key, I fancy: only it's written in cypher. Partly it's a constitutional inability to think plainly, an inability which I pass off as metaphysics, and partly it's funk — or at least a feeling that on no account is it possible for me to think of giving myself quite away.' But in his letter of 23/10/1922 he returns to the matter and analyses his own literary procedure. 'As you, a critic, have seen, the thing (the *Seven Pillars*) is intensely sophisticated, built up of hints from other books, full of these echoes, to enrich or side-track or repeat my motives . . . By avoiding direct feeling I would keep the emotional expression on the plane of the rest of the construction. That's the reason of all that resolution of the personal, the indirectness of which offends you, and my temptation is to go more abstract, more complex, rather more often.' I quote the above passage to show that T.E. knew exactly what he was aiming at, though he had, indeed, miscalculated. 'I thought that the mind I had (and I've matched it competitively often against other fellows, and have an opinion of it) if joined to a revival of the War passion would sweep over the ordinary rocks of technique.' 'I collected a shelf of titanic books, those distinguished by greatness of spirit, *Karamazov*, *Zarathustra* and *Moby Dick*. Well, my ambition was to make an English fourth' (26/8/1922). And in the grip of this ambition and of his War memories he had not understood that as a creative artist he must sublimate or sacrifice large portions of his historic chronicle and saturate it in his own feeling. Hence, later, his disillusionment and distress: 'I had hopes all the while that it was going to be a big thing and wrote myself nearly blind in the effort. Then it was finished (*pro tem.*) and I sent it to the printer, and when it came back in a fresh shape I saw that it was no good . . . Please don't read this as a *cri de cœur*. I'm perfectly cheerful. If I'd aimed low I could have hit my target as squarely as Max Beerbohm or Belloc with it; but their works are only a horrid example and I'm much happier to have gone high and flopped than not to have tried, or to have tried half measures' (26/8/1922). As 'a critic in action' T.E. was remorseless in his judgment of himself: 'Your judgment that the book is in excess as regards length, is also, I judge, true as regards intensity and breadth. I've had no pity on myself writing it — nor on my readers reading it. There's a clamour of force in it which deafens. A better artist would have given the effect of a fortissimo with less instrumentality' (9/10/1922). T.E. had been offered £7000 for his book and he accepted my suggestion in September 1922 that I should abridge the book to 150,000 words, while he should revise the abridgment and only later on decide as to publication. But, fortunately as it turned out, the plan of publishing the abridgment was scrapped early in January 1923, when T.E. had been smelt out at Farnborough Camp by the press, and in the ensuing official row there had been 'a disgusting mess'. T.E. was then free to revise and rewrite the *Seven Pillars* at leisure, and prepare the final version which he sent me in portions, a year and a half later, saying (21/6/1925): 'Twice you have read the thing: once you have abridged it. I've read it twenty times, written it five times. Will there never be an end for either of us?'

A remarkable illustration of T.E.'s power of analysing literary technique is shown in his letter (20/1/1928) on *Tarka the Otter* by Henry Williamson, beginning: 'It is written too hard. There are no flat places where a man can stand a moment. All ups and downs: engines full on or brakes hard on.' And then he proceeds to criticize sixty passages, awarding many very high praise for style, verbal felicity, etc. 'It has kept me sizzling with joy for three weeks' (at Karachi). This letter from one literary craftsman to another, for justice and keenness should become a classic, for such intimate technical analysis is very rare in literary criticism. He complained with justice of the *London Mercury* review of *Revolt in the Desert* (10/6/1927). 'Tommy-rot. Nothing about the literary pretence of my work, and hopeless in the psychology it ascribed to me. The happy warrior! The man of action! Whereas I'm a walking embodiment of the critical temperament ... O'Flaherty is good in what he says ... Odd he should think me English. I thought my native land exuded its brogue all over my prose!' Later (1/8/1927) he complains: 'None of the reviews yet have helped me to write better, yet for all their writers know I might have wanted to.' And (1/12/1927) he devotes several pages to an acute criticism of Herbert Read's 'very excellent note' on *Revolt in the Desert*, in which he passes his reviewer through a mincing machine, with the final complaint that 'Read talks as though I had been making a book and not a flesh and blood revolt'.

What bothered T.E. about literary criticism was 'the lack of an absolute'. He recurred to this point again and again in his talk and his letters, and used it craftily to discount the praise and dispraise by his friends of passages in the *Seven Pillars* and *The Mint*: 'Opinions are not worth much; they are too subjective. There is no absolute and therefore no criticism. As you say, I tend to go Tolstoyan with years. I now like H. G. Wells better than Norman Douglas and call Kipling better than Crackanthorpe', he writes (14/4/1928). He had momentarily swerved in his allegiance to Doughty's great style, and I had charged him with becoming prone to judge books too much by the capacity of the R.A.F. man to understand them. But this Tolstoyan fit was only temporary and he preserved intact his freshness and receptivity to authors new to him till the end. Indeed, of the authors I have known, T.E. possessed, I think, the most responsive and the widest critical taste. He combined the true scholar's sense of literary values with the unconventional judgment of a man of culture who tests books by life. His nature was sympathetic and generous, his heart warm, his mental horizon wide, his power of analysis great, and his individuality responded to talents of marked originality. Of course like all men he had his limitations of taste and his peculiar attitude to women screened off from him in literature, I think, many tracts and aspects of feminine psychology. But apart from this, he was almost sure to appreciate new writers of talent. His judgment of his contemporaries, conveyed in a flying line or so, seemed to me nearly always to find the target. T.E. seemed to me to hold in reserve a standard of literary achievement which preserved him from the deceptive lure of the second rate. It was rarely I disagreed with his verdicts and in sending him books I had greater confidence in his responsiveness than in that of other men. About my particular relations with him in the appreciation of his work generally, I must refer to his letters to me, in one of which (20-11-1928), when acknowledging my volume *Letters from Joseph Conrad* he says: 'There you are, easing him and encouraging him and confirming him. I tell you I recognized every tone and inflection of it,' and then he concludes with one of his habitual self-deprecatory remarks about his own work and about 'having failed you'. It was not always easy to meet and turn the edge of his pessimistic depreciation of himself as an author, but, however, I never ceased growling over his wasting his creative talent in R.A.F. drill and clerking and petty duties, and urging him to go on with and conclude his R.A.F. book, *The Mint*. He was secretly ambitious to achieve *The Mint*. He felt, I think, that he owed it to himself to prove what he could make of a second book and he explains (1/8/1927) why he had not yet sent me the Uxbridge notes: 'I wrote them pell-mell, as the spirit took me, on one piece of paper or another. Then I cut them into their sections and stuffed them, as Joyce is supposed to have stuffed *Ulysses* ... So I am copying them *seriatim* into a notebook as a Christmas (which Christmas?) gift for you.' His plan in writing *The Mint* he explains (22/9/1927), 'I am trying not to rewrite, but I have to rearrange extensively and to cut out repetitions and expand the sentences which are in an esoteric shorthand ... I think the job may be worth its trouble.'

In the above letter he replies to my charge of disingenuousness in his abridgment *Revolt in the Desert*. 'You will not realize the difference between a real book (the *Seven Pillars* being as truthful as I could make it) and an edition for general consumption, put out just to make money and to stop the mouths of those who were crying for word from me ... I cut out all the high emotion. The preface, the murder in the valley, the killing of my camel in the Camel-charge, the scene at Deraa, the worst of the winter-war, the death of Farraj, the Hospital —

all of it.' But later on he styled *Revolt in the Desert* 'a dishonest sweep of a book'.

T.E. sent me the MS. of *The Mint* 'bound in the simplest blue morocco' (15/3/1928), saying: 'This afternoon I am going out into the desert with some paraffin and the original draft, to make sure that no variant survives, to trouble me as those two editions of the *Seven Pillars* do. So before you get it your copy will be unique,' and on receiving a telegram from me to say the book had reached me safely, he wrote (23/4/1928): 'Do not let your enthusiasm for new notes in writing run away over *The Mint*. It is a new note, I fancy: I've never read any other book of exactly the same character. It is fragmentary and has the dry baldness of notes: none the worse for that, for the *Seven Pillars* was prolix, and *The Mint* is not long-winded or not often long-winded . . . also it isn't a book. It's a note for your private eye, a swollen letter.

'It is well written, I fancy, as prose . . . You like the booklet: which I made up to please you . . . So — regard it as a notebook of mine, given to you because you liked my *Seven Pillars*, and because I had no further room for it. I won't tell you it's rubbish, but it's pretty second-rate, like me and my works: it's the end of my attempts to write anyhow . . . I'd so like something of my creating to be very good: and I bask for the moment in the illusion of your praise. Very many thanks therefore.'

To show the variety of T.E.'s reading, after April 1928, there are flying references in his letters, to Miss Hodder's *Pax*, George Moore, Blunt's translation of the *Moallakat*, Stephen Reynolds, Jacobsen's *Marie Grubbe*, Elizabeth Roberts' *My Heart and My Flesh*, Pushkin's stories, Peadar O'Donnell, Macnamara, Liam O'Flaherty, *Red Dust*, Selma Lagerlöf, Stephen Crane, Vansittart's *Singing Caravan*, Butler's translation of the *Odyssey*, *Lady Chatterley's Lover*, Baring's Lament for Lord Lucas, *All Quiet on the Western Front*, *No Love*, *The Grasshoppers Come*, H. E. Bates, Faulkner's *Soldiers' Pay*, 'The new de La Mare', Dunn's poems, Auden, Spender, Archibald Macleish, E. E. Cummings, V. Clifton's

Book of Talbot, Twenty Years A Growing, Manhood's *Night-seed,* Riesenberg's *Log of the Sea,* Hanley's *Captain Bottell,* John Buchan, Grace Black's *A Beggar, Letters from John Galsworthy.*

In a letter on *Red Dust* (27/5/1930) T.E. sums up his attitude to his literary ambition and disinclination thus: 'I will not write a foreword or a backword or a middle piece for any-one for anything I hope. I always say "I hope" because I don't say "never": that would ring down the curtain on too many hopes. I propose to go on fancying that I could in some cir-cumstances write; and so long as I don't disabuse myself by trying to write that makes a nice warm fiction to cherish under one's breath. After the *Seven Pillars* I gave up writing for four years and it will take me longer than that to forget the dis-illusionment of re-reading *The Mint.* So don't suggest my writing anything again. It is not worth while to incur certain missing on the off chance of pleasing somebody's not too critical sense.'

T.E.'s last letter to me (26/11/1934) dwelt on my relation-ship to authors, and spoke, of course deprecatingly, of his own literary achievement: '... your criticisms have always gone personally from you to the artist, instead of being exhibition pieces to catch the public eye on the way. Astonishing, as I have said!' 'I am watching over the refitting of the R.A.F. boats here. After that I plan to go to Clouds Hill ... I'm afraid of what may follow, and of what may not follow. It feels like — not an end which would be welcome I think, but like something interminable. I've always wanted less from life than I've had ... And you? ... If only I had done you credit!'

T.E., indeed, to the end was a critic in action.

DAVID GARNETT, c.b.e. Born 1892. Literary Editor of
New Statesman and Nation, 1933-35. Author of *Lady into Fox*,
A Man in the Zoo, *The Sailor's Return*, *Go She Must!*, *The
Grasshoppers Come*, *A Rabbit in the Air*, *Pocahontas*, *The Golden
Echo*, etc. Edited *The Letters of T. E. Lawrence* and *The Essential
T. E. Lawrence*.

I FLEW down to Southampton in the summer of 1934 and
paid T. E. Shaw a visit one Sunday afternoon, and after he
had taken me out in one of the Air Force boats and told me
of the improvements he had introduced in them, we hunted
round the deserted works of the British Power Boat Company
trying to find a bit of rope which I needed for picketing
my Klemm on the common beside Frensham Pond. Stray ropes
had been tidied away and we scrupled to steal any in use. At
last a length was found and we set out to return to Southampton.
On the ferryboat were two north-country young men in civvies
who recognized Shaw, who immediately turned his back on me
and spoke to them, saying that two boats were being sent up to
Scotland and that there was a chance for them to form part of
the crew. They were eager for the experience; Shaw's tip was
worth a lot; they were breathlessly excited and overwhelmed
with gratitude. Quite suddenly Shaw took the rope out of my
hands and asked one aircraftman to splice an eye at one end and
the other to work a backsplice on the other. Then he turned
back abruptly, ignoring them as completely as he had me, while
they set busily to work with knives and fingers. The job was
beautifully done and the picket-rope handed back to me just
as we reached Southampton. 'They like being asked to do
something', said Shaw. It was a magical arrangement; I had
what I wanted and the young men's pride had been doubly
gratified. No man's approbation was so agreeable as Shaw's.
People were either won immediately, like the aircraftmen, or
mystified and irritated because they could not class him. People
want a colonel to be a colonel and an aircraftman to be an aircraftman; they dislike also a shrinking modesty which draws

338

the fiercest publicity upon itself. Shaw was vain and almost pathologically ashamed of his own vanity, hence his ostrich-like concealments and exposures.

T. E. Shaw was extremely unlike ordinary people; so unlike that none of the labels which serve to 'explain' people will fit. He was well aware of this unlikeness; this is perhaps the chief explanation of his shyness, which was extreme, though it wore off, I think, in later years. Robert Graves, who, of course, knew him far better than I, says: 'Perhaps his most unexpected characteristic is that he never looks at a man's face and never recognizes a face.' But it is the long look, right into one's eyes, followed by a broad grin, which I remember best. When the shy fit was on there was something clerical, celibate, typically Oxford and pedantic about him, and there was a really terrible feeling of having got stuck. And then the shy stiffness of the schoolmaster would be interrupted by his turning into a rather perky schoolboy. Underneath shyness and perkiness was the wish to get rid of them both, forget himself and lose himself in what he was doing or talking about. The red-faced, weather-beaten, thick-set little mechanic, tightening the gland of a propeller-shaft, while the engine was ticking over and the boat lurched in a sea-way, and his yellow hair hung down into the oil-sump, was a very different person, with a boyish intimacy in his laugh and a sharing of one's eagerness as the spray flew and the boat spurted over the waves. He was described as 'a mystic who had lost interest in living'. If that was ever true it did not last long. He was happy in the Air Force not, I think, because he found in it a monastic way of life or a retreat from the world, but because he valued more than anything the intimacy which comes from doing a bit of work with other men. The Air Force gave him that. He was very proud of his boats, explained in great detail all the improvements he had made in them and spoke with enthusiasm of their designer, Scott Paine.

His taste in literature was good, but capricious; he prided himself on book production, but the *Seven Pillars*, to my mind, is a monstrous example of it. While his vanity was engaged by such pretensions he undervalued himself as a writer. His labours in the desert have vanished as fast as those of other soldiers, but they will live for ever in men's minds because of the book he wrote. The unlimited edition of the *Seven Pillars* is the best memorial to Lawrence of Arabia — though not of T. E. Shaw, for whose memorial, *The Mint*, we may have to wait till 1950. As a writer, one of T.E.'s most striking qualities is his relationship with language. He uses English, both in his original writing and in his translation of the *Odyssey*, as an inventor, or a self-trained mechanic, uses familiar materials and tools for quite new purposes. He is completely free from affectation. There is nothing of Yeats, whom Moore records as searching for 'the right language' in which to tell his stories, nothing of Doughty's archaism, and not much of tradition. He is building rapidly and improvising with words, taking classicisms as the Moors took the classic columns from the temples and fitted them into Cordova Mosque with plinths and capitals of varying lengths. This gives his style an astonishing, unexpected richness, which is yet the furthest removed from the sought-after richness of a Pater. One is conscious, in every sentence, that Shaw is searching for accuracy, and one almost feels him snatch up the best words, not for their own sake, but because they are needed in construction to fill a gap. He had also an astonishing sense of design in literature: the structure and sequence of events in the *Seven Pillars* and in the unpublished account of his life in the Air Force, *The Mint*, are like great music. In each of these books Shaw's subject is only comparable, in terrible qualities and penetrating psychology, with Dostoevsky at his greatest. *The Mint* can indeed be closely compared with *The House of the Dead*. Both men had an abnormal capacity for suffering, both had the power of lifting the lid on horror and of describing incidents that are symbolic and stay in the mind for ever. Of course, no two temperaments could be more unlike. For T. E. Shaw was always impish, without a trace of Russian self-pity, full of malicious humour and at the same time matter of fact, while as T.E. said himself: 'Dostoevsky had not a crisp word in him.' Each of Shaw's books is a picture of his own soul, of his motives and agonies, yet in each he appears to be primarily interested in the background, the interest of which is feverish and overwhelming. Each is the record of self-mutilation for an idea, and the record of the triumph of that idea. To capture Damascus, Lawrence had to submit himself to months of agonizing effort and to bear physical torture; to survive the Air Force training Shaw had to have his body broken anew and his instincts violated. Yet the characteristic grin of impish humour is always there.

When judging his military achievements it must be remembered that he had to use the Arabs and the English without taking either into his full confidence; for example, he had to pretend an inability finally to cut the Hejaz railway because English officers would not understand the enormous advantage of keeping it just running. As a soldier he had to deceive his superiors, and as a writer he had to play a similar elaborate game, deceiving his friends and that side of himself which he could not get rid of, even by deed-poll. But he had great literary ambitions, he had matured, and I think he was about to enter on a most creative period as a writer.

JONATHAN CAPE, publisher. Born 1879.

T.E. AS AUTHOR AND TRANSLATOR

Towards the end of 1920, when I was making plans to begin publishing under my own name, Lawrence heard that I was contemplating a reprint of Doughty's *Arabia Deserta*, which had not been available for many years except in an abridged edition. Events in Arabia during and after the War had aroused interest in this classic of travel. But it was a large, not to say a risky, undertaking, and required careful thought. Lawrence came to see me, as he put it, 'to encourage me'.

His view was that, since sums of £20 or £30 were being offered for single copies of the old edition, a new edition of five hundred copies was quite feasible, even if its published price had to be, as I pointed out to him, as much as ten guineas. Eventually he consented to write an introduction to the new edition, and we fixed on nine guineas as the published price. I had included in my estimate a fee of twenty-five guineas for this introduction, but he refused to accept any fee. He did, however, ask me to print two special copies for him on hand-made paper.

During 1921 Lawrence was at the Colonial Office, and sometimes after working hours he would come to my office, and we would talk over books and publishing projects. He met Edward Garnett about this time, and as Garnett read for me this made another link.

In 1922, when he entered the R.A.F., a correspondence began which went on until his death. Publishing, in all its literary and creative aspects, interested him deeply. He enjoyed the fascination of unknown manuscripts, and the adventure of discovery; and he relished the practical delights of dealing with type, paper and binding. He had a small printing-press of his own, and proposed one day to amuse himself by setting type and pulling sheets for himself.

By some of his letters to me, I am reminded of an interest we shared in the works of Herman Melville. *Moby Dick*, *Typee*, and *Omoo* he considered to be works of the greatest significance: as also *White Jacket*, that remarkable document of life in the United States Navy. *Mardi* he considered dull, while *Redburn*, he remarked, 'should have interest for Liverpudlians as a local curiosity'.

In 1923 he wrote to me: 'If you ever have anything in French which needs translating (for a fee!) please give me a chance at it. I have plenty of leisure in the Army, and my French is good, and turning it into English is a pleasure to me: also the cash would be welcome, however little it was.' Later he wrote: 'Thanks for the word about translating. I'd like to make however few pounds, and it will be nice to play with words again. Squad drill is a little heavy on the mind.'

In 1923 I suggested that he might translate from the French Mardrus's version of the Arabian Nights. The idea appealed to him. He referred to Mardrus, 'much the best doing of the Nights in any language (not excepting the original which is in coffee-house talk!) The correctness of Mardrus cannot be bettered. The rivalry in English is not high. Payne crabbed: Burton unreadable: Lane pompous ... I've lots of time, and could do up to two thousand very decent words a day. Anonymous, of course.' Unfortunately, when I went to the French publisher I found that the rights of translation into English had only very recently been disposed of, and the Mardrus version was eventually ably rendered into English by Edward Powys Mathers.

I next offered Lawrence a short French book, *Le Gigantesque*, by Adrien le Corbeau; he was attracted by this unusual book, which is in effect the biography of a giant tree of the Western forests, and started to work on the translation. In July 1923 he wrote: 'This is how *Le Gigantesque* stands. I started gaily, did about twenty pages into direct swinging English, then turned back and read it, and it was horrible. The bones of the

poor thing showed through. I did it again more floridly.
The book is written very commonplacely by a man of good
imagination, and a bad mind, and unobservant. Consequently
it is banal in style and ordinary in thought, and very interesting
in topic. Let me know when you want the completed text, and
it will come signed "J. H. Ross", translator. You will have to
have it typed and deduct this before you pay me.'

A month later he wrote: '*Le Gigantesque* is coming this
week. It has been stiff to do, not because the French was hard
but because the style was banal. I have four chapters yet to
re-write.' And then, on September 13th, 'At last this foul
work, complete. I made a vow I wouldn't write until it was
ended, and now it's ended I'm off for a bike ride, and will hope
to break my neck upon it (or off it).'

His next attempt was on a short French book called *Sturly*,
by Pierre Custot, a depiction of ocean life viewed, as it were,
from beneath the waves. 'It will take a while to do well,
for the wretched man catalogues innumerable French fishes
and my French never extended into scientific icthyology!
Can you give me a long time to do it in? I'm hiring a writing
room, giving up the struggle to write in barracks.' On Christmas Day, 1923, he wrote: 'I did not write, because I wanted
to send you *Sturly* as a Christmas present. He is not ready.'
A month later: 'To-night I have read through my *Sturly*, and I
have burned it page by page. There is something about this
book which I cannot get. I have spent days over a single
chapter and yet not got the essence of any. I enclose a cheque
for £20, add this to what you would have paid me and have a
first-rate version done by a real, proper writer. It [his trans-
lation] was not fair to the author and I like the book for that
hard unsentimental writing. It is the sort of thing I would do
willingly, but cannot.'

I did not accept the cheque, and eventually Richard Alding-
ton translated *Sturly*. When it was printed, Lawrence wrote
the announcement of it which appeared on the jacket of the
book.

During 1924 I was contemplating a plan for a complete English edition of Flaubert, all the books to be newly translated. I suggested *Salammbô* to him, and he was keen on the idea; but the project seemed less attractive after a while and was dropped.

On Armistice Day, 1923, he had week-end leave. It was a Sunday. He went to the service at the Cenotaph and joined me later at lunch. We parted in the evening, and he later went on to Augustus John's studio. There he came across the typescript of Roy Campbell's poem, *The Flaming Terrapin*, and next morning I received a postcard from him with Campbell's address, which he had obtained from John. It was laconic. 'Get after this man. I saw a MS. of a poem by him in John's studio. Great stuff.' I published *The Flaming Terrapin* a few months later.

I asked him to write the announcement for *The Flaming Terrapin*, but he said: 'No, I can't write about that yet. It's such an extravaganza, so exuberant, vital, lavish, that criticism isn't easy; and I don't respect my own judgment enough to put it into words. Normally, rhetoric so loud and bombastic would have sickened me, but I have a dim sight of something big under this storm of words and images . . . but what a profusion, what invention, what a waste of colour! Magnificent, I call it.'

About this time he remarked: 'My own writing is only a dissatisfaction to me: so much disappointment and pain, without any faculty of pleasing myself or anyone else. For that reason I've tried translating, hoping to dodge thereby the creative effort: only to find myself as particular over the reproductive. Consequently I have given it up, and shall manufacture no more books. The trifle I tried to do lately for Garnett was only to pay a little of the debt I owe him for help and kindnesses . . . and even that stimulus didn't carry me to the achievement.' [The 'trifle' was an introduction which he wrote for Edward Garnett to go with a new edition of Richard Garnett's *Twilight of the Gods*.]

In 1926 I published a one-volume edition of Doughty's

Arabia Deserta, a copy of which I sent him. 'Congratulations on the 1-volume edition,' he wrote. 'As regards my introduction. *Arabia Deserta*, as a work of art, is better without the discordance of a preface by a strange hand. Its value doesn't lie in its exactness to life in Arabia (on which I can pose as an authority), but in its goodness as writing.'

About this time I was pressing him to write a life or memoir of Doughty. 'I've thought of that "life" idea, up and down: and I'm sorry that I can't touch it. I would not have delayed so in considering the life of anyone else: but for C.M.D. I had a very real regard. That *Seven Pillars* effort showed me my incompetence with a pen. Rule me "off" in every respect.'

After the publication of *Revolt in the Desert* letters addressed to him were continually being sent in my care. At his request I dealt with these, sending forward only such as seemed to be of importance. He wrote: 'It is good of you to defend me from letters. The stamps necessary for the letters I do get are already a severe tax on my pay. Otherwise things are easy. I'm not going to write another book. Nor will I edit a review.' Then a postscript. 'Why not reprint Coryat's *Crudities* in your travellers series? And add the memoirs of Sergt. Bourgogne: and a translation of the memoirs of Ousama ibn Mankidh.' I followed up the suggestion as to Sergeant Bourgogne, but I did not adopt the others.

Two months after the publication of *Revolt in the Desert* in 1927 he wrote — this is an exact copy: 'I've been sent wild stories of the genesis of "Revolt in the Desert". If you like, make a "third person" note in your Now and Then booklet saying:

'The abridgement of Mr. T. E. Shaw's "Seven Pillars of Wisdom" which we were able to publish by arrangement with him on March 10 last, under title "Revolt in the Desert" by "T. E. Lawrence" was made by him in seven hours at Cranwell in Lincolnshire on March 26 and March 27, 1926, with the assistance of two airman friends, A/A Knowles and A/C Miller. It was received by us (in the form of cut-down proofs of the Seven Pillars) on March 30, three days later, and reprinted immediately as we received it. There were no author's corrections, nor was this text ever submitted to anyone for advice or criticism. The only subsequent alterations were the division into chapters and the writing in (at the publishers' request) of three paragraphs to justify the inclusion of two much desired illustrations from the many in Seven Pillars.

'The author has promised the subscribers to "Seven Pillars of Wisdom" that no further copies of this shall be published during his lifetime: and he will make no additions to the issued text of "Revolt in the Desert".

'"Revolt" was sold to us in order that our advance on its royalties might enable the author to commission extra drawings for the Seven Pillars: and the author's contract with us gives him the option of terminating our sale of the book when this advance is fully met.

'There: short and sweet! Any good? I think so.'

In August 1928 I sent him proofs of Robert Graves' *Lawrence and the Arabs*. He wrote from India: 'The Graves book puzzles me. I do not like the long passages in which he turns *Revolt in the Desert* into sober prose. Something of the original goes, without anything of Graves' excellent own coming to take its place. His independent chapters are good. You were wrong to make him write so quickly. In six months he could have gathered enough stuff from onlookers and participants to have written a fresh story of the Arab Revolt: — which would have put me into a historical perspective, and been valuable for its own sake. However, you want to catch the wave before it is completely flat. I'm enduring this spot, meanwhile, till you have finished. After so great a boom a great slump: that's a comforting thought.'

Early in 1928 he was on the North-West frontier. 'I don't know how it is, but things inside me seem to have shut up very much, lately. So I read very little. I haven't seen either Aloysius Horn or my brother's book, for instance: though they should have interested me. I did read the Greville and Conrad memoirs because Doubleday sent them me. But otherwise I just moon about. As Garnett has mentioned my R.A.F. notes I'd better explain that they are just a fair copy of an informal diary I wrote up every night, nearly, in Uxbridge in 1922. Quite unreadable: quite unprintable. Scotland Yard would have you as well as me, if you tried it. Yet the clean copy (which will be the only copy, the draft being destroyed) is going to be formally offered you for publication, to leave no liability of a contracted nature hanging over my head. My second book, you'll remember, was promised you; and these notes will be it. They will not have any successors. Incidentally they are being sent to Garnett for a Christmas present for 1928: to explode his lingering idea that I ever had in me the makings of a writer. The rest will be silence, I hope.'

In March 1928 he apologized for the paper and ink he was using. 'I am writing in the oily, dirty shop. Will you thank your lady of the chocolates?' (A box of chocolates had arrived at my office, with a letter asking that they should be forwarded to Private Shaw, as the sender understood that soldiers like sweet things.) 'About twenty airmen finished her packet in a few minutes. It was kind of her, but foolish. Our circumstances leave us with appetite for food rather than the frills of food, and expensive chocolates are out of the picture. However, she was very kind, and very extravagant. Dissuade anyone else there may be, please!'

I sent him Alfred Aloysius Horn's *Ivory Coast in the Earlies*. 'I read Horn, right through, but with mixed feelings. Some of it, I suppose, is all right; but I've not been impressed, either by his sincerity or by his observation. Of course it was written years later, which would account for some vagueness of memory. The effect upon me of the book was of gutter-decay: a man who slipped right down, deservedly. That curious credulity, and narrow mind and cheapness. The binding you put on the book is very good. I'd call it the best part. If I'd never heard of it, and had come to it without Galsworthy's introduction, I'd have called it very good. But to describe it as gorgeous! And it's got about as much "stingo" as a feather-bed.'

Later he referred again to *The Mint*, which he described as an agony of the Royal Air Force, 'which he [Garnett] will offer you for publication *as it stands*, soon. This is in accordance with the terms of our *Revolt in the Desert* contract.

'By the way, I'm asking £1,000,000 down in cash, in advance of royalty, on *The Mint*. I hope you will regard that sum as a compliment to the firm. I wanted to make sure that they would refuse it: and I feared that any lesser figure might be within your reach. They say you had five of the six best-selling books of last year.'

A book which called forth his steady admiration was Verner von Heidenstam's *The Charles Men*, a saga of Charles XII, the mad king of Sweden. It is a classic of Swedish literature but little known here, full of glowing pictures of the life of the period, written in a vivid and beautiful style. A translation was published in England in 1920, but it languished and eventually went out of print. In 1933, fired by Lawrence's enthusiasm, I made arrangements to republish it. He wrote: '*The Charles Men* is an exquisite and rare work. It has a good deal of the quality of a frieze in sculpture, and the conversations are so odd. I've read nothing else like it.' He began his letter with an apology for not writing to me about the book earlier. 'I seem able to do only one thing at a time. That one, at present, is motor boats. I do them all day long, and think of them all my spare hours. It's a matter of design, you see. So books play 14th fiddle.

'*Gösta Berling* and the *Charlesmen* are two unusual books. If they sell at all, add the two Jacobsens to your Scandinavian section. I wish I had read some of von Heidenstam's poetry. I knew his brother, years ago: a power engineer, as so many Swedes are. How far, I wonder, is *Charlesmen* just a transcript, sublimed, of the original authorities? I wonder what books he used in writing it. Parts of it are quite historical: but that gallery of crazy portraits must be his own. Sorry: but I oughtn't to puff any more books. It is a vanity. Let us forget

349

books. They are only things meant to read. The publishing them is a form of extravagance.' Lawrence was right about *The Charles Men*: its publication has so far been a form of extravagance!

In September 1933 our letters were concerned with Burton's *Anatomy of Melancholy*. For a long time I had contemplated a new edition. Lawrence's judgment was: 'The worst of Burton is his enormous length: and the second worst his mania for stuffing into his (really very good) prose all the vapid Latin quotations within reach. I like him: but could never read him unless an Arctic night lay at my disposal, and a warm chair. And while in my last R.A.F. year I wish to do nothing.'

Captain Liddell Hart was commissioned by me in 1930 to write a study of T.E. and the Arabian Revolt. Lawrence wrote: 'You make me a figure of fun with all these pompous biographies. I only hope the public go sick, all over the other three sides of Bedford Square.'

The last letter I received from Lawrence was a long one, written in August 1934. I quote from it: 'I've been wanting to write and say how good a book *Winged Victory* is. [*Winged Victory* by V. M. Yeates.] I have persuaded quite a group of people to buy it, and all of them are accepting it as a document and work of art.

'Now I return to find my bed here awash, as usual, under a sea of letters. Your part in the sea is a copy of Peter Fleming's new book on Manchuria (Good: I've meant to read that. His bits in the papers are tempting), a symposium upon Public Schools (missed your aim: I went to day schools only, or convent schools: and all of them were waste of my time) and Nesbitt's *Desert and Forest*. I had given up hope of that, in the time that has passed since we talked of it. I hope it has been well edited and pulled together. I shall read it and write to you as soon as I have had time to get right through it.

'Ah yes, there is a letter too. You'd like a note on the Nesbitt book for *Now and Then*. Can I? I doubt it. One of my major feelings to-day is a shrinking from all sorts of print. No: I'd better say "No", for that at any rate is a promise I can keep.

'Then Burton (*Anatomy of Melancholy*). You mentioned it to me once before. I've picked up the Armstrong often (I possess the only edition I know which translates all the Latin tags) but never got very far with it. I wonder if anybody will ever read it again. As for buying it ... Well, I did, second-hand. Do you really think it would pay to re-set? A huge long book which nothing that I can imagine will ever make vital again. Also I'm 46: before I'd finished it I'd be 66. It wouldn't pay either of us, surely?

'My civil date gallops towards me. March the eleventh. Seven months. But don't conceive of me as needing immediate work then. I am promising myself a huge rest and sample-time, to see if (a) I am happy doing nothing, and (b) if I have money enough for it. Granted (a) and (b) you'll hear no more of me. My heart tells me that I'm finished.'

LATER GENERAL VIEWS

F. YEATS-BROWN

IAN DEHEER

JOHN BROPHY

G. W. M. DUNN

HENRY WILLIAMSON

W. H. AUDEN

MAJOR FRANCIS YEATS-BROWN, D.F.C., writer.
Born 1886. Second Lieutenant, King's Royal Rifle Corps, 1906;
Indian Army, 1907; Royal Flying Corps, in Mesopotamia, 1915;
prisoner in Turkey, 1915; escaped, 1918; retired, 1925. Assistant
Editor of the *Spectator*, 1926-28. Author of *Caught by the
Turks*, 1920; *Bengal Lancer*, 1930; *Golden Horn*; *Dogs of War!*,
etc.

MY acquaintance with T.E. came about when I wrote to
him in the spring of 1926, as Assistant Editor of the
Spectator, asking him to review some books on the
Middle East. I addressed the letter to Colonel Lawrence, at
All Souls, Oxford. He replied in a characteristically cryptic
way: 'I haven't written anything since I enlisted, and hope
sincerely that I won't, so long as I remain in the R.A.F. . . .
T.E.S.'; and enclosed my original letter so that I should be
under no misapprehension as to the identity of the writer.

After further letters (all of which he answered to Miss
Yeats-Brown, insisting, in spite of my protests, that Literary
Editors were always feminine) he agreed to write for the
Spectator occasionally, on any subject except Arabia.

This was the beginning of a correspondence which lasted
for four years. 'Reviewing comes hard to me,' he wrote. 'I
can't do it without trying my best: and if I've ever in my past
written decently it was under dire command of some mastering
need to put on paper a case, or a relation, or an explanation,
of something I cared about. I don't see that happening with
literature and so I don't expect you to like what I write. My
last two employers cast me away very firmly, after a trial.
I am expecting you to do the same.'

However, in the next paragraph (and these are, perhaps, the
most revealing sentences he ever wrote to me, displaying as
they do the conflict in his character) he discussed how his
pseudonym of Colin Dale should be gradually revealed to the
public. 'I'd suggest the first five or six things worth publishing be restrained to their initials. If the miracle continues

after that (surely either your forbearance or my endeavour will break down) we might climb so far as Colin D., keeping the full truth about the D till it was certain that the fellow could write and had a character. In my heart of hearts I know he hasn't. People have been led away by his retinue of extraneous accidents.'

We may well ask what T.E. was really thinking when he wrote this letter? He had, I believe, a desire to astound the world. Would he, he may have been asking himself, be recognized as a brilliant critic? Would the world talk about Colin Dale as it had of Lawrence of Arabia? He knew quite well that he could write, and that he had character, but nothing short of world fame could assuage his inferiority complex. One of his first essays was on D. H. Lawrence. Immediately a firm of publishers wrote to the *Spectator* asking who the reviewer was, and suggesting that he should edit a volume for them. When he wrote of Mr. H. G. Wells' short stories, I sent the article to the author, who was also curious as to the identity of the critic who had written what he described as the most interesting estimate of his work that he had ever seen. However, in spite of laudation on all sides, T.E. continued in his self-depreciation.

One Wednesday afternoon I was correcting proofs in my flat at Adelphi Terrace House, when I heard a knock. A slight figure in a blue suit stood at my door, and apologized for disturbing me. It was T.E., just back from India.

I made him some China tea (he had a palate for delicate flavours, which he rarely indulged) and was plying him with questions when Richard, the office-boy of the *Spectator*, arrived with some galley proofs. Richard was a smart boy, and I remembered that out of his small wages he had bought the recently published *Revolt in the Desert*, so I told him who the visitor was.

Richard was a motor bicycle fan. 'Is it true you ride your Brough at a hundred miles an hour, sir?' he promptly asked. T.E. was delighted. He loved to talk about machines, and told Richard some wonderful stories of tanks and aeroplanes.

That day he was happy, and in reminiscent vein: the printers waited long for their proofs.

On another occasion, when another person was in my flat, T.E. sat very quiet: there was a riddling smile on his lips and a cruel look in the eyes: he was always the soul of courtesy, but he had no small-talk, and an immense capacity for silence. Presently he seemed to fade away like the Cheshire cat: he was no longer there: instead of T.E., I saw a small, polite man, inclined to wring his hands, sitting stiffly on the edge of my sofa.

Twice I met him by pure chance in London, and spent several hours walking about the streets. He told me that he loved London: his comments ranged from cathedrals to the unemployed and from strategy to speedboats. He did not care to talk philosophy and seemed to have a real aversion to India and to the speculations of the Brahmins.

He thought Yoga was nonsense. Curious, that. With all his reading I do not think he can have read much of Monier-Williams or Max Müller. Yoga would have supplied him, it seems to me, through its breath control and its meditative exercises, with something that he lacked. But then he always hated his body: his will must master his flesh: he would not co-operate with it and achieve the Platonic union of the inner and outer man.

In spite of his (maybe only apparent) neglect of philosophy, I was always conscious in him of a latent psychic superiority over me and mankind in general: in fact, of his greatness. That, of course, was not an altogether comfortable feeling. However, he did his best to put me at my ease, and once he succeeded. It was the Easter of 1930, when I had brought down to Cattewater for his perusal the proofs of *Bengal Lancer*. He read the book in three hours, lying flat on Dartmoor. Then he said: 'It's queer, elusive stuff. To-morrow I'll read it again. I always read a book I like twice. I like your writing, but not your philosophy.'

His comments were practical as well as kind and clever: he estimated the probable sales very correctly: he amended an Arabic phrase: he made suggestions as to spelling, punctuation, balance. Afterwards we talked of his campaigns (a rare privilege that) and of his future. 'I'm in perfect health now, but I think I'll crack up suddenly one day.' T.E. was not gloomily anticipating his death: he meant (I believe) that the nervous strain of the War would affect his health in middle age. We spoke of a young airwoman much in the public eye. 'I wonder,' he mused, 'whether she'll make such a mess of her life as I've made of mine?' Again that sounds an unhappy remark, but it was said humorously. Except about writing he had no false modesty. He genuinely disliked newspaper publicity (as who does not who has experienced it, and who has no immediate end to gain by submitting himself to the inquisition of the press?) but he was too sensible and too shrewd not to know the place he occupied in the minds of Englishmen: particularly in the mind of youth.

When I said good-night at the door of his barrack-room, which he shared with fifteen other men, I knew that I had spent one of the happiest days of my life.

He possessed a radiant physical awareness (though he declared that he never noticed anything), an Irish sense of humour, a cool, clear, sparkling wit and had a power of giving happiness such as I have never known another man to possess. Giving happiness is a feminine quality. T.E. was entirely masculine in outlook and appearance, but with all his strength and courage he had also a woman's sensitiveness. His mind, so critical of himself, so charitable to others, had more bright facets than any other I have known. To be with him was to feel that one had bathed in some mountain spring.

Yet in the background, leashed but very much alive, a devil lurked. I had seen it early on this same day.

He had promised to meet me in a R.A.F. launch at the Drake Steps at Plymouth. After waiting an hour, I drove round to Cattewater, since he had not arrived. There I saw him, and it is no exaggeration to say that his appearance was fiendish.

He was bare to the buff, except for a bathing slip, but he

looked a king among men as he strode up to me scowling. Behind him came two shrinking aircraftmen, fully clothed, much taller than he, but obviously under the spell, as I was, of some atmosphere of menace. He carried a small object like a baby in his arms. The sun gleamed on his wet red hair, on his small brown body, in his wrathful eyes.

I was thoroughly uncomfortable. Had I mistaken the rendezvous? Was he angry with me? What could he do to me? My alarm grew. It seemed ridiculous, but I felt paralysed. His temper seemed like lightning, full of the possibilities of destruction: I wanted to avoid this cosmic force, yet was rooted to the spot.

When he spoke, his expression changed. He apologized for having kept me waiting. Something had gone wrong with the launch's engine. The thing he carried was a dynamo. For two hours he had been working — a good part of the time under water — to locate a fault in the ignition system.

He went to dress. I lit a cigarette with a slightly shaky hand. Viewed with the eye of recollection my emotions seem absurd, but I have described the exact effect of his presence on me at the moment.

I believe that I saw then, for the first and only time, the power in T.E. that brought his Arabs to Damascus.

In 1930 he gave me the *Seven Pillars* to read, and the manuscript of *The Mint*. The former is obscure in parts, occasionally dull, occasionally over-elaborated, yet it is a masterpiece: a twisted masterpiece which will endure because it is symbolical of the grandeur and misery of the days in which he lived, and because through it and in it glows an unconquerable spirit. Of *The Mint* he wrote: 'You will realize, when you read it, that it is only notes, of a very scrappy character, never intended for publication, or to be seen by anyone in its present form. Reading it is pretty grim work.' I agreed, and answered that it was a thousand pities he did not expurgate some of the (to me) unnecessarily dirty talk. Had he done so, had he worked at creative writing with the same finesse,

flexibility, enthusiasm that he gave so willingly and enthusiastically to the development of speedboats, he would have
produced other masterpieces. As it is, *The Mint* contains some
of his best, as well as some of his most mannered and tortured
writing.

He was a man set apart for unusual tasks. Literature could
not capture his whole imagination. He gave me the impression
that he was a stranger to himself, that he disliked his sturdy,
compact frame; indeed, that he hated it with a consuming,
subconscious, perhaps pre-natal hatred. Some such complex
was the weak link in his mental armour. He was not human
enough, though so kind and gentle in personal relationships,
to take his place in the smooth and settled worlds of archaeology,
scholarship, or State service: he needed some great, grim background, such as war or revolution, for the full exercise of his
talents, and not finding such a setting in peace-time England
he sought refuge in the monasticism of barrack life.

Had the Air Force been able to use his knowledge and
descriptive skill in the service of what he called 'man's last
and greatest adventure', I believe he would have given all his
powers to the task; and in that event, conscious that he was
playing a big part in the world's work, he might still be alive
to-day. He once told me that he wished that there were a
decent book on the Air Force. 'At present there's only *War
Birds*, which isn't decent. 'Also,' he added, 'Sassoon's unaffected
little *Third Route*, which I put higher than its simplicity appears
to claim.'

T.E. could have written a great book on flying. He told me
that he would have liked to keep the log of the Australia Flight.
What a record it would have been. What opportunities of
service were neglected in keeping him (happily, humbly, a
little wistfully) tapping at a typewriter, or steering a motor
launch.

Others know more than I of his work on speedboats, but I
remember, one evening at Southampton, how his lambent wit
played round the ideas of the Navy with regard to power-
driven craft. In the days of Queen Victoria, he said, steam

launches often broke down, so it was decreed that a pair of oars should be kept in them. Even in 1932 the absence of this accessory occasioned some adverse comment from the nautical experts who sat in judgment upon the seaplane tenders in which T.E. was interested. A memorandum to the Admiralty, which he drafted, ran as follows: 'Objections noted. Oars will be provided according to recommendation. It is submitted that this principle should be extended to the land vehicles of the R.A.F.: a set of harness should be kept in all motor trucks.' Such letters do not endear the writer to Authority, but they sometimes produce results not to be achieved by routine methods.

Already he has passed into legend. Already his spirit ranges beyond his grave at Moreton, inspiring the youth of England. We who knew him, however slightly, are guardians of a sacred fire. He had terrific, indeed terrible energies pent in his small body. They flared up at a great moment in his country's history, and although they are now extinguished something greater than the physical T.E. remains: a tradition to light future ages.

IAN DE HEER, shipbuilder, lighter, tug and salvage contractor. Born 1900. Royal Naval Air Service (in France); Royal Air Force (in Southern Ireland). Rear-Commodore, Royal Yorkshire Yacht Club.

O N T. E. Shaw's first visit to Bridlington he told me that he had tried most things once, but never deep sea diving, and asked if I could give him the opportunity.

An occasion arose when one of the local fishermen had fouled his trawl net on some object on the sea bed, and as was our custom, we went out to clear the net and remove the obstruction.

When we arrived at the position, our diver descended and found that the net was foul of an old anchor; he cleared the net, which was then brought aboard.

The diver descends a weighted rope, called a shot rope, to the bottom of which is attached a small line called a stray rope, which the diver takes with him to lead him back to his shot rope. On this occasion our diver made the stray rope fast to the anchor and then ascended.

T.E. who was to follow him had taken his spell on the diver's pump all the time our diver was down, and realizing that it was not an easy job, told them that he would not be down for more than a few minutes, not wanting them to have to work for long for his pleasure. He got dressed and descended, like an old hand at the game. The water being beautifully clear, we were able to see him; he realized this and waved to us. He proceeded along the stray line until he came to the anchor, spending quite a time examining same and having a look round; he eventually came back to the shot rope and ascended, being under water approximately twenty minutes; we then found that he had disconnected the stray line from the anchor and neatly coiled it up just as if he had been diving for years.

On one occasion, certain Air Ministry representatives were

visiting Bridlington with a view to choosing a site on the harbour top for a boat shed.

We were all on the South Pier when one gentleman saw a shed that had been used as a 'Sailors' Bethel', and remarked that it looked exactly the place for the boats; he said that the dimensions of the shed were so many feet long by so many feet wide. T.E. said 'No, sir, I should say so-and-so by so-and-so'. Everyone proceeded to the shed and it was measured; it was found to be exactly the size T.E. guessed. He turned to me and said, 'I measured it last night'.

He had been at Bridlington quite a long time and had often spoken to me about his motor cycle, then one day after returning from a week-end leave, came to me and said, 'I have brought my bike up, would you like to see it'? 'Most certainly,' I replied. He took me up to the cycle, which with him standing alongside, looked enormous. I was taken aback at the size of it and remarked, 'You will be breaking your blinking neck on it', and his reply was, 'Well, better that than dying in bed'.

On another occasion he had been out on his motor cycle and had been caught in a bad storm and the cycle was covered with mud. He was beginning to clean it when I suggested that one of my men, who was a keen motor cyclist, would be only too pleased to clean it, so T.E. agreed.

I have since heard from my man that when he had finished it T.E. came up and thanked him, and as the man was leaving he was called back; T.E., unscrewing the petrol filler cap, lifted out the gauze strainer and it was seen to contain seven or eight half-crowns. He handed one to the man who received it in amazement.

T.E. then explained, with the remark, 'It saves a lot of trouble getting half undressed to get at your money pocket to pay for petrol, etc., on the road.'

We were discussing auto-suggestion one day and he quoted the following story:

He was at a dinner one night and much to everyone's surprise when the port came round, accepted a glass.

He smelt it, tasted it, then looking at his host he shook his head. His host tasting his, immediately called for another bottle, remarking that the first one was corked.

T.E. said, 'I knew nothing about port and proved that my host did not either'.

JOHN BROPHY, writer. Born 1899. Enlisted 1914; worked in general store; advertising copy-writer. Author of *The Soldier's War*; *Songs and Slang of the British Soldier*; *Waterfront*, etc.

I FIRST met T. E. in Zwemmer's book shop in the Charing Cross Road, soon after his return from India. We were not strangers, for we had been exchanging letters for some time. He was Aircraftman Shaw then, but I doubt if he would have passed anywhere for an ordinary mechanic or clerk in the Air Force. Not that there was anything untoward about his neat blue uniform, but his head, disproportionately large, dominated his short and slight body. The expanse of his weather-reddened face was more noticeable at first glance than the modelling of the features, which was bold and strong. It was only later that you noticed the delicate and subtle changes of his expression. His eyes were a brilliant and clear blue. His voice was low and precise, and his manner had the cloistered containment which one associates with Oxford dons.

I found it difficult, almost impossible, to believe that I was talking to the most individual, successful, and personally courageous soldier of our time. It was not that T.E. was a disappointing and smaller incarnation of the legendary leader of the revolting Arabs: rather, that the two struck me as being great men of different kinds. I was drawn to T.E. first as 'Lawrence of Arabia' and the author of *Seven Pillars of Wisdom*; but I soon learned to like and admire the aircraftman whose ambition was to be an artist in letters and who was never sure if he had the right equipment. I was proud when our friendship ripened to the point when we could address each other by our initials and abuse each other's opinions without restraint. Perhaps I caught an infection of modesty from T.E., for I soon found myself taking undue care not to mention to others that T.E. was numbered among my friends.

We discussed all those discrepant topics which can roughly

be classified as life and letters, through the post, and when we met occasionally during his visits to London. I remember that, having recently read Robert Graves' biography, I was excessively careful never to shake hands with T.E., but my wife either did not know, or had forgotten this supposed distaste of his for physical contact with others. However, he made no bones about it, and indeed I never saw any sign of abnormal shyness in his attitude to my wife, who is, now I come to think about it, the only woman I ever saw him with. He talked and joked with her as easily as with me, and when, as not infrequently happened, she fell out with his opinions and expressed herself bluntly, he seemed to enjoy it. Perhaps he was weary of women who gushed over him. One of the pictures of T.E. which my memory most vividly retains is set in the little semi-detached house in Brentford where we then lived. He had come up from the Mount Batten camp at Plymouth, three hundred miles in six hours, on his motor cycle, and was going on to stay with Mr. Bernard Shaw. I remember he was amused at my directions for finding the house — 'Straight down the Great West Road till you see the sign of Smith's Potato Crisps and then turn left' — and I had a plate of the crisps ready for him. He decided that on the whole they tasted better straight out of the paper bag. He would eat nothing else, except 'a strawberry or two'. But before he went, the two strawberries had increased to a good fifty. He watched my small daughter, Brigid, being bathed, with an air of solemn curiosity which made my wife laugh till the tiny little bathroom reverberated, and he enjoyed being splashed when Brigid grew exuberant.

In my relations with T.E. I was always aware, perhaps too much aware, that behind the immediate personality of Shaw there was looming the legendary 'Lawrence of Arabia'. Shaw was within my scope, but Lawrence had done things which even in my wildest dreams I could not imagine myself doing. Mingled in every discussion I found a subconscious or half-conscious respect for one who had transcended the limitations of human nerves and endurance. Yet Shaw was the same man as Lawrence, or at least a later development. I never claimed to understand him, though this ceased to distress me when I came to the conclusion that he did not understand himself.

The discrepancy between Lawrence and Shaw suggests a dual personality, and that is always too easy a way out of a problem of psychology. But if it is used as a pointer for further investigation, and not as a Q.E.D., it may help to make things clearer. Duality marches through his career. He had two claims to fame, one as a general, organizing and leading the flank attack which overthrew the Turkish Empire in Arabia and Transjordan; and another as the author of *Seven Pillars*. He was successively the most famous colonel and the most famous private soldier in the British Army. He was a contemplative and a man of action. He was classic in his taste and interests, and romantic in the impulses and conduct of his active years. He was an ancient, in love with Greek and the archaeological remains to be found in this country and the Near East: yet he was also a modern, deeply interested in every new movement of contemporary literature, and fascinated by rapid travel and the machinery of motor cycles, speedboats and printing presses.

All this suggests a man at variance with himself, torn by an inward conflict. He never struck me as happy or fulfilled. Two years ago he described himself to me as 'a man who has done all he wants to do'. I have spent odd moments of several years pondering his character, and for what they are worth I give the conclusions I have reached.

As I interpret T.E. he was at twenty-eight a rather eccentric scholarly young man, studying military strategy and tactics with exceptional penetration, but as a hobby. The first two years of the War provided him only with an office job, but suddenly circumstance put him down in Arabia, and he found an opportunity of working out in real life theories he had evolved from books and meditations. The result astonished him, not so much because it brought success and a fame he no longer wanted, as because he discovered in himself a new personality, a resolute and resourceful general and an arbiter of the destinies of nations. But after the War the exultation ebbed away, and the original contemplative was left, a detached observer to analyse and reassess the record of the man of action who for a few years had inhabited his body: and that body was grown older and weary, exhausted by the terrible strains put upon it. It is this exhaustion, physical, nervous, spiritual, which I think accounts for T.E.'s retirement into the ordered life of a private soldier. He needed a long period to recuperate, and towards the end of his period of service he was undoubtedly a reinvigorated man. He sometimes spoke longingly of the approaching end of his service, just as a convalescent, feeling the strength returning to his limbs, desires to be out and about again. It was ironic, and yet not inapt, that T.E. should have met his death two months after returning to civilian life and through his well-loved motor cycle, which he had reckoned would be too big an expense for him to retain. He would have wished to lose consciousness for ever as swiftly as he did, with no awareness of dying.

It seems to me that a good deal of the elusive truth about T.E. lies in the two related words 'conscious' and 'conscientious'.

The so-called mystery which surrounded his later years arose from the fact that he could not and would not fit into the popular conception of a great hero. He was neither flamboyant nor boyishly modest: his good taste forbade the one and his self-consciousness made the other impossible. He was honest, more honest, I think, than anyone I have ever known, but not simple. Most of the paradoxes of his personality were due to his intense and unremitting awareness of his own complexity. He was always attempting to realize objectively and finally who and what he was, both in the past and in the present. His interest in photography is significant of this overpowering desire to catch and fix the truth. It is paralleled by his willingness (despite his 'modesty', which was never of the *Boy's Own Paper*-Drury Lane melodrama kind) to allow others to make portraits of himself. He would have been the last to deny the element of vanity in his motive. But the truth, I think, is more profound and subtle than that. 'It seemed to me,' he said in *Seven Pillars*, 'that every portrait drawing of a stranger-sitter partook somewhat of the judgment of God.' T.E. was a mystery even to himself, and he hoped that mechanical or artistic likenesses of his features might help him towards that perfectly objective view of the self, in striving for which is our only hope of sincerity.

In literature he had an intense interest in, and liking for, realistic accounts of life, especially life spent under stress. 'I want a diary', he wrote to me, 'or record of events to be as near slice-of-life as can be. Imagination jars in such instances. In novels, however, slice-of-life jars because their province is the second remove, the sublimation of the theme. One is eye-witness, the other creative mind. In the first the photograph cannot be too sharp, for it is the senses which record: in the second, you need design. Any care for design renders the record infect'. I could not agree that such precise photography is possible in the human mind, or that design can be avoided, whether the artist was aware of it or not. I would not concede that once the mind has set to work writing, it is the senses alone which record. We agreed to differ, but I have often since thought that T.E's. 'photographic' theory of literature was a significant indication of his lifelong striving to attain objective truth.

His interest in machinery and speed also seems to me significant. Machinery is a human creation and needs human control, but it is completely impersonal. T.E., more than most of us, lived under the burden of modern self-consciousness. He needed temporary reliefs and he found them by losing awareness of himself in engineering problems and in travelling on the road, over the sea, and through the air at such tremendous speeds that his mind was focused to a single point of control and had no margin from which to regard itself.

Closely allied to this self-consciousness was his conscientious responsibility in every task, small or great, which he undertook. Two minor examples came within my own experience. When I tried to persuade him to resume creative writing (for *Seven Pillars* is imagined as well as recorded) he revealed to me in confidence that after the War he had tried free-lance journalism. He could have obtained high fees for anything to which he would sign his name, but rather than trade on his Arabian reputation, and in order to find out the true merits of his writing, he sent out his manuscript to editors always under assumed names. Every one came back to him with a rejection slip. He took this as a verdict, from which there could be no appeal, that he lacked creative ability. He argued that he could only record what happened to him and what he observed, and even that he could do only in a synthetic and unoriginal style. He would not listen to my objections that editors are very rarely competent judges of literary value, and are more concerned with reputations and the business of supplying a market than with the discovery of new ability.

He translated a couple of French books into English, but always under an untraceable name or anonymously. His R.A.F. pay was hardly sufficient to provide oil and petrol for his motor cycle and he relied on quiet literary work of this kind for the remainder of his small income. When I was editing, with Eric Partridge, *Songs and Slang of the British Soldier, 1914-1918*, I sent galley proofs to T.E. for his comments. They came back with the margins filled with emendations in the familiar 'Indian ink', erudite, witty and often ribald. A bookseller, not known to me personally, who in some way heard of this, offered a considerable sum for these corrected proofs, and as I knew T.E. was hard-up just then I wrote and asked if I should sell them for him. He replied that the bookseller wanted to buy only because 'Lawrence of Arabia' had an inflated reputation, and he would not accept any money that Aircraftman Shaw did not earn straightforwardly. He added that if I wanted money for myself I should by all means sell the proofs. This last suggestion infuriated me. I was touchy, perhaps stupidly so at that time, and I answered that I had no intention of trading on my friendship with him. What is more (infected no doubt by T.E.'s overscrupulousness) I sent back the proofs by registered post, and every letter I had received from him to that date, for I knew that his letters also had a price in the collectors' market. I told him to burn them all in the camp incinerator. It was a silly misunderstanding, and it blew over at once, for T.E. in my experience was always tolerant and understanding. He was a man burdened with awareness of himself and with one of the most exacting consciences I have ever known. I never doubted that he was what we call 'a great man', and I never doubted the intensity and completeness of his personal integrity. He was honest, but not simple; a complex, civilized modern, striving at immense cost to himself to attain the simplicity of the ancients.

G . W . M . D U N N , former Aircraftman, Royal Air Force. Born 1908. First met T.E.L. 1929.

TIME after time I've tried to pin T.E. on to paper and each attempt has left a mere succession of words, hard and cold, as incapable of carrying him as a drawn line. For words can give only ideas, suggestions: they must leave out those subtleties of feeling and easy adjustments of mood, the electrics of understanding.

The certainty is that he was short and stocky, with wide eyes, fair hair brushed back, a big face of which the lowest quarter was jaw; a habit of holding his left wrist in the palm of his right hand; a soft voice spoken with lips more than throat. He looked very ordinary, almost coarse, at first glance.

Then one noticed the paleness of his eyes; that they were of an almost transparent light blue, normally as undistinguished and dead as jelly: he became interested and life effervesced into them: he was angry, and they set hard, tempered like knives.

He spoke, and his voice was magnetic, compelling attention. Then there came about a quickened pulse, a heightened sensibility, the cool excitement of friendliness. He charmed by his easy manner, his persuasiveness, the attraction of his whole presence. One felt that he was good in a sense larger than the merely ethical, that he was completely aloof, half removed from earth, that power surrounded him.

The range of his conversation was memorable. Talk might start, say, on Epstein's 'Night' over the Underground building. He would point out the heavy somnolence of the piece viewed in its context from thirty feet beneath its level, compare it with a figure on an Egyptian temple, with an Assyrian carving in the British Museum, then set 'Night' beside Epstein's early work on Agar House to show the architectural value of sculpture, compare this with the Angel choir of Lincoln Cathedral, fling his thought out to Athens via some minor continental cathedral to speak of a caryatid in some place and show, meanwhile, how country and environment affected the quality of art. Now he would return to London again to compare Greek architectural sculpture with Gill's 'Prospero' on Broadcasting House: functional art with decorative art. A mention of Jagger and he would condemn hysteria and overstatement, expanding into an analysis of greatness. Design, form, the sense of scale interested him enormously.

And it was not on sculpture alone that he could range in this way. Politics, history, literature, theology, engineering: he seemed to have wrested the core from everything.

He might be walking in a town and come to a flight of steps. 'Guess how many,' he would suggest. 'Oh, thirty-nine. The original thirty-nine steps'. He would grin and start to talk about Buchan's book and its characters, of John Buchan himself, describing him (not too seriously perhaps) as the modern Walter Scott devoid of Scott's tedium, and branching out, inevitably it seemed, into an analysis of the requirements for a popular story, into speculation on the effect and growth of the twopenny libraries, into . . . who could tell? In a few minutes we would probably be comparing the shops of the Co-operative Society with the International Tea Stores. Or he might be jerked out of this homely topic by the sight of a bastion in a wall and talk about medieval defence schemes, comparing forts in India, thirteenth-century walled towns and early British camps.

Always, unexpectedly, he was making little excursions into speculation on objects and men which suddenly interested him. His whole mind, in friendly conversation, was restless, searching the byways of thought rather than being content with the main track. Yet all these alleyways converged on to the crux of whatever problem was being discussed. It was as though in all things he preferred to stand apart, to be an encouraging spectator rather than a player, watching events with a more certain vision because of his distance from the scene.

He was very sensitive to moods and thought. We might walk along very happily in silence until, swiftly, the light in a square might excite me and T.E., sensing this change, would start to say a little more than had been in my mind. The square in this present fall of light would be compared to a picture by Utrillo. Then in detail he would compare its sides, feasting on the restful cliff of a Georgian terrace, contrasting this elegance with the squalor of its modern red brick counterpart, and so talk about the changed conditions and mentality which caused the difference; drawing on social history, economic relations, and literature to support his ideas.

He could sense the missing of one of his points and explain very carefully what his intention had been. There were few celebrities he had not met. There appeared to be little on which he could not speak with acute judgment. He seemed to have solved most problems for himself; though in the presence of experts he would retire and humorously urge them on.

I can remember only once, on his being asked to join the British Union of Fascists, when he was genuinely distressed; certain of Fascism's incongruity in England, but unhappy at the distinguished support it had at the time, troubled at all this frittering of energy in yet another political shade.

So much knowledge, such a distillation of wisdom, and he spanned it all with an arch of humour, an impish delight in the construction of almost scandalous stories, larger than the truth, about his friends and acquaintances. Once when he came to see me we sat on the aerodrome and talked, a little apart. To a friend he wrote a week or two afterwards: '. . . I saw Dunn in his Squadron . . . He was like a slightly irascible bantam cock in a large harem of hens — who looked up or down to him with vast fluttering respect . . .' It is unfortunate that his enlargements of the truth about other people cannot be told.

He invented fantastic things to do. He thought of building a chute from his upper room across the road to the swimming pool, so that he could slide straight into the water in the morning and swim to his study at the other end where he could be free from importunate interviewers unless they chose to swim up to him. Books and paper were to be transported by a clockwork boat and kept dry in a waterproof bag!

He told (untruly I believe) how, when H.M.S. *Nelson* went aground, he presented himself on board to a paralysed quarter-deck as the man from the British Movietone News wishing to take a close-up of the Admiral: and he planned to paint a boat to look like a red hot boiler and tear through a certain dock-yard on some solemn naval occasion with a great screen of smoke belching from its stern.

He despised himself as a fraud, for legend had built up a person far different from the reality and he thought the legendary person was what he was expected to be. 'An ordinary chap, blown up by a seized War opportunity, easy come, easy esteemed, easy let go. Not an oracle, and not staying up,' he wrote in a letter.

Often I felt that he was dissatisfied with himself. He seemed to be pleased by nothing which he did, unless it was an act of kindness to someone or the surmounting of a difficulty by some simple ingenuity. His larger acts were never suffi-ciently perfect to please him. There was constantly the need for improvement of details, streamlining, simplifying to the uttermost limits to increase efficiency.

He would take no credit for his share in the Arabian Revolt, describing it as a series of fortunate accidents, devoid of any strategic scheme likely to come off merely from his own planning. He regretted *Seven Pillars of Wisdom* as being affected in style and lacking in singleness of purpose. He called it his mental junk shop, with bits of history, archaeology, observations on many subjects all distracting from the main theme. He called his translation of the *Odyssey* a pot-boiler and unsatisfactory from every point of view, although he did confess that it was done as well as he could do it. Yet *The Mint*, his early R.A.F. journal, pleased him by its simplicity, its ease, and because it came nearer to being a creative work than any-thing he had ever written. For he wanted to create a work of art, but only found a shocking incapacity for writing. 'There is nothing left to write about,' he complained, 'not much left for anyone now. You can only go on doing the same thing in a different way.'

If his creative instinct had to have an outlet, it was in the solution of the mechanical difficulties and the gradual refinement of the R.A.F. motor boats. In this work he found the troubled joy which is the artist's happiness: yet he could never realize the sheer impossibility of ultimate perfection. He could not acknowledge that a moment came when one must cry halt, the moment before a book becomes too literary, a painting too photographic, an engine refined to the point of emasculation, a poem pared down to incomprehensibility. Perfection was his goal, the only thing worth striving after.

His tragedy seemed to be that he had reached a peak of attainment on which his peers were few and unbearable and from which he could not climb down in spite of his many attempts. Lawrence of Arabia was always behind Aircraftman Shaw; and no matter how well and equally he came to be accepted by fellow-airmen, the dreaded spectre still lingered, in his own mind at least.

The memory of Arabia which was, I think, largely the remembrance of his huge suffering at Deraa, was the stain from which he wished to be cleansed. He tried to, but could not, cut himself away from its fouling. His ideas of integrity were scrupulous. No man could have been more honest with himself, more desirous of being taken purely, on his present showing alone. 'Advertisement destroys in us the hope that unalloyed merit ever existed. No one can enter affairs and keep his hands clean. Patience. Be indifferent.' He wanted his yesterdays to be things of the past, if they led only backwards. It mattered that he should rebuild himself as a unity, freed from a military and political background which he believed fraudulent. It mattered that he should realize an ideal by doing all things as perfectly as possible and keeping them untainted by his mythical personality. He wanted to start out in many different fields, anonymously, to catch out his imperfections. He did not believe in other people's views of himself. He battled against his real personality — 'What some call my charm', he once sneered at himself to me as though it was an unclean thing — and he was at his most charming when he said that.

This internal conflict seemed to persist throughout his life. He was a scholar who loathed scholarship when it had no bearing on anything else, a mechanic who refused to accept the name and the rewards. He disliked publicity when it interfered with his affairs, yet secretly it seemed to delight him. He was ridden with friends yet he tried to be isolated. By turns and often together he was solemn and puckish, in action as in thought. There was the boyish, lovable T.E., and behind the laughing eyes a dreadful haunting. The mingling made a troubled creature, a rich mind in a hurt body.

Three things stand out in my experience to show him variously. One was his ability to walk past ticket collectors as though they never existed. Once one called after him. Without looking back T.E. said, quite decisively, 'I have not yet decided to travel', and walked on, in glee. He could not bear the officiousness of most minor officials. I remember too how he came to me in a greatly disturbed state because some chance-met N.C.O. had called him 'Sir' and my invented excuse that he had an impediment in his speech and was actually saying 'Shaw' would not mollify him a little. He was troubled for the rest of the morning. I shall remember too with what fear I watched a small boy approaching with an open autograph album; and how charming T.E. was, signing it and saying, 'There you are. It was worth half a crown once, but I've flooded the market.'

A few days before he left the Royal Air Force he lunched with me. We walked through the canteen. We sat talking on my bed in a barrack-room. We stood about the camp for an hour. But it was not until he left on the Brough that anyone guessed who he was. Yet I have seen a crowd of men become silent as soon as he lifted a finger or opened his lips. In those rare moments he seemed detached, fey, greater than his body, a power which flowed out, irresistibly, from that very quiet little figure. With an effort he had switched himself on. I believe it exhausted him. He had given himself away when his great desire was to be whole and intact. *Noli me tangere:* his ideas of chastity transcended those of St. Paul, the only man on whom we could agree in our dislike.

He was not the shadowy 'mystery man' of the popular press. He had no false ideas about himself. He had the moral courage to say and do what he thought was right. He embraced kings and labourers with equal sympathy. He could make fortunes for those who needed them while he was content to live on little.

If he has left any impression on behaviour it is the thought that joy can only come by throwing oneself wholeheartedly into whatever one's present work happens to be; that the only worth-while happiness can come from hungering always after improvement; by working at whatever one feels the urge to do regardless of convention or extraneous influences; and by anonymity.

He was a great writer, a brilliant leader, a greater friend. He was a saint — but with a sense of humour.

HENRY WILLIAMSON, naturalist and writer. Born 1896. Says he 'started career on Christmas Day, 1914, when during the Truce young German soldiers told him Germany couldn't lose because her cause was just'. Author of *Tarka the Otter*; *The Old Stag*; *The Flax of Dream*, etc.

O NE day about ten years ago, while in the train from Red-hill to London, I opened the *Daily Telegraph* and began to read the opening instalment of Col. T. E. Lawrence's much-advertised story of his Arabian adventure. Immediately the first sentence was arresting: 'When at last we anchored in Jeddah's outer harbour, off the white town hung between blazing sky and its reflection in the mirage which swept and rolled over the wide lagoon, then the heat of Arabia came out like a drawn sword and struck us speechless.'

I opened a bag and took out the manuscript of a book about an otter which had been revised and rewritten many times, to show to myself a sentence of the same visual essence: 'For two days and two nights the frosty vapour lay over the Burrows, and then came a north wind which poured like liquid glass from Exmoor and made all things distinct.'

Recently a junior officer in the Royal Air Force had sold to the *Daily Express* the 'story' of Lawrence of Arabia's hiding in the ranks. Lawrence was said to be in the Secret Service; he was a super-spy. Although I did not believe in super-spies, I had almost accepted the fact, like many another member of the public, that Colonel Lawrence was one. Why else was he in the ranks of the R.A.F., calling himself Ross? And why did he go to London occasionally, to receive bundles of letters from somewhere or other? Thus the newspaper stories had vaguely impressed my idle paper-glancing mind.

It seemed to me, sitting in the railway carriage, having read that opening sentence, that I *knew* Lawrence of Arabia. Should I write to him and say so? No.

I knew we saw many things alike. Perhaps he was the friend I had always longed for: with whom even words would be superfluous. Otters and other wild animals knew each other entirely by a glance, an action. They were usually in perfect accord; no energy wasted by words; their life-force was shared. They were simple. Dare I send Lawrence my book about an otter when it was published?

And yet I was not really surprised, in the following winter of 1927, to open a bulky registered letter from Edward Garnett and to see enclosed another letter in a minute and meticulous handwriting, covering several foolscap sheets and signed — I knew it before looking — T. E. Shaw. I called Loetitia, who had brought the letter with my morning tea. 'Here you are, I told you so. From T. E. Shaw'. 'Oh.' 'You know who he is, don't you?' 'Do I?' She was listening to the baby beginning to whimper downstairs. 'I told you. It's from Lawrence of Arabia! — all about *Tarka*. I knew he would see it as I saw it! Look, he finds all these faults!! I've found some myself, since it was printed. I knew it, I knew it!!'

That morning I wrote a long letter to 337181 A.C. Shaw, R.A.F., Karachi, thanking him and saying that what I had known from reading the first sentence of his book, Everest to my Snowdon, had at last materialized. I sent him off a copy of *The Old Stag*, begging him not to consider it sent for criticism: but only for (perhaps) an occasional entertainment. He wrote back another long letter; and thus began an acquaintanceship which was never complete on either side because, I think, each was conscious of his own deficiencies towards the other. Incredibly, Lawrence thought I was a better writer than himself: whilst I knew myself for a pretty poor specimen compared with himself, a world-famous man. *The Old Stag* was the only book I sent him, not wishing to appear to be taking advantage of an acquaintanceship.

I met Lawrence in the early summer of 1929, after his forced return from India. The *Sunday Express* had printed a 'sensational' news-story about his presence on the North-West frontier, and he had been recalled to England, dreading lest he be turned out of the R.A.F. again, because of it. (I wonder if Lord Beaverbrook realizes how miserable the newspapers under his direction, by their very policy of 'news', made T.E., so persistently unsure of his job, and home, and therefore so unhappy?) But Lawrence's embarrassment was my good fortune; for one wet Sunday in early summer a shy, smiling, nodding, bird-quick, red-faced young man, with a soft and pleasing voice, with faint Irish brogue, padded into my cottage, dressed in a rubber mine-sweeping one-piece suit. He pulled this off in the wash-house, nodded and smiled at the little maid in the kitchen, and then, while a meal of tomatoes and bananas and salads was being prepared, we went upstairs. The nickel-plated twin-cylinder Brough Superior stood in the lane below the small writing-room of ships'-timbers and plaster and tarred corrugated iron roof. It rained steadily outside. He must leave in an hour's time, he said. The journey from Plymouth to Georgeham, about a hundred miles, through continuous rain, had taken three hours, and he was on duty again at 5 o'clock. Our lunch, with Loetitia and our small son Windles, was the best meal I had ever eaten. Never before and never since have I felt so free from myself, so without body: happiness beyond the consciousness of happiness. This man understood a thought before it was uttered. We were like otters, or Arabs. This was the first person I had met, other than ephemeral or social contacts, in thirty years conscious living, who had not criticized, or objected to, or denied some part or other of the world I saw. I felt an immense easy power within myself; as though one could, and would, live for ever. Afterwards, when he had gone, I wondered if he had unconsciously assumed from me, chameleon-like, my usual manner of hesitancy and shyness — symptom of delayed adolescence, too much mother-love in childhood. He had been me; and I had felt so strong and calm and sure of myself. When he had gone, the world was dull and flat, and once more one was alone, with no one to talk to, for days and weeks and months.

I thought much about him in the time that followed. His letters made me sad. He had come to the end of one world; and the new world was not yet born. Like other hypersensitive youths in the War, he was exhausted, not so much by the physical action, but by the knowledge of human stupidity. What a fight he must have had, to convince Arabs and Englishmen! I had met some Englishmen who had known him at Cairo, before he went into the desert; they had thought him a conceited little outsider. He had exhausted himself by trying to convert the unimaginativeness of the ordinary man into imaginativeness. In one of his letters he had written that he did not believe in heroes: 'didn't believe the yarns they tell about me'. He said that the 'Arab business was a freak in my living': that 'in normal times I am plumb ordinary'. He wanted to be; he wanted to be happy; but he wasn't plumb ordinary; so he wasn't happy.

But, until the real human cause of war, or stupidity, or unhappiness, was generally recognized, such men as T. E. Lawrence would continue to be solitaries; and being solitary, would be romantic — for the solitary dreams of, or is always subconsciously searching for, the one perfect companion. I felt I could be that friend to Lawrence; but I did not like to offer friendship, lest I be wrong in thinking his lack was similar to my lack. So although often I was near Plymouth, a few miles south of my village, during the years he was there, I never saw him.

Now that he is dead and I am older, I think I understand him better. What I imagined was true. He was not happy. Much of his despondency (which he never permitted to affect others) came from the very simple cause of semi-starvation. A man's thoughts are his feelings, either of the past or the present; and every man's thoughts arising from physical exhaustion are often entirely opposed to those of his vital well-being. Even if a man knows this to be true of himself at any time, it is difficult for him to believe it, especially if he be an 'original' or true thinker, whose thoughts are the feelings of his subconscious mind brought uppermost. The mental struggle exhausted Lawrence in Arabia; and again he exhausted himself in the written recreation of his Arabian life. He mortified himself, by his expense of spirit or vitality, in the desert; and yet again, in the prolonged labour of writing his book. Once he wrote more than 30,000 words at a sitting, burning his brain like a magnesium flare to light the shades of that olden turmoil. He overstrained himself, while also starving himself. That is the truth, as I see it. And he did not do this for personal gain or glory. He worked, and he wrote, for the glory of God — to use an old idiom to express what in a more modern sense is, perhaps, a conception of integrity and honour. He wrote, and lived, for the glory of life itself — not for personal glory. He couldn't help doing otherwise — he was born a poet. To me he was and is the personification of honour, which is clear sight, and the courage to maintain it. Clarity is rare among men as charity is common. When all men have clarity, there will be no need for charity. I believe that age is being forged now.

There is little more to tell. Many times he set out to visit me; and as many times turned back. He thought I had lots of friends; I thought he had lots of friends.

The new age must begin: Europe was ready for peace: Lawrence was the natural leader of that age in England. I dreamed of an Anglo-German friendship, the beginning of the pacification of Europe. Hitler and Lawrence must meet. I wrote thus to him, shortly after he had left the R.A.F. He replied immediately by telegram, asking me to come the next day, wet or fine; but while returning from writing the telegram, swiftly on his motor-cycle, he saw suddenly before him over the crest of the narrow road across Egdon Heath two boys on bicycles, and braked and turned off lest he hurt them; and the temples of his brain were broken.

Those who knew him have thought and spoken much of this man since; and of those friends many must find it hard to avoid, even within their own minds, phrases of esteem which are usually used to describe the lives of good men. Of Lawrence it can be said that he was that rare kind of good man: one whose goodness gave no offence to any of his fellows.

'T. E. LAWRENCE'

By W.H. AUDEN

I f this article is very little about Captain Liddell Hart's book, it is because he has presented his matter so clearly and convincingly that the reader forgets all about him. Excepting the almost mythical *Seven Pillars* there is no better account of the Arabian campaign than this, and no more living portrait of Lawrence: nor is there likely to be.

Thinking of Lawrence, I am reminded of two stories; the first Turgenev's *A Desperate Character*, particularly the incident of him 'Anyone who wishes to flip a nobleman on the nose may do so for two rubles,' and how he nearly killed one who tried to take two flips for his money. The second, which I read I believe in MacDougal's *Abnormal Psychology* was the statement made by a man after he had cut the throats of his wife and family. 'No, I am not the truly strong man. The truly strong man lounges about in bars and does nothing at all.'

To me Lawrence's life is an allegory of the transformation of the Truly Weak Man into the Truly Strong Man, an answer to the question 'How shall the self-conscious man be saved?' and the moral seems to be this; 'self-consciousness is an asset, in fact the only friend of our progress. We can't go back on it. But its demands on our little person and his appetites are so great that most of us, terrified, try to escape or make terms with it, which is fatal. As a pursuer it is deadly.' Only the continuous annihilation of the self by the Identity, to use Blake's terminology, will bring to us to the freedom we wish for, or in Lawrence's own phrase, 'Happiness comes in absorption.'

But a misinterpretation of absorption is one of the great heresies of our generation. To interpret it as blind action without consideration of meaning or ends, as an escape from reason and consciousness; that is indeed to become the Truly Weak Man, to enlist in the great Fascist retreat which will land us finally in the ditch of despair, to cry like Elijah: 'Lord take away my life for I am not better than my fathers.'

From Lawrence's own account of himself, no one has found this temptation harder, nor conquered it more resolutely, better demonstrated the truth that action and reason are inseparable; it is only in action that reason can realize itself, and only through reason that action can become free. Consciousness necessitates more action not less, and *vice versa*.

To the problem of human relations he has an equally important contribution to make. Different as they appear on the surface, both he and his namesake, D. H. Lawrence, imply the same, that the Western-romantic conception of personal love is a neurotic symptom only inflaming our loneliness, a bad answer to our real wish to be united to and rooted in life. They both say 'noli me tangere.' It is at least doubtful whether in our convalescence sexual relations can do anything but postpone our cure. It is quite possible that the way back to real intimacy is through a kind of asceticism. The self must first learn to be indifferent; as Lenin said, 'to go hungry, work illegally and be an anonymous.' Lawrence's enlistment in the Air Force and Rimbaud's adoption of a trading career are essentially similar. 'One must be absolutely modern.'

I mentioned Lenin. He and Lawrence seem to me the two whose lives exemplify most completely what is best and significant in our time, our nearest approach to a synthesis of feeling and reason, act and thought, the most potent agents of freedom and to us, egotistical underlings, the most relevant accusation and hope.

(1934)

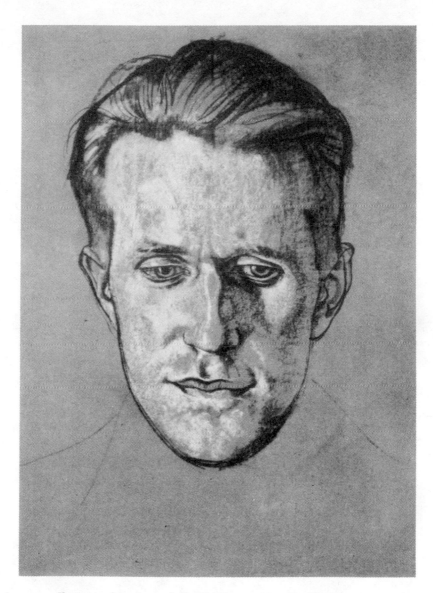

From a drawing of T. E. Lawrence by Kennington
"The Cheshire Cat", 1921

EDITOR'S POSTSCRIPT

A. W. LAWRENCE

A . W . L A W R E N C E , Reader in Classical Archaeology, Cambridge University. Born 1900 (youngest brother of T.E.L.). Excavated in Greece 1920, 1921; at Ur, 'Iraq, 1922. Author of *Classical Sculpture*; annotated Herodotus, etc.

I END this book with my own article, because I alone have written with knowledge of the other contributions, because I am the only writer who met my brother at regular intervals from his boyhood to his last few months, and because I shared with him the same inheritance, the same environments and education, and to a large extent the same interests and the same attitude towards them.

I was influenced by him from my infancy: he was extremely fond of children and I was twelve years younger. His anti-quarian interests became a natural part of my life when I was between five and ten. He took me to the Ashmolean Museum, gave me bits of old pottery and iridescent glass, towed me in a trailer behind his bicycle on excursions outside Oxford; on one of these I was helped to rub my favourite brass, a comic one. I slept in a room papered with his black rubbings of knights, and I read without surprise the many story-books he possessed, such as translations of the romances of Huon of Bordeaux or the Four Sons of Aymon, the Kalevala and tales by William Morris. Later, when he lived chiefly in the East, the antiquities and contemporary state of the places he saw were present to my imagination. Lucian's *True History*, a story I read frequently, now had a special attraction because Lucian was born at Samsat on the Euphrates, not far above Carchemish. Perhaps for the same reason, Ned bought a complete set of his works, in Greek and Latin, on one of his last homecomings before the War, and I fancy that his philosophy of life may have owed something to Lucian's interpretation of the doctrines of the Cynics — abstention from honour and power with their attendant temptations, and satisfaction with the simple life of the righteous poor.

After the War, his interest in Hellenized Syria led him to study the philosophy of Apollonius of Tyana, and to plan an edition of the Gadarene poets and a book on the society into which Christ was born. These men had belonged, as he himself now did, to a two-fold civilization, European and Asiatic. Lucian and Apollonius especially combine with their western education a trace of the oriental carelessness about the trappings of life. I have no doubt that the young T. E. Lawrence greeted it at his first sight of the East, not with the usual western revulsion, but as a disciple. He would recognize the similarity to medieval Europe, in which he was learned. The similarity goes deeper than the mere surface of life; the definitive structure of our feudal society can be paralleled in the tribes, and Hamoudi's narrative illustrates a spirit that would appeal to such a lover of the *Morte d'Arthur*. His medieval researches were, I think, a dream way of escape from bourgeois England as well as a detached study of another civilization, and I doubt whether he continued them when he lived in the East. I do not know whether he had read deeply about any aspect of the Middle Ages other than the military, the chivalrous and the social. His history 'coach' at Oxford, the late L. C. Jane, wrote to Robert Graves: 'He would never read the obvious books . . . He had the most diverse interests historically, though mainly medieval. For a long time I could not get him to take any interest in later European history and was very startled to find that he was absorbed by R. M. Johnstone's *French Revolution*.' (In later life the methods of any revolution aroused his professional curiosity: the Irish were bunglers.) Jane, like Barker, says he was not a scholar by temperament. Indeed both medieval history and medieval archaeology — perhaps he made no distinction — ceased to hold his attention when he knew enough to obtain a general view of the subject and had extracted what he wanted for the benefit of his own personality. The same applies to every academic study which he took up. His application to oriental archaeology ceased a few years after the War, though with Feisal as king of Syria he had wished to continue the excavation of Carchemish and when the kingdom of 'Iraq was established he determined to clear the Assyrian palace underneath Jonah's Tomb; at Feisal's instigation some popular saint would have a revelation that the prophet had really been buried elsewhere on a site of no archaeological importance. But this plan lapsed, ostensibly because his political notoriety would have caused embarrassment in 'Iraq, and he told me about the same time that he could not face the labour of research involved by his projected *Background of Christ*. As a matter of fact his only learned publications were his share of reports, the compilation of which was unavoidable. Contrary to general practice, he wrote no articles in archaeological journals, although he must have had ample material: he said not long ago that he knew a Norman capital in France with carvings of pots of a shape the museums always dated two centuries later.

In languages too he was satisfied without a scholar's knowledge. He could read primitive Arabic poems from his experience of desert speech but he never troubled with classical Arabic. He could learn in a few days enough of any Latin or Teutonic language to read its literature and did not care to know more, and though he wished to extract the full meaning of such Greek authors as he liked, he emphasized the fact that he was no Greek scholar by omitting all the accents with which texts are habitually sprinkled. Before the War he used to practise translating epigrams from the Greek Anthology (a copy of which and an Aristophanes he carried with him in the campaign), and he discloses a high standard of translation from the French in the letters quoted by Jonathan Cape. With his *Odyssey* too he took immense care, sacrificing correct wording to correct feeling. I am not qualified to judge how often he mistook the sense; some who profess a complete knowledge of the dead language assure us that he was blatantly inaccurate, but slips would rarely have passed his checking of his version by previous translations and I do not see why departures from the traditional rendering should necessarily be wrong. Rothenstein's article shows how he perverted his English to reproduce what he believed to be the characteristics of the original: there remain too few specimens of early Greek to prove or disprove his contention that the original is decadent, and on this point the judgment of his trained literary mind seems to me to carry more weight than that of a professional scholar.

The ambitions to write and to print books remained with him all his life and were very real. When editors rejected his unsigned articles, as Brophy and Liddell Hart describe, he felt bitter disappointment, though he could also display the comic side of the story to Rothenstein. The editors' verdict did in fact confirm his own conviction that he was no literary artist but only an occasional workman with words. Graves says that he thought the secret of poetry lay in the technique, while Thomas Hardy, after reading one paragraph of the *Seven Pillars*, declared that its author knew all the technique of writing. To my mind, his concern with all the arts was more often that of a craftsman than of an artist or a critic, though at times he was each of these, and brilliantly. He was exceptionally able with his hands and had the craftsman's appreciation of sound work in sound material, irrespective of aesthetic merit: the wrought-iron flowers that a smith made for the fender at Clouds Hill (plate facing page 572) are of very remarkable workmanship, but the design seems to me poor and unpleasant, while David Garnett's condemnation of the *Seven Pillars* as a printed book expresses a widespread opinion. In his teens he had spent much effort upon wood-carving and burnt poker work, using designs he collected from various sources, and he hammered out in brass and fitted with an electric lamp a lantern copied from one in Holman Hunt's picture 'The Light of the World', an engraving of which hung in his parents' drawing-room. Such boyish activities were succeeded by a project for coating the walls of the bathroom at Carchemish with soft Roman glass melted by a blowlamp, and by ventures in drawing and sculpture.

Of his early drawings I need only say that those now extant are technical and imitative; the best are reproduced in a limited edition I have issued of *Crusader Castles*, an essay which the publishers rejected when he wrote it, in 1910, and which he afterwards refused to publish because of an incompleteness he had no opportunity to rectify. As the basis for a suggested illustration by Kennington to the *Seven Pillars*, he drew a sketch of himself laying out dead Turks, which is remarkable for power of expression and sense of composition. It seems to me to show strong feeling but to make no appeal to the emotions; the conscious subjection of his senses to his intellect may have deprived him of the ability to create artistically. Yet in 1935 he had thoughts of taking to sculpture.

The only example of his sculpture with which I am acquainted, a device on the Carchemish house, reproduces the winged sun-disc found in ancient oriental carvings such as he was then busy excavating and piecing together. In this connection I may recall his earliest sculptural interest — at least the earliest I can remember — when as a boy he traced Layard's drawings of Assyrian reliefs. Next, he had developed an appreciation of Greek sculpture that was not confined to the well-known show-pieces; he went to the trouble of obtaining a permit in the British Museum and photographing a male torso from the Parthenon pediments which, though it attracts little attention, is almost unequalled for the combination of realistic and monumental nudity. In his undergraduate days the statues of Chartres cathedral moved him to rapture.

In general his attitude to the major arts was that of an exceptionally appreciative onlooker — exceptionally appreciative for an adult. Ardent enthusiasm of a similar quality is common enough at twenty, but it is unusual for a middle-aged man of great achievements to believe that the production of works of art forms the only valid title to fame, or even justification of existence. But great artists stand eternally beyond comparison, each on his own undisputed pinnacle, whereas anything that he himself did seems to have become almost valueless to him once he had achieved it: no complaisance prompted the strange discussion with Hall, and he could accept only unfavourable judgments upon his work.

The reason for this attitude I should trace to a fundamental distrust of himself and consequent need for self-justification, of which Cherry-Garrard writes — I have no doubt, with complete accuracy. He had, I believe, a diffident, perhaps weak core, so controlled by his colossal will-power that its underlying presence was rarely suspected. The sketch reproduced on p. 190, a portrait which deliberately distorts the features far from their natural shape, may reveal the conflict between diffidence and will, the torture of nerving the self to action. Perhaps it is significant that he worked on the psychology of Fear; he gave this as his reason for buying a dozen or two of psychological books which I helped one Sunday to carry from his room at All Souls across to a Bank, where he pushed them through the letter-box — the jest was one he could repeat any time in the next fifteen years with equal pleasure, as Sims reveals.

His diffidence probably arose from a sense of isolation, of a barrier set by his own oddness between himself and the rest of mankind; he said, in middle-age, that it prevented any thought of marriage. The feeling may well have been slow of growth. A difference in kind from those with whom the accident of birth associates him will not immediately twist a child into self-consciousness, but the habit, once formed, will overwhelm him. I am told by John Snow, his great friend at school, that at first he seemed to be just a rather shy boy who differed from other boys chiefly in not being interested in games — he so infected me with this sentiment that I was embarrassed, a dozen years later, when he asked me about such a fatuous thing as how I had run in a race. It was not till the end of his time at school that it came to be realized that he was remarkably unconventional, when, for instance, he would work out a problem in algebra in a way that would not have occurred to a mathematician. But his most prominent action at school was no more unorthodox than a collection from all the boys for a present to the headmaster when he reached his twenty-first year of service. At college he made fun for himself by eccentricity, riding his bicycle up hills and walking it down them, or sitting through the prescribed dinners in the hall without eating anything. In these conscious demonstrations of his peculiarity we may perhaps see a passing sense of irritation at his accentuated self-consciousness as well as his permanent taste for baiting the conventional. A good instance of that is his scheme for an issue of Syrian stamps in which those of each value should be backed with a gum of a different taste, to help distinguish them in the dark and to popularize use of the post.

His self-consciousness would naturally be intensified by his assumption of another civilization — one might say, of several other civilizations, for his quick reading (a sentence or a paragraph at a glance) and almost faultless memory had set him mentally at home in biblical Palestine, in medieval France and ancient Greece, and to a lesser extent in ancient Egypt and Mesopotamia, before his submergence in Arab nationality. Indeed, in certain respects he persistently appeared to be book-learned rather than life-learned.

He may have owed some of his facility for seeing through the eyes of others to inner lack of confidence. When he had just been with someone or was just going to see someone he tended to take on the characteristics of that person. Helped by this weakness (if such it were) and by the loneliness which kept him eager for human contact, he usually succeeded in evoking the best that lay in his companions and bringing them to realize to the full their own capacities. If he gave his trust and it were betrayed, then, provided he understood the reason for the failure, he felt no rancour — and this seems to me the greatest of his successes. For he valued truth as much as he enjoyed fiction!

His friendships were comparable in intensity to sexual love, for which he made them a substitute. He could not compromise easily with Nature but rejected its government as far as was humanly possible; he thought it better to die than submit to growing old, and against sex in particular he rebelled unceasingly. His hatred of sex was an irrational instinct which went far beyond reason's limits, as he himself recognized. While he may have been endowed in childhood with a realization of sin in this respect, I think that its action was seldom perceptible before the War and held dominance only during the following years of ill-health and turmoil. In 1925 he could write half-seriously of prostitution being marriage *à la carte*, as though he admitted no distinction of kind between relationships into which sex entered. It was this horror of the physical intimacies that he never experienced with anyone — we have his word for it — which inspired his abstinent habits. 'A one-man monastery' he has been called by a philosopher who did not know him, and his subjection of the body was achieved by methods advocated by the saints whose lives he had read. One of his friends, a desert explorer, holds that he was a man perfectly clear in his way of life, who had achieved a balance between spirit, intellect and body to a degree few even imagine, and that in spite of an extremely high evolution of the spirit, as a result of which the balance was so unusual as to appear to most people unbalanced. Certainly the details of his life were consistent to his plan, but in my opinion he neglected the body's claims unfairly. He maintained this 'balance' at a cost so terrible in waste and suffering, that its author would himself, I believe, have agreed that it was a failure. Towards the end of his life he wrote with tender envy of the happy marriage of a contemporary and there was plainly no fate he would have more gladly accepted for himself.

Here I may add the suggestion that the poem which serves as dedication to the *Seven Pillars* is somewhat of a literary exercise, in memory of his own youth, as well as a tribute to the person who had roused him to appreciate the potentialities of the Arab race. The style seems a compromise between Semitic form and the sentiment of English poets of the 'nineties, whom he read during his years at Carchemish, and on his own statements the poem has little personal application, whether or not its reputed subject were his long-lost companion, Sheikh Ahmed, who is called in this book by his nickname, Dahoum (pp. 80, 89, 97, 98).

In 1922 I came home from 'Iraq, horrified, after conversations with the British advisers whose advice the infant state was not over-inclined to heed and whom it dismissed without notice or pension on grounds not always unquestionable.

Putting their case, I asked my brother what good he thought he had done by fomenting Arab nationality. He replied that he saw no reason why Arabs should govern worse than the former Turkish Empire and they might do better; also that he had wished to lay no burden of pension (as in Egypt) upon the 'Iraq revenue, which indeed did not suffice then to continue with the most urgent projects of public utility.

His conscience was satisfied by the creation of autonomous Arab states with provision for their ultimate independence in connection with the British Empire; he wished this connection to endure, envisaging Egypt and 'Iraq as virtual Dominions. His duty thereafter was to leave Asia to muddle through in its own inexperience. I say 'Asia' advisedly, for his friendliness had not been confined to the Arabic-speaking peoples. He had helped to secure a peaceful frontier to the Kemalists during their struggle for the new Turkey and afterwards advocated British support for their Turkish Republic. His attitude to Zionism is explained in this book, unfortunately with no record of how he would have adjusted his policy to the tremendous spurt in colonization caused by Jewish emigration from Nazi Germany. When he left the Colonial Office he anticipated a long-protracted British administration of Palestine, ending in a comparatively amicable solution of the problem, in favour, I think, of a Jewish majority in the distant future.

Feeling now absolved of any further responsibilities in that direction, he proceeded to lose interest in the East, not simply with that satiated curiosity with which he turned from his medieval and archaeological interests. For he looked back upon his subjection to the East with horror. His memories too were the more painful because of the vividness with which he recollected sights and smells and sounds, creating again in all their poignancy scenes he would have preferred to forget.

In Arabia he had anaesthetized his emotions and turned himself from a man into an instrument of victory. Thereafter his life seemed negative, even futile, though he so filled his days with little things as to conceal their emptiness. He might have justified his continued existence by artistic creation, but he could not create. After selling his soul for the success of an alien cause he could work with no great conviction for the cause of his own people. Personal freedom became a passion and his whole philosophy turned upon it. To maintain his independence he would hold no office, accept no responsibilities, would satisfy his body with the barest essentials while demanding the richest sustenance for the intellect; forming no habits of mind, he would keep himself ever fresh and receptive. Only towards other individuals would he have obligations, and in giving himself unstintedly to enrich their lives he must sometimes have felt that his survival was worth while.

The years in the ranks enabled him not altogether to repair the damage he sustained in the War and the peace settlements, but at least to regain physical and mental health. Religious by temperament and without a creed, he found some happiness in working with others, for they helped him to lose sight of the ogre personality he had substituted for himself and become an ordinary human being like themselves.

Towards the end of his service his work on speed boats showed a renewal of activity. Characteristically it came in an unexpected field, though his pre-War concern with the detailed design of bicycles and cameras points the way. But again he grew tired, and on his discharge he looked forward — not without misgiving — to a long peace. Through a former aircraftman he bought a second-hand set of carpenter's tools with which to remake the interior of his cottage. He would have music, books and company at Clouds Hill and in London, and by means of a pedal bicycle and Youth Hostels would explore the by-ways of England at leisure, for he was equally fond of country and of buildings. The smallness of his income was not alarming, although on past occasions he had spent with the utmost freedom. Cheap clothing was a luxury after private's uniform. He would keep bread, butter and cheese under glass bells and go out occasionally to spend a few pennies on bacon and eggs or fish and chips; to one who ate only when hungry the plainest fare was more desirable than the strange mixtures of ingenious chefs. Besides, while his generosity to those who needed money more than himself had no bounds, he was equally ready to receive from those who possessed a superfluity; accordingly he gladly accepted the offer of a new motor bicycle and searched for the loan of a room in London.

But the Press pestered him still. His retirement was not credited. One reporter had been issued with a written questionnaire starting: 'Do you plan to make yourself Dictator of England?' He found Clouds Hill so besieged that he entered his cottage only by ruses concerted with his neighbour, even after the newspapers had at his request withdrawn their authorized reporters, upon assurances that he was indeed doing nothing of any interest. And that was true: after oppressed hesitation he saw means to avoid an active participation in the replanning of national defence—which began immediately with a great expansion of the Air Force. A longing for quiet dominated him. The despondency which naturally overshadowed him, on the completion of the last great task of his life, had not lifted, when, to forget himself for a few seconds, he rode at what to him was no immoderate speed into a catastrophe which the normal quickness of his brain might possibly have averted; as it was, he saved others from injury.

He would have thought it funny as well as moving that we should so mourn the close of a life which, since its sacrifice eighteen years before, had lost its fullness and joy.